Econometric Modelling of European Money Demand

AF810371

Contributions to Economics

http://www.springer.de/cgi-bin/search_book.pl?series=1262

Georg Bol/Gholamreza Nakhaeizadeh/
Karl-Heinz Vollmer (Eds.)
Risk Measurements, Econometrics and Neural Networks
1998. ISBN 3-7908-1152-1

Joachim Winter
Investment and Exit Decisions at the Plant Level
1998. ISBN 3-7908-1154-8

Bernd Meyer
Intertemporal Asset Pricing
1999. ISBN 3-7908-1159-9

Uwe Walz
Dynamics of Regional Integration
1999. ISBN 3-7908-1185-8

Michael Carlberg
European Monetary Union
1999. ISBN 3-7908-1191-2

Giovanni Galizzi/
Luciano Venturini (Eds.)
Vertical Relationships and Coordination in the Food System
1999. ISBN 3-7908-1192-0

Gustav A. Horn/Wolfgang Scheremet/
Rudolf Zwiener
Wages and the Euro
1999. ISBN 3-7908-1199-8

Dirk Willer
The Development of Equity Capital Markets in Transition Economies
1999. ISBN 3-7908-1198-X

Karl Matthias Weber
Innovation Diffusion and Political Control of Energy Technologies
1999. ISBN 3-7908-1205-6

Heike Link et al.
The Costs of Road Infrastructure and Congestion in Europe
1999. ISBN 3-7908-1201-3

Simon Duindam
Military Conscription
1999. ISBN 3-7908-1203-X

Bruno Jeitziner
Political Economy of the Swiss National Bank
1999. ISBN 3-7908-1209-9

Irene Ring et al. (Eds.)
Regional Sustainability
1999. ISBN 3-7908-1233-1

Katharina Müller/Andreas Ryll/
Hans-Jürgen Wagener (Eds.)
Transformation of Social Security: Pensions in Central-Eastern Europe
1999. ISBN 3-7908-1210-2

Stefan Traub
Framing Effects in Taxation
1999. ISBN 3-7908-1240-4

Pablo Coto-Millán
Utility and Production
1999. ISBN 3-7908-1153-X

Frank Riedel
Imperfect Information and Investor Heterogeneity in the Bond Market
2000. ISBN 3-7908-1247-1

Kirsten Ralf
Business Cycles
2000. ISBN 3-7908-1245-5

Michele Bagella/Leonardo Becchetti (Eds.)
The Competitive Advantage of Industrial Districts
2000. ISBN 3-7908-1254-4

Frank Bohn
Monetary Union and Fiscal Stability
2000. ISBN 3-7908-1266-8

Jaime Behar
Cooperation and Competition in a Common Market
2000. ISBN 3-7908-1280-3

Michael Malakellis
Integrated Macro-Micro-Modelling Under Rational Expectations
2000. ISBN 3-7908-1274-9

Stefan Baumgärtner
Ambivalent Joint Production and the Natural Environment
2000. ISBN 3-7908-1290-0

Henri Capron, Wim Meeusen (Eds.)
The National Innovation System of Belgium
2000. ISBN 3-7908-1308-7

Tobias Miarka
Financial Intermediation and Deregulation
2000. ISBN 3-7908-1307-9

Chisato Yoshida
Illegal Immigration and Economic Welfare
2000. ISBN 3-7908-1315-X

continued on page 205

Engelbert Plassmann

Econometric Modelling of European Money Demand

Aggregation, Cointegration, Identification

With 16 Figures and 24 Tables

Physica-Verlag
A Springer-Verlag Company

Series Editors
Werner A. Müller
Martina Bihn

Author
Dr. Engelbert Plassmann
Dresdner Bank
RCO RMT
Jürgen-Ponto-Platz 1
60329 Frankfurt/M.
Germany
engelbert.plassmann@dresdner-bank.com

zzgl. Diss., Univ. Konstanz

ISSN 1431-1933
ISBN 3-7908-1522-5 Physica-Verlag Heidelberg New York

Cataloging-in-Publication Data applied for
Die Deutsche Bibliothek – CIP-Einheitsaufnahme
Plassmann; Engelbert: Econometric modelling of European money demand: aggregation, cointegration, identification; with 24 tables / Engelbert Plassmann. – Heidelberg: Physica-Verl., 2003
(Contributions to economics)
ISBN 3-7908-1522-5

This work is subject to copyright. All rights are reserved, whether the whole or part of the material is concerned, specifically the rights of translation, reprinting, reuse of illustrations, recitation, broadcasting, reproduction on microfilm or in any other way, and storage in data banks. Duplication of this publication or parts thereof is permitted only under the provisions of the German Copyright Law of September 9, 1965, in its current version, and permission for use must always be obtained from Physica-Verlag. Violations are liable for prosecution under the German Copyright Law.

Physica-Verlag Heidelberg New York
a member of BertelsmannSpringer Science+Business Media GmbH

© Physica-Verlag Heidelberg 2003
Printed in Germany

The use of general descriptive names, registered names, trademarks, etc. in this publication does not imply, even in the absence of a specific statement, that such names are exempt from the relevant protective laws and regulations and therefore free for general use.

Softcover Design: Erich Kirchner, Heidelberg

SPIN 10887632 88/2202-5 4 3 2 1 0 – Printed on acid-free and non-aging paper

An solchen Feiertagen mußte man auf die Marina blicken,
um zu ahnen, was Leben heißt.

Ernst Jünger, *Auf den Marmorklippen*

Preface

The introduction of a single European currency constitutes a remarkable instance of internationalization of monetary policy. Whether a concomitant internationalization can be detected also in the econometric foundations of monetary policy is the topic dealt with in this book. The basic theoretical ingredients comprise a data-driven approach to econometric modelling and a generalized approach to cross-sectional aggregation. The empirical result is a data-consistent structural money demand function isolated within a properly identified, dynamic macroeconomic system for Europe.

The book itself evolved from a research project within the former Sonderforschungsbereich SFB 178 "Internationalization of the Economy" at the University of Konstanz. Its finalization entails a due amount of gratitude to be extended into several directions:

I am personally indebted, first of all, to my academic supervisor, Professor Dr. Nikolaus Läufer, for originally inspiring this work and for meticulously perusing its eventual result. Professor Dr. Winfried Pohlmeier, as a second supervisor, provided valuable confidence bounds around an earlier draft. The comments of both supervisors contributed substantially to the present shape of the book.

I am institutionally indebted to the University of Konstanz, notably its Faculty of Economics and Statistics, for continuous provision of an excellent research environment, and to the Deutsche Forschungsgemeinschaft in Bonn for generous sponsorship of the former SFB, whose financial support during that period is gratefully acknowledged. I am also indebted to Dresdner Bank AG Frankfurt, Risk Methodology Trading, for benign tolerance of all distractions associated with the preparation of the final manuscript.

Frankfurt am Main,
May 2002

Engelbert Plassmann

Table of Contents

1 Introduction

Money demand and its supposed stability are certainly a perennial topic in econometrics. Indeed, *"rarely have such varied data purporting to proxy the same concept - money - been subjected to such persistent torture, with such ingenious and innovative devices, in the hope that it will confess the secrets of some golden rule ..."* (Podolski 1986, p.218). The reason earning money demand this dubious distinction is twofold. First, the existence of an empirically stable relation to prices and output renders the quantity of money a potentially useful tool for economic policy. Second, the widespread disagreement on the first point renders money demand a natural testing ground for new econometric models and methods.

The present study cannot hope to finally settle these points, but it adds a new motivation to each. As to the golden rule, it is asked whether an empirical money demand function supporting a policy of monetary targeting can be established for aggregated data covering the recently formed European Monetary Union. As to the innovative devices, it is asked whether this money demand function can be established within a so-called structural error-correction model (SECM). This recently proposed model class, essentially an extension of a cointegrated vector autoregressive system (VAR), allows to combine economic and statistical theory in a methodologically attractive fashion.

The present introduction delineates the economic considerations motivating an econometric interest in money demand in Europe. The statistical considerations motivating an interest in VAR's and SECM's are then expounded in chapter 2. The precise design of these models, and the present approach of isolating data-consistent economic relations, are detailed in chapter 3 and chapter 4. Possible links between the aggregated European money demand relation and its constituent national money demand relations are explored in chapter 5. Chapter 6 applies the preceding theoretical arguments to an empirical analysis of money demand in Europe. Chapter 7 finally concludes. The precise content of all chapters will be outlined in due course.

1.1 Motivation

In economic theory, the label 'money demand' denotes one side of a real balance mechanism which simultaneously equates money with its long-run demand, and nominal output with its potential supply. In its basic form, this mechanism regards money as a medium to transact nominal output and as an asset to substitute interest-bearing bonds. Splitting nominal output into a price component (price level p) and a quantity component (output y), and the interest rate into money's own return (short rate is) and a proper return on bonds (long rate il), this assertion is formalized as a mathematical relation[1]

$$m - m^* \overset{!}{=} 0 \quad , \qquad m^* \equiv f\,(\overset{+}{p}, \overset{+}{y}, \overset{-}{il}, \overset{+}{is}, \varepsilon) \quad , \tag{1.1}$$

where m denotes the actual quantity of money, m^* its long-run demand, and ε some stochastic shock. A disequilibrium $m > m^*$ in the money market now triggers portfolio shifts from money into bonds until the falling interest rate lifts output demand. Likewise, an opposite disequilibrium in the goods market induces price- or quantity adjustments until the increased transaction volume lifts money demand. Both effects collaborate to restore equilibrium. The precise design of this mechanism is however disputed, and so is the role of money therein. Loosely, there are two camps. A currency-school maintains the existence of an exogenous money stock which is controllable by the central bank via some time- and policy invariant money-supply function, and via money demand causal for fluctuations in nominal output. A banking-school in contrast maintains the existence of an endogenous money stock which via money demand merely reflects economic activity, and via financial innovation eludes unwanted policy control. This originally 19th-century currency/banking controversy continues in modern macroeconomics: Monetarism or New Classical Macroeconomics belong to the first camp, whereas for example Real Business Cycle Theory (King/Plosser 1984) or Inflation Targeting (Bank of England 1999) represent the second.[2]

In applied economics, central banks usually lean towards the currency camp, for good reason: if a money demand relation is indeed existent, and if the money stock is controllable by available policy instruments, then the quantity of money may serve as an *intermediate target* within a procedure of monetary targeting. In practice, this procedure involves two separate stages. At the beginning of a period, the central bank determines a reference value of the intermediate target (money) which according to some empirical money

[1] Above each argument is indicated the sign of the first derivative of $f(\cdot)$ with respect to that variable.

[2] The deliberately simplified characterization is of course not meant to imply that this controversy divides macroeconomic theory in but two irreconcilable camps. Other important disputes concern, in particular, the subdivision of movements in nominal output into price- and quantity effects.

demand relation seems ex-ante consistent with the desired value of the ultimate target (nominal output or price level). Over the period, the central bank then controls its proper policy instruments (short interest rate) according to some empirical money supply relation as if achieving the intermediate target were in itself the policy objective. Besides efforts to protect the money supply relation from erosion through financial innovation, central banks therefore devote considerable scientific and rhetoric attention to the empirical link between money and nominal output (cf Issing 1992, Bundesbank 1992, König 1996, Bundesbank 1997).

In addition, an empirically stable money demand relation renders the quantity of money also a useful *information variable* for policy reaction functions. For the currency camp, the actual quantity as compared to the target quantity constitutes a simple indicator for the current stance of monetary policy and for likely future movements of the ultimate target. For the banking camp, the actual quantity of money constitutes a timely indicator for yet unobservable movements in nominal output, given that monetary data are available sooner than national account data (cf Bank of England 1997).

After the break-down of Bretton-Woods, a policy of monetary targeting geared towards the ultimate target of price stability was adopted in several European countries (cf Bundesbank 1998). The implied conviction that national money causes national inflation can be characterized as *domestic monetarism* (McKinnon 1984, p.10). Monetary independence, however, is not necessarily a sensible paradigm in open economies. If money and bonds denominated in foreign currency become available to domestic agents, then domestic and foreign currency compete for the delivery of monetary services (transaction services, store-of-value services). Agents may then respond to a perceived shift in relative monetary services by reducing their demand for 'bad' money and increasing their demand for 'good' money, a process known as *currency substitution* (Giovannini/Turtelboom 1994). For example, a perceived devaluation of the domestic currency may trigger a flight from domestic into foreign money.[3] In this way national money demand relations

[3] This flight may occur as direct or as indirect currency substitution (McKinnon 1982, 1996). Direct substitution occurs if the ability of domestic money to provide monetary services is expected to decrease, so that agents simply switch from domestic into foreign money. Indirect substitution occurs if the ability of domestic bonds to provide monetary services is expected to decrease, so that domestic interest rates rise to compensate for the relative loss, and foreign interest rates fall to compensate for the relative gain. The rate changes trigger an intra-currency money-bond substitution: domestic money demand falls to buy domestic bonds, and foreign money demand rises to sell foreign bonds. The gaps are closed by bond arbitrageurs who sell domestic bonds, convert the proceeds from domestic into foreign currency, and then buy foreign bonds. Both cases lead to a decrease in domestic money holdings and a corresponding increase in foreign money holdings.

become interdependent, even if flexible exchange rates preserve national independence on the money supply side. Currency substitution therefore leads to international demand-swings which may render national money demand relations individually instable and thus unsuitable for national monetary targeting (McKinnon 1982, Giovannini 1990, Mizen/Pentecost 1996). Currency substitution also leads to exchange rate instability, in that shifts in relative monetary services produce larger exchange rate fluctuations with greater degrees of currency substitution (Girton/Roper 1981). Exchange-rate fluctuations in turn, if battled by asymmetric central-bank interventions, may induce an inflationary bias in flexible exchange-rate systems (Claassen 1977). These theoretical implications - inflation, exchange rate fluctuations, and instable national money demand relations - are prominent empirical characteristics of the post-Bretton-Woods era.

To stabilize prices and exchange rates within a group of countries plagued by currency substitution, two concepts for monetary policy coordination have been proposed which resort to targeting the group-wide money stock and may hence be described as *international monetarism.* In a concept formalized by Parkin (1977) and later verbosely advocated by McKinnon (1982, 1984), each country targets but the domestic component of its national money stock via its own national money demand relation, and lets the foreign component vary freely through unsterilized interventions stabilizing the exchange rate. Since these variations in national money stocks cancel out in the aggregate, the whole arrangement is equivalent to targeting the group-wide money stock via a group-wide money demand relation, stabilizing the average price level (cf Parkin 1977, Russo/Tullio 1988).[4] In a second concept, described by Brunner (1984), the participating countries unilaterally stabilize their exchange rate vis-a-vis some leading country, which in turn anchors the whole system by targeting its national money stock via its own national money demand relation. Since the money stock in each peripheral country is determined by the unsterilized interventions maintaining the peg, the whole arrangement is equivalent to targeting the group-wide money stock via the leading country's national money demand relation, and aligns the group-wide price level with that of the leading country (cf Bini-Smaghi/Vori 1991).

In the course of the 1980's and early 1990's, the European Monetary System (EMS), albeit originally designed in a symmetric spirit similar to the

[4] The precise argument involves, however, a number of subtleties. In the derivation of national targets, allowance must be made for a country's departure from the group's average productivity. Second, simple aggregation theory shows that the aggregate money stock is invariant to the distribution of base money only if money supply functions are equal across countries. Finally, dynamic sustainability of the system requires some agreement on the desired common price level. The lack of such a pre-agreed 'nominal anchor' constitutes a basic fault in the originally symmetric design of the EMS.

McKinnon concept, gradually developed the distinctive asymmetric features characterizing the Brunner concept (cf Giavazzi/Giovannini 1987). The alleged German 'hegemony' in the EMS was however criticized for a number of reasons, indeed, the Bundesbank's exclusive focus on its national monetary target was even blamed for having contributed to the 1992 EMS crisis (Portes 1993, Eichengreen 1997). In order to restore some symmetry to the EMS, and to reduce the dependency of the whole system on but German money demand, several proposals have been made which essentially revive the McKinnon concept (Russo/Tullio 1988, Läufer 1990 and 1992b, Sardelis 1993, Monticelli/Papi 1996). The precise arguments of these proposals depend on the chosen analytical framework, but their central message is the same. First, if an European money demand relation were existent and more stable than the German money demand relation, then a symmetric monetary policy coordination would be advantageous for all participating countries. Second, due to a certain portfolio gain possibly effective in the money demand shocks, it is not unreasonable to believe that the European relation is more stable than the German relation.[5]

The proposed European dimension of monetary policy coordination has become reality in the meantime, albeit in a radically different institutional framework: in January 1999 the majority of EMS countries ceded national monetary policy control to the newly founded European Central Bank (ECB). Firmly enshrined in the Bank's charter is the ultimate target of price stability. This relieves the participating countries from a basic problem of the McKinnon concept, namely to constantly and multilaterally negotiate a target value for the common price level. However, the exclusive responsibility of the ECB for achieving price stability intensifies another problem, namely to devise a coherent European monetary policy strategy. This but reinvigorates the interest in an aggregate European money demand relation. Indeed, the ECB (1999a, 1999b) itself seems, so far, undecided between two different policy strategies, namely one of intermediate monetary targeting and one of direct inflation targeting. Empirical evidence for or against European money demand may help to tip that balance.

Unfortunately, this empirical evidence crucially depends on the chosen methodological spectacles. And here the statistical considerations motivating this study enter the scene. To begin with, a clear distinction must be drawn between a theoretical and an empirical money demand relation (section 2.2). The theoretical relation denotes a set of freely chosen assertions describing the design of some controlled thought experiment. An example is (1.1). The

[5] Technically, this gain comprises a reduction in the principal variance of a macro function (cf chapter 5). Its precise conditions however depend on the chosen aggregation structure. The gain is demonstrated by Läufer (1992b) for a quasilinear and by Monticelli/Papi (1996) for a linear aggregation structure.

empirical relation, which is of interest for monetary policy, denotes a set of assertions describing the unknown mechanism governing the actual evolution of observed data series. Obviously the mere postulation of the former does not entail the validity of the latter. Instead 'the' econometric problem arises of "*bridging the gap between the isolated system projected by a theory and the actual DGP*[6] *giving rise to the observed data*" (Spanos 1986, p.664).

A straightforward method to bridge this gap would be to turn (1.1) into a static log-linear regression, estimate its parameters by OLS from some suitably chosen data set, and confirm this empirical relation's significance via some t-statistics or R^2-measures. A number of early studies on aggregate world money demand actually proceed in this fashion (Gray/Ward/Zis 1976, Frowen/Kouris 1977). However, under today's methodological spectacles this procedure can at best be regarded as naive, and at worst yields what is now known as a spurious regression. The reason is that the simple regression model does not really attempt to bridge the cited gap: no effort is made to account for the statistical properties of the observed data to ensure validity of the chosen inference procedure. And no effort is made to check the truly interesting properties of the estimated empirical relation, namely its time-invariance and the direction of causality. The recognition of such failures triggered an essentially data oriented 'revolution' in macroeconometrics, briefly sketched in section 2.3. The present state of this development marks the cointegrated vector-autoregressive model, which is outlined in chapter 3.

A failure to let 'the data speak' may thus lead to invalid inference about the mechanism governing economic reality. A telling example is the evaporation of Milton Friedman's alleged money demand evidence in the light of new econometric methodology (Hendry/Ericsson 1991). However, even under the favourable assumption that the employed model is statistically valid, the gap between theoretical and empirical money demand contains yet another problem: the variables in (1.1) could likewise be linked by a number of other equilibrium relations, e.g., money supply or output demand. In this case the observed data constitute but a solution of some underlying simultaneous system of structural relations. The problem of disentangling money demand from the reduced form of a whole system is known as the identification problem. Unfortunately, "*there is no obvious way to formulate models of equilibrium in financial markets in which the demand for money is identified*" (Cooley/LeRoy 1981, p.840). The present vector-autoregressive model, which returns a system of statistically determined 'equilibrium' relations, cannot escape this problem. This motivates its extension into a structural error-correction model, introduced in chapter 4. The incorporation of a-priori economic theory then allows an at least hypothetical isolation of money demand, and a plausible assessment of its stability.

[6] The abbreviation stands for Data Generation Process (see section 2.1.1 below).

1.2 Outline

Between the present introduction (chapter 1) and the summarizing conclusions (chapter 7) this study contains the following, relatively self-contained chapters.

Chapter 2 traces the recent methodological debate in econometrics and motivates the particular approach taken in this study. The starting point is the interpretation of any given sample as a realization from some unknown stochastic data generation process. An econometric model then performs a double task. First, it constitutes a probability model designed to account for salient statistical properties of the data (section 2.1). Second, it constitutes a testing ground designed to expose the data to the implications of some economic theory (section 2.2). Failing on the first task may render statistical inference invalid or spurious, whereas failing on the second task may render econometric modelling an unduly 'atheoretical' exercise. Various methodological camps can be distinguished by the importance attached to either task (section 2.3). The combined approach taken in this study involves a 'statistical' vector autoregressive probability model, which is subsequently developed into an 'economic' structural error correction model. Both models are detailed in the next two chapters.

Chapter 3 introduces the autoregressive probability model. In its scalar version, the model provides a framework for the discussion of 'integration' as a special form of nonstationarity arising from unit roots in the characteristic polynomial of an autoregressive sequence (section 3.1). Such unit roots induce peculiar asymptotic properties in estimators and statistics, a foretaste of which is given by the intricate menu of statistical tests checking for integration in a scalar autoregressive model. In the vector version of the model, the notions of 'cointegration' and 'error-correction' are introduced (section 3.2). These dual notions formalize the observable tendency of some individually nonstationary time series to trend together in the long-run, and arise from a certain combination of unit and stable roots in the polynomial matrix governing the underlying vector sequence. A comprehensive method to simultaneously determine the order of integration and the rank of cointegration in multivariate time series is the Johansen maximum-likelihood procedure. Owing to the many possible constellations of unit roots and their interactions with a deterministic regressor, this comprehensiveness involves, as its price, a certain complication of estimation methods and testing procedures. Moreover, the Johansen procedure operates within a 'closed' autoregressive system and thus avoids untested exogeneity assumptions. This fits nicely into the present methodological stance, but impedes an economic interpretation of the estimated equations. A solution is to split the system into interpretable submodels, which is done in the next chapter.

Chapter 4 starts with a split of the vector autoregressive model into a conditional and a marginal submodel. The conditional submodel allows an operational definition of 'stability' (section 4.1). Under stability, the dynamics in (hence) endogenous variables correct the equilibrium errors implied by static cointegration relations without contributing to these errors themselves. This suggests to reparameterize the conditional submodel into a system of 'economic' or 'structural' error-correction equations (SECM). In a first step, the systemwide cointegration relations are just-identified into structural equilibrium relations resembling some economic theory of interest. In a second step, the adjustment dynamics are just-identified such that each endogenous variable explicitly adjusts only to deviations from its own equilibrium value. The resulting adjustment coefficients provide a sensible measure for the stability of an economic relation. To assert its statistical validity, some crucial properties of the SECM are formulated as over-identifying restrictions (section 4.2). Specifically, the properties of constancy, weak exogeneity, and noncausality are formulated as likelihood ratio tests within the Johansen procedure. The hypothesis of instability is formulated as a Wald test on the SECM itself.

Chapter 5 explores the behaviour of static equilibrium relations under cross-sectional aggregation. Given a set of national relations holding between national variables (micro relations), it is asked to what extent a similar relation may hold between European variables (macro relation). The properties of the macro relation depend on the chosen aggregation rules. Conventional aggregation theory employs linear aggregation rules, e.g., simple summation. Under stationarity this setup yields tractable conditions for consistent aggregation into a 'perfect' macro relation (section 5.1.1). Unfortunately, it bears but little relevance to money demand where the interesting relations are log-linear and cointegrated. Therefore the analysis is extended in two directions. Under quasilinear aggregation rules, a distinct portfolio effect appears in the macro relation, but consistent aggregation is no longer possible (section 5.1.2). Under cointegration, the micro level passes this property to the macro level under conditions resembling those for consistent aggregation. A violation of these conditions biases the adjustment coefficient feeding an 'imperfect' static macro relation into a dynamic macro ECM (section 5.1.3). These theoretical results are illustrated by a simulation experiment (section 5.1.4). In its second part, the chapter explores the economic interpretation of macro variables. A result from index number theory shows that genuine European price- and quantity indices can be obtained by summing available national Paasche- and Laspeyre indices, and that rival indices do not exist (section 5.2.1). Both the national and the aggregate variables may, however, suffer from measurement errors induced by cross-border activities, and competing choices exist for the exchange rate converting national variables into a common denomination (section 5.2.2).

Chapter 6 finally applies the outlined methods to actual data series. In order to compare the two concepts of monetary policy cooperation described in section 1.1, namely a hegemonic EMS based on German money demand and a symmetric EMU based on European money demand, the empirical analysis includes one data set for Germany (section 6.1) and two data sets for Europe (section 6.2). In a first step, the respective bodies of empirical literature are reviewed, and some stylized facts of German and European money demand are replicated from the present data sets. Since the large majority of the literature employs but single-equation error-correction models, these replications provide an interesting reference to check the validity of earlier 'evidence' within the present framework of less restrictive multi-equation models. In a second step, the individual data series are modelled as scalar autoregressions to check for stochastic and deterministic trends. As a by-product, models for velocity in Germany and in Europe are obtained. In a third step, one vector autoregressive model (VAR) is formulated for each data set. Since these statistical models provide the basis for later structural analysis, considerable care is taken in the determination of a cointegration rank and a deterministic degree. In particular, vector I(1)-tests are conducted sequentially over all possible submodels and also recursively over time, the possible influence of dummies is evaluated, the constancy of the cointegration space is tested, and vector I(2)-tests are conducted to rule out higher order integration. As one result, the presence of 3 cointegration relations is established for the German as well as the European data set.

In a subsequent structural analysis, properties relating to the existence and stability of money demand are implemented into the statistical VAR models for Germany and Europe (section 6.3). To this end, the VAR's are systematically tested for exogeneity and causality restrictions. The resulting conditional models are subsequently identified into SECM's, which reformulate statistical cointegration relations as structural equilibrium relations (long-run identification), and then insert these static relations into separate dynamic adjustment equations (short-run identification). Such dynamic equations, describing the reaction of some conditioned variable to the deviations ('errors') from a single structural equilibrium relation, are finally used to compare the stability of empirical money demand in Germany and Europe.

The estimation and testing procedures described in chapters 3 and 4, and the simulations described in chapter 5, have all been programmed in the statistical software package RATS 4.20 (Doan 1995) as menu-driven subroutines which are available from the author upon request. The package PcFiml 9.00 (Doornik/Hendry 1997) has been used for several misspecification tests in chapter 6.

2 Econometric Modelling

In the previous introduction, the problem of econometric modelling was quoted as "*bridging the gap between the isolated system projected by a theory and the actual DGP giving rise to the observed data*" (Spanos 1986, p.664). In the present chapter this bridge is discussed using two pillars, namely the transition from sample to population (section 2.1) and the transition from population to structure (section 2.2).

2.1 Data Generation and Statistical Inference

Going beyond the mere description of empirical phenomena requires some theory about the actual mechanism governing the behaviour of observables under study. One approach is to suppose a chance mechanism and to invoke the theory of probability and statistical inference as a tool for deriving statements about observable economic variables. In order to analyze economic reality such a *probability approach*[7] would start from the untestable fundamental assumption that economic variables represent draws from a population obeying some (unknown) probability law, or realizations of random variables with some (unknown) joint distribution.[8]

To set this stage some concepts of probability theory are briefly reviewed: Let $\omega \in \Omega$ be states-of-the-world in some abstract space, and $\mathcal{F}$ the σ-field of event-subsets $E \subseteq \Omega$. The measurable event space $\{\Omega; \mathcal{F}\}$ represents the proper source of randomness. Probabilities are assigned to events via a measure $P : \mathcal{F} \mapsto [0, 1]$, the triple $\{\Omega; \mathcal{F}; P(\cdot)\}$ is called a *probability space*. The actual observation of randomness is in a measurable sample space $\{\Xi; \mathcal{B}\}$. Usually Ξ is a real product space $\mathbb{R}^{p\mathbb{T}} \equiv \times_{t \in \mathbb{T}} \mathbb{R}^p$ over a discrete index set $\mathbb{T}$, and $\mathcal{B}(\mathbb{R}^{p\mathbb{T}})$ a σ-field from Borel cylinders with finite-dimensional base.

[7] The approach was first comprehensively advocated in a monograph *The Probability Approach in Econometrics* by Haavelmo (1944), whom to 're-read' has become quite fashionable recently.

[8] Whether 'probability' actually exists and actually governs the variables is of no concern. Probability theory is primarily a mathematical tool. It can for example usefully be applied to analyze actually deterministic series, like 'random numbers' generated from a computer or 'white noise' generated from a logistic function.

Any $\mathcal{F}/\mathcal{B}(\mathbb{R}^p)$-measurable point function $x : \Omega \mapsto \mathbb{R}^p$ from an event space into a sample space is called a (vector) *random variable*. A jointly measurable family of such functions, $X(\omega) \equiv \{x(\omega, t)\,; t \in \mathbb{T}\}$, forms a composite $\mathcal{F}/\mathcal{B}(\mathbb{R}^{p\mathbb{T}})$-measurable point function $X : \Omega \times \mathbb{T} \mapsto \mathbb{R}^p$ or equivalently $X : \Omega \mapsto \mathbb{R}^{p\mathbb{T}}$. This family of indexed random variables is called a (vector) *stochastic process*. For each index $t \in \mathbb{T}$, the function $X(\omega, \cdot)$ constitutes a random variable $x_t : \Omega \mapsto \mathbb{R}^p$. For each elementary event $\omega \in \Omega$, the function $X(\cdot, t)$ constitutes a real function $X_\omega : \mathbb{T} \mapsto \mathbb{R}^p$ called a *realization* of the process. For a discrete index set the process is called a *random sequence* and its realization a *time series*, interpreting the indices as equidistant points in time. A stochastic process and its realization are both denoted by $\{x_t\,; t \in \mathbb{T}\}$, or shortly $\{x_t\}$, leaving the distinction to the context.

The probability law governing the behaviour of a random variable is formalized as a measure $G_p : \mathcal{B}(\mathbb{R}^p) \mapsto [0,1]$ on a finite-dimensional sample space. This *distribution* is derived from the original probability measure by setting $G_p(B) = P(E_x)$ over all Borel sets $B \in \mathcal{B}(\mathbb{R}^p)$ and their inverse image sets $E_x \equiv \{\omega : x(\omega) \in B\} \in \mathcal{F}$. Moreover, via the Radon-Nikodym Theorem there exists a point function $g_p : \mathbb{R}^p \mapsto [0, \infty]$ such that $G_p(B) = \int_{b \in B} g_p(b)\, d\nu$ over all Borel sets B and real vectors $b \in \mathbb{R}^p$ for a suitably chosen measure $\nu(\cdot)$, usually the Lebesgue-measure. This function is called the *density* of $x(\cdot)$ with respect to $\nu(\cdot)$. The density is measurable and integrates to one over $\mathbb{R}^p$. Since the point function $g_p(\cdot)$ embodies the same information as the set function $G_p(\cdot)$, the concepts of density and distribution equivalently characterize the behaviour of a random variable. The probability law of a stochastic process is similarly formalized as a measure $G : \mathcal{B}(\mathbb{R}^{p\mathbb{T}}) \mapsto [0,1]$ on an infinite-dimensional sample space. This measure can be constructed by extending a consistent family of distributions $G_p(\cdot)$ via Kolmogorov's Extension Theorem.[9]

2.1.1 Definition of Probability Models

Let v_i^* denote the vector of all variables appearing in a somehow defined 'economic reality' at some point $i \in \mathbb{R}$ in continuous time. The family $\{v_i^*\,; i \in \mathbb{R}\}$ then denotes the whole economic reality over time and space. This reality is filtered by a measurement system generating vectors of observations v_t at equidistant points $t \in \mathbb{Z}$ in discrete time. The family $V \equiv \{v_t\,; t \in \mathbb{Z}\}$ then

[9] Precisely, let $G_{pT} : \mathcal{B}(\mathbb{R}^{pT}) \mapsto [0,1]$ denote the distribution of some finite collection $\{x_t\,; t = 1, ..., T\}$ of p-dimensional random variables. Let such a distribution exist for each finite subset $(t_1, ..., t_T) \subset \mathbb{T}$ of indices, and let the collection of all such distributions satisfy two consistency conditions. The theorem then asserts the existence of a stochastic process $\{x_t\,; t \in \mathbb{T}\}$ with a unique distribution $G(\cdot)$ on $\{\mathbb{R}^{p\mathbb{T}}; \mathcal{B}(\mathbb{R}^{p\mathbb{T}})\}$, having for each $T < \infty$ the measure $G_{pT}(\cdot)$ as its restriction to $\{\mathbb{R}^{pT}; \mathcal{B}(\mathbb{R}^{pT})\}$ in that $G(C_B) = G_{pT}(B)$ for all Borel-cylinders $C_B \in \mathcal{B}(\mathbb{R}^{p\mathbb{T}})$ with Borel-sets $B \in \mathcal{B}(\mathbb{R}^{pT})$ as their finite-dimensional base.

denotes economic reality as an empirical phenomenon. The entire reality is of little interest. Only those aspects deemed relevant by some investigator for some given problem receive attention. Accordingly, the variable set v is partitioned into the relevant variables $x \in \mathbb{R}^p$, the data, and its complement w, the irrelevant variables. Likewise, the index set $\mathbb{Z}$ is partitioned into a presample period $(-\infty, ..., -1, 0)$, a relevant sample period $\mathcal{T} = (1, 2, ..., T)$, and a postsample period $(T+1, T+2, ..., +\infty)$. A set of variables over a certain time period is denoted by upper case letters with sub- and superscripts indicating bounds, so that $X_1^T \equiv \{x_1, ..., x_T\}$ denotes a sample.

The actually chosen sample is the basis of subsequent analysis. In his probability approach to econometrics, Haavelmo (1944, p.48,69) proposed as "*fundamental assumption about the nature of economic data*" that these pT observations $X_1^T \in \Xi = \mathbb{R}^{pT}$ be interpreted as realizations of random variables obeying some "*joint integral probability law*". Later authors therefore called the pT-dimensional distribution $H_T(X_1^T)$ defined on a sample space $\{\mathbb{R}^{pT}; \mathcal{B}(\mathbb{R}^{pT})\}$ the *Haavelmo distribution*[10]. The associated density $h_T(X_1^T)$ is called the *data density*, with respect to some suitably chosen measure $\nu(\cdot)$. Given the axiomatic existence of a Haavelmo distribution for every finite $\mathcal{T} \subset \mathbb{Z}$, and provided this family is consistent, then by Kolmogorov's Extension Theorem there exists on some probability space a random sequence $\{x_t\, ;\, t \in \mathbb{Z}\}$ with a unique probability distribution $H(\cdot)$, having $H_T(\cdot)$ as marginal distribution with respect to finite sample periods. This random sequence is called the *data generation process (DGP).*[11] Its infinite dimensional distribution $H(X)$ provides a complete description of the true stochastic relationships holding among the data, both contemporaneously within a vector x_t and serially over the set $\mathbb{Z}$.

In uncontrolled nonexperimental settings the DGP is unknown, and only one out of many possible realizations is actually observed. Inferring interesting aspects of an unknown population from a single sample thereof is the

---

[10] The terminology is not uniform. The present definition is used in Spanos (1989). Cook/Hendry (1994) define as Haavelmo distribution the unknown conditional parametric density $d_T(X_1^T \mid V^0; \delta)$. Clements/Mizon (1991) call a 'good' *model* of the data density the Haavelmo distribution, interestingly by reference to the (different) definition in Spanos (1989). Aldrich (1994) calls the *known* distribution implied for X_1^T by some economic theory a Haavelmo distribution.

[11] The terminology is not uniform. The present definition is used in Spanos (1986) and White (1994). Other definitions of a DGP include $\{v_t\, ;\, t \in \mathbb{Z}\}$ or $\{v_t \mid V^0\, ;\, t \in \mathcal{T}\}$. The latter is used in Hendry (1987) and Cook/Hendry (1994), despite its name it does not constitute a stochastic process. Strictly speaking, the DGP does not actually *generate* the data since 'probability' need not exist in reality. Rather, the DGP *imitates* the data generating reality. By definition the DGP is a perfect imitation. Models of the DGP in contrast constitute approximate imitations, unless correct specification occurs.

subject of statistical inference. Its main tool is the *probability model*[12], set up by specifying a family of distinct probability distributions on the respective sample space such that one of its members hopefully characterizes the unknown distribution from which the sample was drawn. A parametric probability model of the DGP accordingly specifies a certain family $\{F(X,\theta)\,;\ \theta\in\Theta\}$ of distributions on $\{\mathbb{R}^{p\mathbb{Z}};\mathcal{B}(\mathbb{R}^{p\mathbb{Z}})\}$ for some parameter space Θ. A parametric probability model of the Haavelmo distribution is obtained by restricting the measures $F(\cdot,\theta)$ to the sample space $\{\mathbb{R}^{pT};\mathcal{B}(\mathbb{R}^{pT})\}$, giving a family $\{F_T(X_1^T,\theta)\,;\ \theta\in\Theta\}$. If a σ-finite measure $\nu(\cdot)$ dominating the $F_T(\cdot,\theta)$ for all $\theta\in\Theta$ can be defined on the sample space, then there exists via the Radon-Nikodym theorem a corresponding family of densities. Consequently a parametric probability model of the data density comprises a family

$$\mathcal{P}_0 \equiv \{f_T(X_1^T,\theta)\,;\ \theta\in\Theta\} \tag{2.1}$$

of probability densities, each characterized by some vector θ of statistical parameters. Mathematically, this model is a point function $\mathcal{P}_0 : \Xi\times\Theta\mapsto[0,\infty]$. For each parameter $\theta\in\Theta$, the model $\mathcal{P}_0(X_1^T,\cdot)$ constitutes a parametric density $f_T:\Xi\mapsto[0,\infty]$ called *population.* For each sample $X_1^T\in\Xi$, the model $\mathcal{P}_0(\cdot,\theta)$ constitutes a real function $f_T:\Theta\mapsto[0,\infty]$ called *likelihood function.* The model assembles all densities which (according to an investigators opinion) could possibly describe the behaviour of the data over the sample period. For example, $\mathcal{P}_0$ could comprise all pT-dimensional Gaussian densities.

Let $\mathcal{P}$ denote the family of all conceivable probability densities defined on the sample space. The axiomatic existence of some data density translates into the trivial statement $h_T(\cdot)\in\mathcal{P}$. A statement $h_T(\cdot)\in\mathcal{P}_0\subset\mathcal{P}$, postulating the true probability law to be contained in some specified family, is called a *(statistical) hypothesis.* A parametric hypothesis is true if $h_T(\cdot)=f_T(\cdot,\theta^*)\in\mathcal{P}_0$ for some $\theta^*\in\Theta$. The particular vector θ^* is called the *true parameter* or the *population parameter*, the whole probability model is said to be *correctly specified.* If $h_T(\cdot)\neq f_T(\cdot,\theta)\in\mathcal{P}_0$ for all $\theta\in\Theta$ the probability model $\mathcal{P}_0$ is said to be *misspecified.* Since the data density is unknown one can only guess whether a model is misspecified. Formalized guesses are for example the misspecification tests conducted in chapter 6.

Statistical inference comprises estimation and testing. Any $\mathcal{B}$-measurable point function $S:\Xi\mapsto\Theta$ from the sample space into a (measurable) parameter space is called a *statistic.* Since the composite function $S\circ X:\Omega\mapsto\Theta$ is

---

[12] The terminology is not uniform. The term *statistical model* is used synonymously. White (1994) defines a probability model as a family of infinite dimensional distributions. Spanos (1986) defines a statistical model as a family of finite dimensional parametric densities plus a sampling model. Hendry/Richard (1982) define a statistical model as a family of finite dimensional parametric conditional densities.

$\mathcal{F}$-measurable, a statistic is again a random variable. A statistic arising as solution to some optimization problem related to a probability model is called an *estimator*. An important example is the maximum likelihood estimator $\hat{\theta} : \Xi \mapsto \Theta$, the solution to $max_{\theta \in \Theta}\ \mathcal{P}_0(X_1^T, \theta)$. A statistic discriminating between members of a probability model is called a (Neyman-Pearson) *test statistic*, denoted $\hat{\tau} : \Xi \mapsto (\Theta_0; \Theta_1)$ for complementary subsets in Θ. The stochastic properties of a statistic depend on the underlying DGP and on the specified probability model. This feature complicates, for example, the scalar and vector unit root tests presented in chapter 3.

The parameters $\theta \in \Theta$ appearing in (2.1) are *statistical parameters* whose purpose is to characterize the densities assembled in a probability model.[13] This characterization is not necessarily unique. A parameterization of a family of densities of same functional form is therefore called *sufficient* if $f_T(\cdot, \theta_1) \neq f_T(\cdot, \theta_2)$ implies $\theta_1 \neq \theta_2$, and *(statistically) identified* if in turn $\theta_1 \neq \theta_2$ implies $f_T(\cdot, \theta_1) \neq f_T(\cdot, \theta_2)$, for some sample $X_1^T \in \Xi$. A sufficient and identified parameterization ensures a unique correspondence between parameters and densities. Without identification, distinct parameters $\theta_1 \neq \theta_2$ could imply observationally equivalent populations $f_T(\cdot, \theta_1) = f_T(\cdot, \theta_2)$, and thus deprive the likelihood function of a unique maximum. For a probability model to be statistically identified it is usually sufficient that the information matrix of its likelihood function be of full rank, see e.g. Rothenberg (1971) or Spanos (1990). Sometimes, however, this condition fails, namely in models where the parameter θ is restricted to some subspace of Θ. In such cases additional a-priori restrictions on θ are necessary to achieve statistical identification (see Rothenberg 1971, Theorem 2). One example is the reduced rank regression model used in chapter 3: The parameter $\Pi_1 \in \mathbb{R}^{p \times p}$ appearing in (3.36) is restricted to a subspace of matrices satisfying the rank condition $\operatorname{rk} \Pi_1 \leq \widehat{r} < p$. Hence the orthogonality restrictions (3.41) are invoked to achieve statistical identification of $\widehat{\alpha}$ and $\widehat{\beta}$. The intrinsic arbitrariness of these restrictions complicates the identification of a long-run money demand function later on in chapter 4.

The probability model expresses an investigators opinion about the chance mechanism governing the behaviour of variables and statistics. It does so, however, in a somewhat obscure fashion: The conjectured design of the DGP is mainly hidden in the parameter vector θ controlling the moments of $f_T(X_1^T, \theta)$. In order to explicitly state the dependencies assumed by a probability model for some data, an equivalent concept called *statistical generating mechanism (SGM)* is introduced. The SGM is defined as an identical

[13] Apart from their genuine statistical purpose of characterizing densities, the parameters θ may also be fed into an inverse mapping $h^{-1}(\theta) = \sigma$ in order to generate structural parameters σ characterizing economic structures. This additional purpose is discussed in section 2.2.

decomposition of each random variable x_t into a systematic part $E_F[x_t \mid \mathcal{I}]$ plus an orthogonal innovation $e_t \equiv x_t - E_F[x_t \mid \mathcal{I}]$; see Spanos (1986).[14] The expectation is conditioned on a σ-field $\mathcal{I} \subset \mathcal{F}$ representing some available information, and taken with respect to the measure $F_T(\cdot, \theta)$. Thus a systematic part and its innovation are relative concepts, namely relative to a particular information set. The latter often comprises the history of x_t, namely $\mathcal{I}_{t-1} = \sigma(X_1^{t-1})$. In this case the analysis of an arbitrary sequence $\{x_t\}$ can be conveniently reduced, via the SGM, to that of a sequence of conditional expectations and that of a martingale difference sequence. An example for the construction of a SGM is given in the following section.

2.1.2 Interpretation of Probability Models

Given the interdependent and dynamic nature of economic data, the chances of some probability model to capture the data density seem but small. Indeed, the very existence of some correct specification and hence the very sense of probability models may be questioned: "*The 'correct' formulation of the [probability] model is not just highly uncertain, it may not even be a sensible concept*" (Hendry/Wallis 1984, p.4). One conclusion, adopted by many economists in the 1930's, is to altogether reject the use of statistical inference as a 'crime in economic research' on grounds that the properties of economic data cannot be properly captured in any tractable probability model.[15] In the present section this scepticism is cast into a formal framework, which leads to an interpretation of probability models as possibly invalid simplifications of the data density.

The chosen sample $\{x_t\,;\, t \in \mathcal{T}\}$ is a subset of the reality $V \equiv \{v_t\,;\, t \in \mathbb{Z}\}$, with respect to variables $x \subset v$ and to time $\mathcal{T} \subset \mathbb{Z}$. If the family V is given the axiomatic status of a stochastic process, and if in addition the behaviour of V is regular enough to sustain a description by some time-invariant entities (i.e., parameters), then the 'reality generating process' V constitutes a parametric joint density $d_V(V;\psi)$, of which $h_T(X_1^T)$ is a marginal density with respect to x and $\mathcal{T}$. The problem now is to statistically isolate the DGP within $d_V(V;\psi)$ such that inference can validly be based on $h_T(X_1^T)$, or its model-counterpart $f_T(X_1^T;\theta^*)$. To obtain appropriate conditions, the joint density $d_V(V;\psi)$ is identically factorized as:

[14] This definition isolates a systematic part only in the level of x_t. Of course it could be extended, letting also higher moments of x_t depend on the conditioning information. Examples are the ARCH-model conditioning the variance on $\mathcal{I}$, and the ARCD-model conditioning all moments on $\mathcal{I}$; see Hansen (1994).

[15] The famous question "*What is the use of testing, say, the significance of regression coefficients, when, maybe, the whole assumption of a linear regression equation is wrong?*" is cited (not posed, as many believe) by Haavelmo (1944, p.66,81) to illustrate this attitude. A historical account is given by Morgan (1987).

$$\begin{aligned} d_V(V;\psi) &= \prod_{t=-\infty}^{\infty} d_v\left(v_t \mid V^{t-1};\varphi\right) \\ &= \prod_{t=-\infty}^{\infty} d_{w|x}\left(w_t \mid x_t, V^{t-1};\varphi_c\right) \cdot d_x\left(x_t \mid V^{t-1};\varphi_m\right) . \end{aligned}$$

The first term sequentially factorizes $d_V(\cdot)$ into a product of independent conditional densities $d_v(\cdot)$ by conditioning every variable v_t on its entire history V^{t-1}, resembling the evolution of reality over time. The second term separates out the relevant variables x by contemporaneously factorizing each $d_v(\cdot)$ into a conditional density $d_{w|x}(\cdot)$ and a marginal density $d_x(\cdot)$. Note that neither factorization involves any restriction on variables or parameters.

An isolated DGP is now obtained from the marginal densities $d_x(\cdot\,;\varphi_m)$ by suitably restricting the interdependent and dynamic nature of the data. First, the parameter space Φ_m is required to not depend on the value taken by φ_c, so that φ_c and φ_m are *variation free* or in a sense *likelihood independent.*[16] Second, any dependence of present x_t on past W^{t-1} is eliminated by requiring Granger-noncausality of the irrelevant w-variables for the relevant x-variables, rendering the DGP a self-causal subprocess within reality.[17] Third, the dependence of present x_t on past X^{t-1} is reduced by requiring k-th order Markovness for the DGP.[18] This produces:

[16] Let $\theta_1 \in \Theta_1$ and $\theta_2 \in \Theta_2$. Let Θ denote the domain of variation possible for the combined vector $[\theta_1, \theta_2]$. If $\Theta = \Theta_1 \times \Theta_2$, then θ_1 and θ_2 are called *variation free.* Let $f(\cdot,\theta)$ be a likelihood function defined on Θ. If there exist likelihood functions $f_1(\cdot,\theta_1)$ and $f_2(\cdot,\theta_2)$ defined respectively on Θ_1 and Θ_2 such that $f(\cdot,\theta) = f_1(\cdot,\theta_1)\, f_2(\cdot,\theta_2)$ at every point in the sample space, then θ_1 and θ_2 are called *likelihood independent* (cf Barndorff-Nielsen 1978). To obtain the ML-estimator for θ_1 it then suffices to maximize $f_1(X_1^T,\theta_1)$ rather than $f(X_1^T,\theta)$. For example, the parameters of a conditional and marginal Gaussian density are variation free, whereas those of a conditional and marginal Student density are not variation free (cf Spanos 1986, p.471).

[17] Granger-noncausality can be defined with unbounded or with bounded memory: A variable w is said to be *noncausal* for variable x if $f(x_t \mid X^{t-1}, W^{t-1}\,;\theta) = f(x_t \mid X^{t-1}\,;\theta)$, and said to be *k-th order noncausal* for variable x if $f(x_t \mid X^{t-1}, W^{t-1}\,;\theta) = f(x_t \mid X^{t-1}, W_{t-k}^{t-1}\,;\theta)$. In the first case, present x do not depend on any past variables w, whereas in the second they depend on only the last k variables w.

[18] There is a trade-off between Markovness and noncausality: The (strong) restriction of noncausality with unbounded memory allows for the (weak) restriction of Markovness on only $\{x_t\,;\,t \in \mathbb{Z}\}$. Conversely, the (strong) restriction of Markovness on $\{v_t\,;\,t \in \mathbb{Z}\}$ allows for the (weak) restriction of only bounded noncausality. The noncausality-condition moreover ensures that the subprocess indeed inherits the Markov-property from the superprocess. The relationship between the two concepts is studied in detail by Florens/Mouchart/Rolin (1993).

$$d_x\left(x_t \mid V^{t-1}; \varphi_m\right) \overset{\text{GNC}}{=} d_x\left(x_t \mid X^{t-1}; \varphi_m\right)$$
$$\overset{\text{Markov}}{=} d_x\left(x_t \mid X_{t-k}^{t-1}; \varphi_m\right) \quad , \quad \varphi_m \in \Phi_m .$$

These three conditions restrict reality severely enough to isolate the marginal densities $d_x(\cdot\,; \varphi_m)$. The DGP described by these densities then constitutes a *complete true mechanism* for x in the spirit of Granger (1982). The Markov condition moreover ensures that this DGP can be reconstructed from its members over a finite sample window, provided of course $T > k$.

Statistical inference thus hinges on two strong (criminal?) priors: First, some discoverable regularity exists in the underlying reality. Second, this reality condescends to satisfy the conditions of likelihood independence, non-causality, and Markovness for the process generating the chosen data. Under these priors an isolated data density $h(X_1^T) = \Pi_{t=1}^T d_x(x_t \mid X_{t-k}^{t-1}; \varphi_m)$ exists, and renders a probability model sensible in that correct specification is possible. Otherwise a data density $h(X_1^T)$ also exists, but any probability model thereof is bound to suffer from parameter-nonconstancy or predictive failure.

A probability model attempts to model the unknown data density. Since any model hypothetically restricts the behaviour of its variables, one interpretation of a probability model is that of a *reduction* or *simplification* of the data density. Since the latter constitutes a perfect description, or summarization, of the stochastic properties shown by a chosen sample, another interpretation of a probability model is that of a *summary of sample information.* The two interpretations are of course intrinsically related: Invalid simplifications result in a loss of information. The extent of this information loss can be measured by the 'distance' between $h_T(X_1^T)$ and $f_T(X_1^T, \theta)$ as defined for example by the Kullback-Leibler information criterion. Indeed, an estimator $\hat{\theta} \in \Theta$ maximizing the likelihood function can be shown (White 1994) to also minimize this information criterion, i.e., to establish the closest possible correspondence between the actual properties of the sample and the properties implied for it by the specified probability model.

The interpretation as a summary of sample information emphasizes an inference aspect (Spanos 1989): The probability model constitutes a maintained hypothesis for estimation and subsequent specification testing, i.e., a basis for deriving statements about the behaviour of the empirical variables in a given sample. The quality of these statements obviously improves with the amount of sample information captured by the model. Conversely, inference based on an inadequate sample summary can be entirely futile. A famous example is the spurious regression model (cf Phillips 1986), where a probability model (i.e., the regression) is derived from static economic theory without reference to the dynamic properties shown by the data the model is supposed to explain. Other examples are discussed in Spanos (1990, 1995).

The interpretation as a reduction of the data density emphasizes a model-building aspect (Hendry 1987, Cook/Hendry 1994): A probability model $\mathcal{P}_0$ is arrived at by formulating certain simplifying assumptions about the data density. One set of assumptions, tacitly implied by the mere specification of $\mathcal{P}_0$, concerns the isolation of the DGP within the entire reality. Another set of assumptions, testable by misspecification tests, concerns memory, functional form, or time heterogeneity of the densities contained in $\mathcal{P}_0$. For example, assuming joint normality gives a probability model with members

$$f_T\left(X_1^T\,;\,\theta\right) \;=\; n_T\left(X_1^T\,;\,\theta\right) \;=\; n_i(X_1^k\,;\,\theta_i)\prod_{t=k+1}^{T} n_x\left(x_t|X_{t-k}^{t-1}\,;\,\theta_c\right). \quad (2.2)$$

This specification is well suited for modelling linear dynamic phenomena: the joint normal density $n_T(\cdot)$ can be sequentially factored into an initial normal density $n_i(\cdot)$ and a number of conditional normal densities $n_x(\cdot)$. For the latter, the assumption of joint-normality implies linear conditional expectations and nonrandom conditional variances. Defining the σ-field $\mathcal{I}_{t-1} = \sigma(X_{t-k}^{t-1})$ allows to express these conditional moments explicitly as

$$E_N[x_t|\mathcal{I}_{t-1}] \;=\; m_0 + \textstyle\sum_{i=1}^{k} A_i\, x_{t-i} \quad , \qquad V_N[x_t|\mathcal{I}_{t-1}] \;=\; E_N[e_t^2] \;=\; \Omega\,,$$

for some parameterization $[A_1, ..., A_k, m_0, \Omega] \equiv \theta_c \in \Theta$. In terms of the SGM concept introduced in section 2.1.1, the conditional expectation constitutes a systematic part and the conditional variance is that of an innovation. In this more accessible formulation the model now resembles the autoregressive probability model which is detailed in chapter 3 below. Note that expectation and variance are here taken with respect to the specified normal density rather than the true data density.

The innovations $e_t \equiv x_t - E_N[x_t\,|\,\sigma(X_{t-k}^{t-1})]$ returned by the above SGM are likewise defined but relative to an information set chosen by the investigator. This has serious implications for the interpretation of 'errors' in econometric models: arising from some potentially invalid reduction, they generally constitute "*a compound of many reduction losses and cannot sustain claims to be a 'demand shock' or a 'monetary innovation'* " (Hendry 1995, p.359). The only situation where the SGM-innovation coincides with a random shock from nature, i.e., with an innovation $u_t \equiv x_t - E_H[x_t\,|\,\sigma(V^{t-1})]$ relative to reality, is that of correct specification, that is, if all simplifying assumptions are valid. Otherwise the SGM-innovations also capture every information loss incurred over the various reduction steps. Different reductions may therefore result in different innovation sequences.

2.2 Statistical Inference and Economic Theory

The probability approach to econometric modelling, as outlined so far, relied exclusively on probability theory in order to analyze economic reality. This seems surprising given the large body of economic theory apparently developed for exactly the same purpose. The gap is closed now.

2.2.1 Definition of Economic Models

Economic theory usually explains reality in terms of certain *structural* relationships describing the postulated behaviour (e.g., decision taking, expectation formation, error correction) of economic agents (cf Hendry/Richard 1983). Precisely, allowing for interdependent behaviour, such structural relationships might form a system $g(x;\sigma)$ of simultaneous stochastic equations in some interesting observable variables $x \in \mathbb{R}^p$ governed by some vector $\sigma \in \Sigma$ of *structural parameters.* Such a system or *structure* is characterized by the alleged property that the parameters in any equation could actually change without any change taking place in any of the parameters of the other equations. The true structure of the underlying economy is of course unknown, though assumed to exist. In analogy to (2.1), an economic model for some given sample is therefore defined as a family of structures

$$\mathcal{E}_0 \equiv \{g(X_1^T,\sigma)\,;\; \sigma \in \Sigma\} \quad , \tag{2.3}$$

such that one of its members hopefully characterizes the unknown true structure. The relevance of an economic model hinges on the isolation of a true structure within economic reality, in analogy to the argument developed for the data density in the previous section. An economic model may comprise rival economic theories insofar these are nested in a common functional form. For example, an economic theory could be cast into the dynamic linear form

$$B_0\, x_t - \textstyle\sum_{i=1}^k B_i\, x_{t-i} \;=\; u_t \quad , \qquad u_t \sim i.i.n(0,S) \quad , \tag{2.4}$$

where B_0 is nonsingular. The parameter vector $\sigma_1 \equiv [B_0, ..., B_k, S]$ of course allows for judiciously placed zero- or unit elements in order to generate distinctive features of the respective theory, like homogeneity- or causality assertions. The system (2.4) can be transformed by premultiplying an arbitrary nonsingular $p \times p$ matrix T. This gives a new system

$$\mathrm{T}B_0\, x_t - \textstyle\sum_{i=1}^k \mathrm{T}B_i\, x_{t-i} \;=\; v_t \quad , \qquad v_t \sim i.i.n(0,TST') \quad , \tag{2.5}$$

which could express another economic theory. Provided T is not simply diagonal, the parameters of the new system are linear combinations of those in the old system. Therefore (2.5) is not truly structural if (2.4) is, and vice versa. An important transformation is T$= B_0^{-1}$, which yields the reduced form of the system.

An economic model also has stochastic implications. Over its reduced or final form, each structure $g(\cdot, \sigma)$ uniquely implies some probability density $f(\cdot, h(\sigma))$, whose statistical parameters are a function $\theta = h(\sigma)$ of the structural parameters. This association from structure to population establishes a useful though ambiguous role for economic theory in the formulation of probability models (cf Spanos 1990). Useful because probability theory offers but little guidance as to the selection of interesting variables or sample periods. Ambiguous because the converse association from population to structure is not unique: A given density $f(\cdot, \theta)$ can be implied by several underlying structures $g(\cdot, h^{-1}(\theta))$, or equivalently, a vector of statistical parameters θ can be given alternative economic interpretations $\sigma = h^{-1}(\theta)$. For example, the conditional densities in (2.2) could be implied by either (2.4) or (2.5), since both structures are linked by[19]

$$n_x(x_t \,|\, \mathcal{I}_{t-1}) \;=\;$$

$$n_v(v_t)\; |\det \mathrm{T}B_0| \;=\; n_u(\mathrm{T}^{-1}v_t)\; \left|\det \mathrm{T}^{-1}\right|\; |\det \mathrm{T}B_0| \;=\; n_u(u_t)\; |\det B_0|\;.$$

Thus, all systems obtained as linear transformations of (2.4), including the true structural form and the reduced form, are *observationally equivalent* in that they generate a same population of observable variables. Conversely, judging from a known population $f(\cdot, \theta)$ there exist infinitely many systems qualifying as candidates for the true structural form producing this density. This problem is known as *structural identification.*[20] It reappears in chapter 4 in the context of identifying a short-run money demand function. Here it suffices to call a structure *(just-)identified* if there is enough economic a-priori information concerning $h(\cdot)$ such that a vector of structural parameters can be uniquely determined from a given vector of statistical parameters via the inverse function $\sigma = h^{-1}(\theta)$.

[19] Let $x(\cdot)$ be a vector random variable with distribution $F_x(\cdot)$ and density $f_x(\cdot)$ w.r.t. the Lebesgue-measure, such that $F_x(B) = \int_{b \in B} f_x(b)\, db$ for Borel-sets $B \in \mathcal{B}$ and real vectors $b \in \mathbb{R}^p$. Transform $x(\cdot)$ into a new random variable $y(\cdot)$ through a bijective point function $H : \mathbb{R}^p \mapsto \mathbb{R}^p$. The inverse $H^{-1}(\cdot) \equiv G(\cdot)$ produces Borel-sets $A \equiv \{a : G(a) \in B\} \in \mathcal{B}$ for real vectors $a \in \mathbb{R}^p$. For the density of $y(\cdot)$ w.r.t the Lebesgue-measure then holds $f_y(a) = f_x(G(a))\; |\det G'(a)|$.

[20] A nice illustration is given, unwittingly, by Mercenier/Sekkat (1988) and Muscatelli (1988): In nearly identical notation both papers employ Nickell's (1985) procedure for minimizing an intertemporal quadratic loss function describing the adjustment from an actual to a target money stock. The first-order conditions produce a dynamic linear regression model for money explained by prices, output, and interest rates. This probability model is interpreted as a money supply reaction function of some central bank in the first paper, and as a buffer-stock money demand function of some representative agent in the second paper.

2.2.2 Theoretical and Empirical Models

In nonexperimental situations, the data generating reality might actually not behave as assumed by the statistical or economic theory employed to analyze it. Or plainly: Probability models might be misspecified. This often ignored triviality leads to the distinction of empirical models and theoretical models. Following Haavelmo (1944), Hendry/Richard (1982), and Spanos (1995), a decisive criterion for this distinction is knowledge of the experimental design generating the observed variables.

Theoretical models formalize isolated thought experiments, shielded from unspecified influences and controlled by ceteris paribus conditions. Indeed, theoretical models *are* the design of a known experiment. As free creations of the human mind they explore the implications of a freely chosen set of initial assumptions, and postulate relationships between theoretical variables under the constraint of logical consistency. In this sense economic models and probability models are both theoretical: The former study implications (e.g., the neutrality of money) of hypothetically known structures, while the latter study implications (e.g., the consistency of OLS) of hypothetically known DGP's. In this sense also Monte Carlo simulations (e.g., the effects of aggregation simulated in chapter 5) are theoretical.

Empirical models postulate relationships between data series generated by uncontrolled experiments of unknown design. Arising from the imposition of some probability model on a given sample, they explore the implications of an actually unknown DGP for some theoretical framework under the constraint of data consistency. They constitute a theory-induced reconstruction of whatever experiment generated the data, or alternatively the representation of some theoretical model under the actual DGP (Hendry/Richard 1982). In this sense econometric models are empirical: The density $f(X_1^T, \hat{\theta}) \in \mathcal{P}_0$ estimated over some sample, and the structural model identified from it, both postulate certain relationships among actual economic data series.

Empirical and theoretical models are linked by interpreting some probability model as correctly specified for a given sample. Under correct specification, the empirical variables of the sample coincide with theoretical variables of the probability model. Inferring the true statistical parameters from an observed sample is then a problem of statistical inference. Probability models and economic models are linked by interpreting some probability model as representing the reduced form of an economic model. The theoretical variables appearing in a probability model then coincide with the hypothetical observations generated by some model economy, i.e., the solution of some simultaneous equation system. Converting statistical into economic parameters then amounts to inferring the parameters of an equation system from its solution, which is a problem of structural identification.

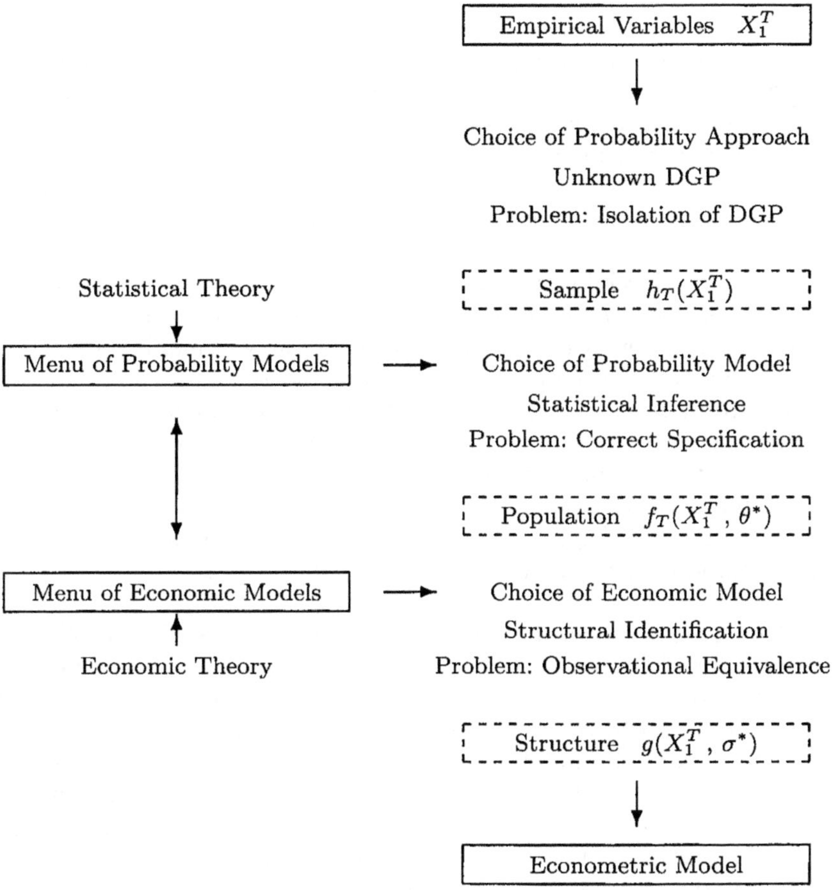

Table 2.1. Econometric Modelling

Summary: The process of econometric modelling outlined in the present chapter is summarized in table 2.1. The workflow highlights the interpretation of an econometric model as a theory-induced reconstruction of an unknown DGP. The relevant theory enters at two different stages: Statistical theory at the transition from sample to population, and economic theory at the transition from population to structure. In this study, the relevant statistical theory is contained in chapter 3, and the entrance of economic theory is discussed in chapter 4. Of course these two bodies of theory are strongly interrelated: The choice of a certain probability model restricts the class of admissible economic models, and vice versa. The next section examines several econometric methodologies in terms of table 2.1.

2.3 Econometric Methodologies

Several methodological approaches to (macro-)econometrics prevail in the literature. In idealized form they can be distinguished, in terms of table 2.1, by the emphasis put on either economic or statistical theory in the formulation of an econometric model. While far from being exhaustive, the following discussion details the statistical considerations alluded to in chapter 1 in order to motivate the present interest in VAR's and SECM's.

An approach relying primarily on economic theory is what Spanos (1989) calls the *textbook approach* to econometrics. In its pure form, this approach would proceed from some economic model of interest, manipulate this model by suitable transformations into an estimable reduced form, estimate the reduced-form parameters by OLS from some data set, and finally recover the original parameters by some clever identifying restrictions. One example for this approach are the static money demand regressions already mentioned in chapter 1. Other examples include dynamic rational-expectations models (e.g., Cuthbertson/Taylor 1992), or the large-scale macroeconometric models which still form a backbone of economic policy evaluation.

Consequently, under the textbook approach a probability model is derived as the estimable implication of some economic theory. This is a perfectly legitimate procedure as long as the resulting probability model, besides being theory-consistent by construction, is also data-consistent. The imminent danger of the textbook approach now is to solve also this problem by recourse to economic theory, that is, to assume it away. The widespread indulgence into this practice led Leamer (1978) to characterize the textbook approach as tacitly resting on the 'axiom of correct specification'. Under this axiom, statistical theory may proceed as if the data were experimental and concern itself with inference about the reduced-form coefficients. Econometric modelling then reduces to the identification of structural parameters.[21] The methodological problem is of course that this axiom immunizes economic theory from empirical criticism: Anomalous properties of the data are interpreted as a problem impeding estimation, not as problem invalidating the model.[22] Indeed, the obsession of most econometric textbooks with efficient and consistent estimation of axiomatically true models earned the approach its name.

[21] Lucas/Sargent (1981) for example, firmly rooted in the textbook approach, brandish the failure of certain identification schemes to properly account for expectations about future policy actions as 'the' failure of *Keynesian macroeconometrics* (sic!), and propagate New-Classical principles for structural identification as a solution.

[22] A meanwhile classic example is the inclination of many textbooks to interpret residual serial correlation not as a sign of general misspecification, but as a nuisance impeding efficient estimation of the true model.

The textbook approach has been dominant in applied research for quite a long time. Serious flaws became apparent in the 1970's and 1980's : A multitude of published regression equations, necessarily relying on roughly the same data but corroborating conflicting theories, unhappily co-existed. Moreover, empirically significant relationships were also obtained from 'nonsense regressions' relating economic variables to non-economic mock variables.[23] This predicament considerably increased susceptibility to the methodological aspects of econometrics in general, and to the shortcomings of the textbook approach in particular. Succinctly, "*simply writing down an economic theory, manipulating it to a [reduced] form and calibrating the resulting parameters using a pseudo-sophisticated estimator based on poor data which the model does not adequately describe constitutes a recipe for disaster ...*" (Hendry 1980, p.25). The recognition of these failures prompted an essentially data-oriented 'revolution' in macroeconometrics.

As a prime example of this data-orientation, a *time series approach* relying primarily on statistical theory attempts to model the typical intertemporal dependencies found in economic time series. Such dynamic models allow to study the behaviour of data-based functions, like estimators or forecasts, within a well defined stochastic environment. An important model class is that of integrated scalar autoregressive sequences, popularized by Box/Jenkins (1976), Fuller (1976), and Dickey/Fuller (1979, 1981). These models explicitly account for a trending behaviour combined with long-run unforecastability, and soon proved a good approximation of many macroeconomic variables (cf Nelson/Plosser 1982). A distinctive feature of such unit-root-models is the non-standard behaviour of otherwise familiar estimators and test-statistics, even in the limit (cf section 3.1).

This feature quickly exposed the inferential shortcomings of the textbook approach. Phillips (1986) showed the non-consistency of OLS in static regressions relating actually independent but integrated variables. These 'spurious regressions' offered an explanation for nonsense regressions and seriously undermined confidence about alleged empirical evidence. Confidence was soon restored when Engle/Granger (1987) showed even super-consistency of OLS in static regressions relating dependent integrated variables. These 'cointegrating regressions' formalize an interesting tendency of some macroeconomic variables, namely to trend together over the long-run, as a simple time-series property, namely that a linear combination of integrated variables be not integrated. Subsequent generalizations (cf Sims/Stock/Watson 1990, Phillips 1991, Johansen 1988, 1991, 1995a, Watson 1994, Haldrup 1998) virtually exploded into the model class of cointegrated vector autoregressive sequences (VAR's). Although inheriting the non-standard inference procedures associ-

[23] Hendry (1980) for example runs regressions 'confirming' the hypothesis that rainfall causes inflation.

ated with unit roots, the decisive advantage of this model class is that it utilizes actual statistical properties rather than economic presuppositions to discover long-run equilibrium relations (or other common features, for that matter) that possibly prevail between some given economic time series.

Thus, under the time series approach a probability model is derived from statistical theory, designed to detect interesting statistical properties of the data and to ensure appropriate inference methods. Letting 'the data speak for themselves' however implies cutting links to economic theory. An approach attempting to incorporate both the implications of economic theory and the statistical properties of the data is known as *general-to-specific approach.* Usually associated with the name of D.F. Hendry or the London School of Economics (cf Gilbert 1989), this approach was originally understood as an alternative modelling strategy to both the 'simple-to-general' textbook approach and the 'atheoretical' time series approach.

As a basic methodological tenet, Davidson/Hendry/Srba/Yeo (1978) argue that any economic model whose stochastic implications do not match the statistical properties of the observed data can not possibly claim to explain reality. As indicated by its label, the geenral-to-specific approach therefore starts from a multivariate dynamic model which is designed to nest rival economic theories *and* to capture time-series properties shown by the data. Given its statistical adequacy, this 'general unrestricted model' (GUM) then serves as a maintained hypothesis against which subsequent simplifications can be validly tested as parameter restrictions. In this way the underlying DGP is, in principle, free to produce either an univariate time series model or an 'economic' static regression model as the final result of these simplifications. Besides ensuring empirical acceptability, the 'neutral' baseline of the GUM therefore also allows to discriminate between rival models on a same data set. Succinctly, the message is to "*restrict the model but not the data*" (Davidson/Hendry/Srba/Yeo 1978, p.690).

This feature quickly exposed the modelling shortcomings of the textbook approach: The textbook approach uses econometrics to *illustrate* theories whose truth is believed independently. The general-to-specific approach instead allows to *discover* which views of the economy are tenable and to test rival views (cf Gilbert 1986). The virtues of this alternative modelling strategy are extolled in a series of papers from Hendry (1979) to Hendry/Doornik (1994). A sufficiently general GUM model class, capable of combining a flexible dynamic specification with static equilibrium relations suggested by economic theory, is the error-correction model (ECM) which duly became the workhorse of the general-to-specific approach.

Interestingly, this ECM model provides an albeit debated link to the textbook approach: In its basic form an ECM comprises static long-run equilibrium relations drawn from economic theory, and explains the observed dynamics in the data as adjustments caused by the deviations of actual from equilibrium values. Succinctly, current-period changes in the data are perceived as correcting some proportion of last period's equilibrium error. This 'feedback mechanism' underlies the general-to-specific approach. However, an ECM may also arise because economic agents forecast rather than react to movements in the targeted equilibrium values. This 'feedforward mechanism' underlies sophisticated versions of the textbook approach, which derive dynamic models from intertemporal optimization under rational expectations. The debate between the two approaches is yet unresolved (Hendry 1988, Cuthbertson/Taylor 1992), and serves as a useful reminder that a single empirical ECM can be given several observationally equivalent theoretical interpretations with possibly different policy implications (cf Alogoskoufis/Smith 1991).

Besides its link to the textbook approach, the ECM model also provides an extremely elegant link to the time-series approach: The famous Granger-representation-theorem (Engle/Granger 1987, Johansen 1991) states that any ECM of integrated variables can be represented as a cointegrated VAR, and that conversely any cointegrated VAR can be given an ECM representation. As a consequence of this theorem, the two previously distinct approaches quickly merged. The general VAR model hence allows to combine the interesting features of both while avoiding the respective flaws: On the one hand, it provides a statistically adequate framework to test for integration and cointegration in the data. These properties establish interesting long-run relations by a neutral statistical criterion. On the other hand, these equilibrium relations can be inserted into a multivariate ECM. This allows to reformulate the atheoretical property of cointegration in terms of adjustment towards economic equilibrium relations. Subsequent simplifications, in particular statistically acceptable exogeneity or causality restrictions, may then help to empirically discriminate between rival economic theories.

The initial enthusiasm about reparameterizing a cointegrated VAR into a multivariate ECM somewhat obscured the fact that neither model is uniquely identified. Precisely, while the cointegration relations lack statistical identification (as defined in section 2.1), the embedding ECM equations lack structural identification (as defined in section 2.2). This lack of identification holds even in conditional VAR models protected by valid exogeneity restrictions, and severely impedes the economic interpretation of estimated cointegration relations (cf Wickens 1996). The recognition of these 'atheoretical' remnants in the multivariate ECM now prompted the recent development of structural error-correction models (SECM's). Proceeding from a well defined probability model, namely a conditional VAR, this model class allows to combine the identification of cointegration relations (Johansen 1995b) with an identification of the individual ECM equations (Boswijk 1994). While acknowledging that alternative ways to construct 'structural' conditional models exist (cf Ericsson 1995), these SECM's certainly constitute promising methodological spectacles for interpreting empirical data in the light of both statistical and economic theory.

Summary: The workflow in table 2.1 highlights the interpretation of an empirical econometric model as a theory-induced reconstruction of some unknown DGP. The first piece of theory entering this reconstruction is statistical theory. Its task is to account for the observed time-series properties of the data. In the available menu of probability models, the VAR model described in chapter 3 below is general enough to account for important dynamic properties of macroeconomic data, and to cover a wide range of interesting submodels without recourse to untested economic presuppositions. The second piece of theory in the DGP reconstruction is economic theory. Its indispensability derives from the fact that any probability model constitutes, at best, but the reduced form of some unknown structural model. This identification problem likewise plagues the present VAR model, whose decisive cointegration parameters are neither statistically (p.15) nor structurally (p.21) identified without a-priori theory. To resolve this problem, suitable just- and overidentifying restrictions have to be chosen from a menu of economic models in order to convert a 'statistical' VAR into an 'economic' SECM. The associated statistical and structural identification procedures will be described in chapter 4 below. The underlying data are then, eventually, interpreted as being linked by a system of structural dynamic adjustment equations within a data- and theory consistent econometric model.

3 Autoregressive Probability Models

Proceeding from the interpretation of a given sample as a realization from some Haavelmo distribution, chapter 2 discussed the role of probability models as a basic tool for modelling this unknown distribution. To be empirically acceptable, such a probability model should summarize all relevant sample information, i.e., account for important statistical properties of the data. A class of models suitable for the dynamic trending properties typically found in macroeconomic data is that of autoregressive (AR) probability models. The present chapter discusses these models, basically linear stochastic difference equations. Section 3.1 deals with the scalar case, section 3.2 then generalizes to the vector case.

The material contained in the following sections is, of course, to some extent also considered in textbooks on time series analysis, e.g., Banerjee et al. (1993), Hamilton (1994), or Hatanaka (1996). Besides setting the stage for later chapters, the following exposition therefore emphasizes two aspects which are routinely neglected in textbooks. First, the autoregressive probability model is here understood as a unifying general model which generates different statistical properties as submodels via suitable parameter restrictions (general-to-specific approach). Second, the particular submodel representing best a given sample is not assumed known (unknown DGP). Both aspects together lead to a sequential model-reduction and model-testing procedure, working down from I(2)-models along precisely defined combinations of unit-roots and deterministic regressors. This procedure allows to adequately address topics such as stochastic I(2)-trends or deterministic cointegration in the empirical analysis of macroeconomic data, presented in chapter 6 below.

3.1 Scalar Sequences

The general scalar autoregressive model, denoted AR(k), is given by a stochastic sequence $\{x_t\,;\ x \in \mathbb{R}\,,\, t \in \mathbb{Z}\}$ satisfying the difference equation

$$x_t \;=\; a_1 x_{t-1} + \ldots + a_k x_{t-k} \;+ e_t + d_t \;\;, \tag{3.1}$$

where a_i are real parameters. The autoregressive sequence is driven by a stochastic sequence $\{e_t\,;\, t \in \mathbb{Z}\}$ of white noise errors $e_t \sim wn(0, \omega^2)$, and by a deterministic sequence $\{d_t\,;\, t \in \mathbb{Z}\}$ generated as a polynomial in time, as $d_t = m_0 + m_1 t$ for example. The AR(k) model is conveniently manipulated by defining and factoring its k-th order characteristic polynomial

$$a(z) \;\equiv\; 1 - \textstyle\sum_{i=1}^{k} a_i\, z^i \;=\; \prod_{i=1}^{k} (1 - l_i^{-1} z) \;, \qquad (3.2)$$

where $l_1, ..., l_k$ are the (possibly complex) roots of the polynomial.[24] These roots control the nature of temporal dependence within the autoregressive sequence. Roots outside the complex unit circle, $|l_i| > 1$, are called *stable.* Roots inside the unit circle, $|l_i| < 1$, are called *explosive.* Roots on the unit circle, $|l_i| = 1$, and notably *unit roots,* $l_i = 1$, will turn out to be of particular interest. Using the lag-operator L as argument the polynomial $a(z)$ becomes an AR-operator $a(L)$.[25] The model (3.1) is then compactly written as

$$a(L)\, x_t \;=\; e_t + d_t \;, \qquad e_t \sim wn(0, \omega^2) \;, \qquad \forall\; t \in \mathbb{Z} \;. \qquad (3.3)$$

This model is general enough to generate, as special cases, a fairly wide range of scalar sequences with distinct statistical properties. Several interesting submodels are discussed in the sequel.

3.1.1 Stationary AR Model

A stochastic sequence is called *strictly stationary* if the joint distribution of any subset of its members is invariant to shifts over time, and called *(weakly) stationary* if the first and second moments of the joint distribution of any subset of its members are finite and invariant to shifts over time. Stationarity implies identical marginal distributions and a time-invariant dependence structure. A weakly stationary sequence therefore consists of random variables with identical expectation and identical finite variance, whose autocovariances may vary with the distance τ between points in time, but not with time t itself. Consequently the realizations of a stationary sequence appear to be 'tied down' around its unconditional expectation. This property of *mean reversion* is likewise shown by forecasts of the sequence, which settle down to the unconditional expectation as the forecast horizon increases. Stationarity thus restricts the unconditional moments of a sequence, whereas its conditional moments may well depend on time - as for example in AR models.

[24] A point $l \in \mathbb{C}$ is called a *root* if $a(z) = 0$ for $z = l$, and called a *pole* if $a(z) \to \infty$ for $z \to l$. Any polynomial $a(z) = a_0 - a_1 z - ... - a_k z^k$ can be identically factored using its k roots l_i. For $a_0 \neq 0$ the factorization is $a(z) = (-a_k)\,(z - l_1) \dots (z - l_k)$ or equivalently $a(z) = a_0(1 - l_1^{-1} z) \dots (1 - l_k^{-1} z)$, using $(-1)^k a_0 / (-a_k) = l_1 l_2 ... l_k$.

[25] The lag-operator is defined by $L^\tau x_t = x_{t-\tau}$, $\tau \in \mathbb{Z}$. The difference operator Δ is defined by $\Delta = (1 - L)$. Note that $\Delta^2\, x_t = (1 - L)^2\, x_t \;=\; x_t - 2x_{t-1} + x_{t-2}$, whereas $\Delta_2\, x_t = (1 - L^2)\, x_t \;=\; x_t - x_{t-2}$.

A sequence of white noise errors is a simple example of a weak stationarity. Another example is a sequence whose members are generated as an infinite weighted sum of white noise errors,

$$x_t \; = \; \sum_{s=0}^{\infty} c_s \, e_{t-s} \; . \tag{3.4}$$

The equality sign here denotes convergence of the partial sum sequence $x_{nt} \equiv \Sigma_{s=0}^{n} c_s e_{t-s}$ to a limiting random variable x_t. If the parameter sequence $\{c_s\}$ is square summable such a limit is in fact existent and, hence, the sequence $\{x_t \, ; \, t \in \mathbb{Z}\}$ weakly stationary.[26] Indeed, choosing $\{e_t \, ; \, t \in \mathbb{Z}\}$ to be a 'fundamental white noise' of linear prediction errors, any weakly stationary sequence can be given such a representation (Wold's theorem[27]). A stochastic sequence whose members are generated according to (3.4) is called a *linear process* if its parameters are square summable and also satisfy $0 < |c(1)| < \infty$ (Phillips/Solo 1992). The additional condition precludes roots and poles at unity, so that a linear process is neither overdifferenced nor underdifferenced.[28] The linear process is a useful benchmark for stationarity.

Sequences of the form (3.4) are conveniently manipulated by defining and expanding the scalar power series[29]

$$c(z) \; \equiv \; \sum_{s=0}^{\infty} c_s \, z^s \; = \; c(1) \; + \; (1-z) \, c^*(z) \quad , \tag{3.5}$$

where $c^*(z) = \Sigma_{j=0}^{\infty} c_j^* z^j$ with parameters $c_j^* \equiv -\Sigma_{s=j+1}^{\infty} c_s$ (see appendix A.1). Evaluation at $z = 1$ gives $c(1) = \Sigma_{s=0}^{\infty} c_s$ and $c^*(1) = -\Sigma_{s=1}^{\infty} s \, c_s$, which is the first derivative of $c(z)$ at this point. The expansion (3.5) will be useful below for isolating stationary components in integrated sequences.

---

26 Let $u_s \in L_2$ be zero mean square-integrable random variables satisfying $\Sigma_{s=1}^{\infty} E[u_s^2] < \infty$. Define the partial sum sequence $x_n \equiv \Sigma_{s=1}^{n} u_s$. If the u_s are pairwise uncorrelated this partial sum sequence is Cauchy in the L_2-norm. Since L_2 is a Banach space there exists a random variable $x \in L_2$ such that $x_n \to x$ in quadratic mean. If the u_s are pairwise independent then $x_n \to x$ in quadratic mean and also almost surely; see Lukacs (1975, p.84). Here set $u_s = c_s e_{t-s}$, so that $\Sigma_{s=1}^{\infty} E[u_s^2] = \omega^2 \, \Sigma_{s=1}^{\infty} c_s^2$ which is finite under square summability.

27 Precisely, this theorem states that (i) every weakly stationary stochastic process can be *decomposed* into two mutually orthogonal components, one stochastic and one deterministic, and (ii) the stochastic component can be *represented* as an backward infinite moving average of linear prediction errors. The theorem also holds for the vector case; see Hannan (1970, p.137,158).

28 Roots at unity imply factors (1-z) in $c(z)$ so that $c(1) = 0$ (overdifferencing). Poles at unity imply factors $(1\text{-}z)^{-1}$ in $c(z)$ so that $c(1) = \infty$ (underdifferencing).

29 The function $c(z) : \mathbb{C} \mapsto \mathbb{R}$, given by the power series expansion (3.5), is also called a *transfer function.* It allows to calculate the *autocovariance-generating function* as $s(z) = c(z) \, c(z^{-1}) \, \omega^2$. Setting $z = e^{-i\varphi}$ this produces a function $s(\varphi)$ of angular freqencies $-\pi \leq \varphi \leq \pi$ called the *spectrum* of the sequence. Restricting $c(z)$ at $z = 1$ thus amounts to restricting the spectrum at zero frequency, i.e. at trend behaviour. Since $|e^{-i\varphi}| = 1$ the periodic behaviour of the sequence is determined by its other roots on the unit circle.

Stationarity restrictions for the present general AR(k) model are derived by inverting the polynomial (3.2). An inverse $c(z)$ is obtained by multiplying out the defining relation $c(z)\,a(z) = 1 \;\forall\; z$, and collecting terms of equal power in z. Representing the inverse by a power series (3.5) this gives parameters c_s evolving according to a homogenous difference equation

$$c_0 = 1 \quad , \quad c_s = \sum_{i=1}^{\min(s,k)} a_i\, c_{s-i} \quad , \quad s = 1, 2, ..., \infty\,. \tag{3.6}$$

If this equation is stable, if $a(z) \neq 0$ for $|z| \leq 1$, then the parameters c_s decay to zero exponentially. The sequence $\{c_s\}$ is then l-summable, and the inverse $c(z)$ well defined in that it satisfies the conditions for a linear process.[30] Premultiplying this inverse in (3.3) allows to write the autoregressive sequence as an infinite convergently-weighted sum of the driving sequences:

$$x_t \;=\; \sum_{i=1}^{k} a_i\, x_{t-i} + e_t + d_t \;=\; \sum_{s=0}^{\infty} c_s\,(e_{t-s} + d_{t-s})\;. \tag{3.7}$$

This causal *moving-average representation*, denoted MA(∞), allows to split the sequence into a stochastic component $\{c(L)e_t\,;\, t \in \mathbb{Z}\}$, which is a linear process, and a deterministic component $\{c(L)d_t\,;\, t \in \mathbb{Z}\}$. Moreover, while its conditional moments are easily derived from the AR(k) representation, the MA(∞) representation quickly gives the unconditional moments

$$E[x_t] \;=\; \sum_{s=0}^{\infty} c_s\, d_{t-s} \quad , \quad Cov[x_t, x_{t-\tau}] \;=\; \omega^2 \sum_{s=0}^{\infty} c_{\tau+s} c_s\;. \tag{3.8}$$

The variance ($\tau = 0$) is obviously constant, and the autocovariance ($\tau \neq 0$) varies only with the distance τ between points in time. The expectation is constant for $d_t = m_0$, namely $E[x_t] = c(1)m_0$. Therefore a scalar autoregressive sequence is weakly stationary with a causal moving-average representation (3.7) if its lag-operator polynomial $a(L)$ has only stable roots (ruling out stochastic trends and cycles), and the driving deterministic sequence is time-invariant (ruling out deterministic trends and cycles). The absence of explosive roots merely ensures a *causal* moving-average representation.[31]

[30] Since $a(z)\,c(z) = 1$, roots in $a(z)$ correspond to poles in $c(z)$ and conversely. The restriction $a(z) \neq 0$ for $|z| \leq 1$ (all roots outside unit circle) thus corresponds to $c(z) < \infty$ for $|z| \leq 1$ (all poles outside unit circle). The sequence $\{c_s\}$ is then l-summable, i.e., satisfies $\Sigma_{s=0}^{\infty} s^l\,|c_s| < \infty$ for all finite $l \geq 0$ (cf Brillinger 1975, p.77). For $l = 0$ this amounts to absolute summability, which is a decisive condition for a linear process.

[31] The inverse could be represented by a Laurent series rather than a power series. In this case the defining relation $a(z)\,c(z) = 1$ gives parameters evolving as $c_0 = 1$ and $c_s = \Sigma_{i=1}^{k} a_i\, c_{s-i}$ for $s \in \{-\infty, ..., -1, 1, ..., \infty\}$. If all roots of the polynomial $a(z)$ are inside and outside the unit circle, $a(z) \neq 0$ for $|z| = 1$, then an inverse is well defined in that both parts of the Laurent series converge. Basically, all stable roots of $a(z)$ are solved 'backwards' into $\Sigma_{s=0}^{\infty} c_j z^j$, and all explosive roots are solved 'forwards' into $\Sigma_{s=1}^{\infty} c_{-j} z^{-j}$. Thus the restriction of only stable roots in $a(z)$ is not necessary for the existence of an inverse.

3.1.2 Nonstationary AR Model

A stochastic sequence is called *nonstationary* if the joint distribution of any subset of its members is somehow dependent on time. Nonstationarity can arise for many reasons. Examples include stochastic trends in expectation (integrated AR) or in variance (integrated ARCH), deterministic trends in expectation, deterministic or stochastic cycles in expectation (seasonality), or singular changes (breaks). An important source of nonstationarity in autoregressive models are roots of the polynomial $a(z)$ lying on the complex unit circle ($|l_i| = 1$). *Seasonal roots*, unequal to 1 and evenly spaced on the unit circle, produce stochastic cycles. *Unit roots*, equal to 1, produce stochastic trends. The nonstationarities of interest here are stochastic and deterministic trends in expectation. This is expressed in the following assumption:

Assumption 1 *The polynomial (3.2) has $d \geq 0$ roots equal to 1 (unit roots) and all remaining roots outside the complex unit circle (stable roots).*

An otherwise stable AR(k)-operator containing one or more unit roots can not be inverted anymore. However, using (3.2), it can be factored as

$$a(L) \quad = \quad (1-L)^d \, (1 - g_1 L - \ldots - g_q L^q) \quad , \tag{3.9}$$

where $d + q = k$ and the AR(q)-operator $g(L)$ is stable with inverse $c(L)$. Premultiplying this inverse in (3.3) shows that now the sequence of d-th differences can be given a causal MA(∞)-representation

$$\Delta^d x_t \quad = \quad \textstyle\sum_{i=1}^q g_i \, \Delta^d x_{t-i} + e_t + d_t \quad = \quad \textstyle\sum_{s=0}^{\infty} c_s \, (e_{t-s} + d_{t-s}) \ . \tag{3.10}$$

The stochastic component of this sequence is a linear process. The stochastic component of the (d-1)-th differences is underdifferenced and hence not stationary, whereas that of the (d+1)-th differences is overdifferenced and hence not a linear process. Setting $d = 0$ reproduces the sequence in levels (3.7) as a special case. This motivates the following general definition: a scalar autoregressive sequence is called *integrated of order* $d \geq 0$, denoted $x_t \sim I(d)$, if it satisfies assumption 1, or equivalently if the stochastic component of its d-th differences is a linear process.[32]

The autoregressive representation (3.1) can be rewritten such that unit roots appear explicitly as testable parameter restrictions. To this end the general model is identically reparameterized as (see appendix A.1):

---

[32] More generally, a sequence $\{x_t \, ; \, t \in \mathbb{Z}\}$ can be defined as integrated of order d if it satisfies $(1-L)^d x_t = u_t$, where $\{u_t \, ; \, t \in \mathbb{Z}\}$ is a zero mean innovation sequence showing, to some extent, temporal dependence and heterogeneous distribution. This general specification is considered in Phillips (1987) or Perron (1988). An ARMA specification for u_t corresponds to the original definition of Box/Jenkins (1976), an AR specification $g(L)u_t = e_t + d_t$ gives the present framework.

$$\Delta^d x_t = \sum_{j=1}^{d} \pi_j \, \Delta^{j-1} x_{t-1} + \sum_{i=1}^{q} g_i \, \Delta^d x_{t-i} + e_t + d_t \ . \tag{3.11}$$

The unit root restriction $l_1 = ... = l_d = 1$ on the original model (3.1) is now equivalent to the parameter restriction $\pi_1 = ... = \pi_d = 0$ on the transformed model (3.11). Under this restriction, all regressors x_{t-i} in the original model are integrated with the same order I(d), while in the transformed model the regressors $\Delta^{j-1} x_{t-1}$ are integrated with different orders from I(d) down to I(1) and the remaining regressors $\Delta^d x_{t-i}$ are I(0).

A sequence with a stochastic I(1)-trend in expectation is produced from the general AR(k) model by restricting $a(L)$ to contain a single unit root and specifying $d_t = 0$. The sequence then has a MA(∞)-representation (3.10) with $d = 1$ and $c(L) = g(L)^{-1}$. Using expansion (3.5) its levels therefore evolve as[33]

$$x_t = \tilde{x}_0 + c(1) \sum_{j=1}^{t} e_j + c^*(L) \, e_t \ , \tag{3.12}$$

where $\tilde{x}_0 \equiv x_0 - c^*(L) \, e_0$. In such *difference-stationary* models the levels x_t form a linear process $c^*(L) \, e_t$ around a stochastic trend $\tilde{x}_t = \tilde{x}_{t-1} + c(1) e_t$. The latter comprises the optimal long-run forecasts $\tilde{x}_t = E[x_\infty \,|\, x_t]$ possible at any given point in time. The representation (3.12) explicates the famous decomposition of Beveridge/Nelson (1981) in that any single shock e_{t-j} splits into a permanent and a transitory effect. The permanent effect $c(1) e_{t-j}$ stays always the same, whereas the transitory effect $c_j^* \, e_{t-j}$ is gradually 'forgotten' as the weights c_j^* decrease with time. The stochastic trend now accumulates ('integrates') the permanent effects, which renders an integrated sequence unforecastable over the long-run. This is a natural property of many macroeconomic time series.

A sequence with a linear deterministic trend in expectation is produced from the general AR(k) model by restricting $a(L)$ to be stable and specifying $d_t = m_0 + m_1 \, t$. The sequence then has a MA(∞)-representation (3.10) with $d = 0$ and $c(L) = a(L)^{-1}$. Using expansion (3.5) its levels evolve as

$$x_t = \mu_0 + \mu_1 t + c(L) \, e_t \ , \tag{3.13}$$

where $\mu_0 \equiv m_0 c(1) + m_1 c^*(1)$ and $\mu_1 \equiv m_1 c(1)$. In such *trend-stationary* models the levels x_t consist of a linear process $c(L) e_t$ around a deterministic linear trend $E[x_t] = \mu_0 + \mu_1 \, t$. Any shock in the stochastic component therefore has only transitory effects. This renders the sequence I(0), and generates a tendency for the levels x_t to revert to their unconditional expectation $E[x_t]$ which hence constitutes a perfect forecast. This long-run forecastability is a fundamental difference to integrated sequences. Note that the differences Δx_t are here likewise stationary, but not a linear process.

[33] Note that $x_t = x_0 + \Sigma_{j=1}^{t} \Delta x_j$. Replacing Δx_j by its moving average representation (3.10) with $d = 1$ and applying the expansion (3.5) gives $x_t = x_0 + c(1) \, \Sigma_{j=1}^{t} e_j + c^*(L) \, (\Sigma_{j=1}^{t} e_j - \Sigma_{j=0}^{t-1} e_j)$; rearrangement gives (3.12).

Both sources of nonstationarity can be combined, so that x_t is driven by a deterministic and a stochastic trend: under one unit root in $a(L)$ and with intercept $d_t = m_0$ the levels evolve as

$$x_t \;=\; \tilde{x}_0 \;+\; c(1)\sum_{j=1}^{t} e_j \;+\; c(1)\, m_0\, t \;+\; c^*(L)\, e_t \quad , \tag{3.14}$$

where now $c(L) = g(L)^{-1}$. The simplest version of (3.14) is a random walk with drift. The representation shows that unit roots generally integrate both the stochastic and the deterministic sequence. Thus the above definition of integration covers both *stochastic integration* and *deterministic integration* as special cases.

3.1.3 Estimation and Testing

The general AR(k) model contains submodels characterized by different types of nonstationarity. Estimation within these submodels, and tests to discriminate between them, are discussed in this section. Regressions over the original model (3.1) face the problem that each regressor contains all different types of nonstationarity prevailing in the model. This problem can be circumvented by linearly transforming the original regressors into asymptotically uncorrelated 'canonical regressors' which isolate terms of different order in probability. The asymptotic properties of OLS-estimators in the transformed model indirectly determine those in the original model. This approach is used in Kawashima (1980) for scalar and in Sims/Stock/Watson (1990) for vector autoregressive sequences. Here the transformed model for (3.1) is (3.11), isolating terms of different order of integration. Define their respective regressor-sets as

$$\begin{aligned} x_{or} &\equiv [x_{t-1}, \ldots, x_{t-k}] \quad , \\ x_{tr} &\equiv [\Delta^0 x_{t-1}, \ldots, \Delta^{d-1} x_{t-1}\, ;\, \Delta^d x_{t-1}, \ldots, \Delta^d x_{t-q}] \quad . \end{aligned}$$

Estimation: The property of consistency does not pose much of a problem: Lai/Wei (1983) show that, in a regression of x_t on $[x_{or}]$, the deviations $[\hat{a}_i - a_i]$ between OLS-estimators and corresponding DGP-parameters converge to zero almost surely (strong consistency) for any sequence $\{x_t\}$ generated by (3.1) with $d_t = 0$, irrespective of the location of the roots of the polynomial $a(z)$. Unfortunately this generality does not pertain to the rates of convergence and the limiting distributions of estimators and test statistics, as detailed in the sequel.

The stationary submodel requires k stable roots and $d_t = m_0$, alternatively $d_t = m_0 + m_1 t$ for the trend-stationary submodel. Let $\{x_t\}$ be generated by a stationary model. The properties of OLS-estimators obtained from regressing x_t on $[x_{or}, 1]$ are derived in Mann/Wald (1943): The deviations $[\hat{a}_i - a_i\, ;\, \hat{m}_0 - m_0]$ converge to a zero mean normal distribution if scaled by

$\sqrt{T}$, and the usual t-statistic converges to a zero mean unit variance normal distribution. However, pending on the magnitude of the roots and thus the amount of temporal dependence within the sequence, the estimators may nevertheless show substantial finite sample bias (Nankervis/Savin 1987).

The simply integrated submodel requires $d \geq 1$ unit roots, $q \geq 0$ stable roots, and $d_t = 0$. Let $\{x_t\}$ be generated by a simply integrated model. The properties of OLS estimators obtained from regressing x_t on $[x_{tr}]$ are derived in Chan/Wei (1988): For the integrated regressors $\Delta^{j-1}x_{t-1} \sim I(d\text{-}j{+}1)$ the deviations $c(1)\,[\hat{\pi}_j - 0]$ converge to certain non-standard distributions[34] if scaled by T^{d-j+1}. Thanks to this *superconsistency* the deviations $[\hat{g}_i - g_i]$ can be treated as if the π_j were known to equal zero, that is, as if estimation took place in the stationary world of d-th differences. Accordingly, for the stationary regressors $\Delta^d x_{t-i}$ the deviations $[\hat{g}_i - g_i]$ converge to a zero mean normal distribution if scaled by $\sqrt{T}$. As special cases, Fuller (1976) covers $d = 1$, $q \geq 0$, and Hasza/Fuller (1979) cover $d = 2$, $q \geq 0$. The properties of OLS estimators obtained from regressing x_t on $[x_{or}]$ are derived in Kawashima (1980) and Choi (1993): Under $d \geq 1$ unit roots and $q \geq 1$ stable roots the deviations $[\hat{a}_i - a_i]$ converge to a zero mean normal distribution if scaled by $\sqrt{T}$. Moreover, the usual t-statistic converges to a zero mean unit variance normal distribution.

The integrated submodel around a deterministic trend requires $d \geq 1$ unit roots, $q \geq 0$ stable roots, and $d_t = m_0$. The intercept induces a drift $E[\Delta^d x_t] = c(1)m_0$ in the d-th differences, and thus a d-th order deterministic trend in the levels. Let $\{x_t\}$ be generated by an integrated trend model. The properties of OLS estimators obtained from regressing x_t on $[x_{tr}, 1]$ are derived in Chan (1989): For the constant and the I(0) regressors the deviations $[\hat{g}_i - g_i\,;\, \hat{m}_0 - m_0]$ converge to a zero mean normal distribution if scaled by $\sqrt{T}$. For the integrated regressors $\Delta^{j-1}x_{t-1} \sim I(d\text{-}j{+}1)$ the deviations $c(1)\,[\hat{\pi}_j - 0]$ converge to a zero mean normal distribution if scaled by $T^{d-j+3/2}$. The presence of an intercept in the model thus 're-normalizes' the limiting distribution and increases the rates of convergence for the coefficients on the integrated regressors. Fuller/Hasza/Goebel (1981) and West (1988) cover the special case $d = 1$, $q \geq 0$.

Testing an I(1) Null: Several testing procedures exist to check for unit roots in a realization of a scalar autoregressive sequence. The *augmented Dickey-Fuller (ADF)* strand of these procedures is discussed here. The ADF-tests are based on the transformed model (3.11) which isolates unit roots as testable

[34] Several possibilities exist to express these non-standard limiting distributions. Fuller (1976) or Dickey/Fuller (1979, 1981) used a ratio of two quadratic forms. Phillips (1986, 1987) introduced the meanwhile usual expression in terms of (functionals of) stochastic integrals involving standard Wiener processes.

parameter restrictions. If at most one unit root is suspected, the maintained hypothesis is (3.11) with $d = 1$ and $d_t = m_0 + m_1 t$. Therein, the null of first-order-integration ($\pi_1 = 0$) is tested against the alternative of non-integration ($\pi_1 < 0$). This simple setup, however, requires some modifications to account for possible deterministics. Therefore two distinct null hypotheses are formulated: Simple integration ($\pi_1 = 0$, m_0=m_1=0) and integration around a linear trend ($\pi_1 = 0$, $m_0 \neq 0$, $m_1 = 0$). Table 3.1 summarizes a number of statistics testing these nulls against a range of non-integrated alternatives.

Case	Restriction	Regressor	Statistic	Distribution (H_0)	
I	$H_0 : \pi_1 = 0,\ m_0 = 0,\ m_1 = 0$ $H_A : \pi_1 < 0,\ m_0 = 0,\ m_1 = 0$	$[x_{tr}]$	$t(\pi_1{=}0)$	$\hat{\tau}$	Cheung/Lai (1995a)
II	$H_0 : \pi_1 = 0,\ m_0 = 0,\ m_1 = 0$ $H_A : \pi_1 < 0,\ m_0 \neq 0,\ m_1 = 0$	$[x_{tr}, 1]$	$t(\pi_1{=}0)$ $t(\pi_1{=}0)$ $t(m_0{=}0)$ $F(H_0)$	$\hat{\tau}_\mu$ GLS_μ $\hat{\tau}_{\alpha\mu}$ Φ_1	Cheung/Lai (1995a) Cheung/Lai (1995b) Dickey/Fuller (1981) Dickey/Fuller (1981)
III	$H_0 : \pi_1 = 0,\ m_0 = 0,\ m_1 = 0$ $H_A : \pi_1 < 0,\ m_0 \neq 0,\ m_1 \neq 0$	$[x_{tr}, 1, t]$	$t(m_1{=}0)$ $F(H_0)$	$\hat{\tau}_{\beta\tau}$ Φ_2	Dickey/Fuller (1981) Dickey/Fuller (1981)
IV	$H_0 : \pi_1 = 0,\ m_0 \neq 0,\ m_1 = 0$ $H_A : \pi_1 < 0,\ m_0 \neq 0,\ m_1 = 0$	$[x_{tr}, 1]$	$t(\pi_1{=}0)$	$N(0,1)$	Schmidt (1990)
V	$H_0 : \pi_1 = 0,\ m_0 \neq 0,\ m_1 = 0$ $H_A : \pi_1 < 0,\ m_0 \in \mathbb{R},\ m_1 \neq 0$	$[x_{tr}, 1, t]$	$t(\pi_1{=}0)$ $t(\pi_1{=}0)$ $F(H_0)$	$\hat{\tau}_\tau$ GLS_τ Φ_3	Cheung/Lai (1995a) Cheung/Lai (1995b) Dickey/Fuller (1981)

General Model: $\Delta x_t = \pi_1 x_{t-1} + m_0 + m_1 t + \Sigma_{i=1}^{k-1} g_i \Delta x_{t-i} + e_t$

ADF-Regression: Δx_t *on* $x_{tr} \equiv [x_{t-1}\,;\, \Delta x_{t-1}, ..., \Delta x_{t-k+1}]$

Table 3.1. Tests for Integration of Order $d = 1$.

The various regression-specifications in table 3.1 are summarily known as *ADF-regressions*. Estimating these regressions by OLS produces the t- and F-statistics shown in the fourth column. For the interpretation of table 3.1 it is important to distinguish the DGP that actually generated a sample and the regression (probability model) that is run to calculate a statistic. In case I - III the underlying DGP is always a random walk. The regressions test this null against the alternatives I(0) around zero, I(0) around constant, and I(0) around linear trend. In case IV - V the underlying DGP is a random walk with drift. The regressions test this null against the alternatives I(0) around constant and I(0) around linear trend. In all cases the underlying random walk ($d = 1$, $q = 0$) can be replaced by a higher order DGP ($d = 1$, $q > 0$) without changing the limiting distributions.

The limiting distributions of the test-statistics are referenced in the last column of table 3.1. For the classic Dickey-Fuller statistics $(\hat{\tau}, \hat{\tau}_\mu, \hat{\tau}_\tau)$ also finite-sample critical values are available, which are therefore referenced here. The limiting distributions themselves depend on the underlying DGP and on the specified regression: an intercept in the DGP changes the t-statistic's distribution from $\hat{\tau}$ (random walk) to standard normal (random walk with drift), whereas an intercept in the regression changes that distribution from $\hat{\tau}$ (correct specification) to $\hat{\tau}_\mu$ (misspecification). A plausible specification of the regression and hence the alternative hypothesis is crucial. Suppose a regression including only an intercept is run over an actually trend-stationary DGP. Forced to decide between two erroneous answers, namely integration or stationarity, the test opts for the lesser evil and indicates integration to somehow account for the linear trend in the data. Indeed, West (1987) shows the t-statistic $t(\pi_1 = 0)$ to converge to zero in such circumstances.

A more powerful modification of the standard ADF-test is proposed by Elliott/Rothenberg/Stock (1996). Their *GLS*-statistic tests the null $\pi_1 = 0$ against the local point alternative $\bar{\pi}_1 = c/T$, with T denoting the sample size and c some constant. The corresponding modification of the ADF-statistic $\hat{\tau}_\tau$ is derived in two steps. First, using $d_t \equiv [1,\ t]$ the 'near differenced' series $Dx_t = [1 - (1{+}\bar{\pi}_1)L]\ x_t$ and $Dd_t = [1 - (1{+}\bar{\pi}_1)L]\, d_t$ are defined. Regressing the former on the latter gives an estimate $\hat{m}$. Second, on the locally detrended series $x_t^\tau \equiv x_t - \hat{m}d_t$ an ADF-regression (without constant or trend) is run and the t-statistic on the lagged level regressor computed. The limiting distribution of this GSL_τ-statistic depends on the choice of the constant c, for which a value $c = -13.5$ is recommended by Elliott/Rothenberg/Stock (1996). A similar procedure using $d_t \equiv [1]$ and a recommended value $c = -7$ for a locally demeaned series x_t^μ characterizes the GLS_μ-statistic, a modification of the ADF-statistic $\hat{\tau}_\mu$. An extensive set of critical values for both *GLS*-statistics is provided, via response surface regressions, by Cheung/Lai (1995b) as referenced in table 3.1.

Testing an I(2) Null: If at most two unit roots are suspected, the maintained hypothesis is (3.11) with $d = 2$ and $d_t = m_0 + m_1 t$. Therein, the null of second-order-integration ($\pi_1 = \pi_2 = 0$) is tested against the alternative of first-order-integration ($\pi_1 = 0,\ \pi_2 < 0$) or non-integration ($\pi_1 < 0,\ \pi_2 \in \mathbb{R}$). This setup of hypotheses is again modified to account for deterministics. Table 3.2 summarizes a number of statistics testing the null of simple integration ($\pi_1{=}\pi_2{=}0,\ m_0{=}m_1{=}0$) against a range of alternatives.

In all cases shown in table 3.2 the underlying DGP is a random walk in first differences ($d = 2,\ q = 0$). The various regressions test this hypothesis either directly by formulating an I(2)-null on the sequence of levels (cases Ia, IIa, IIIa), or indirectly by formulating an I(1)-null on the sequence of first differences (cases Ib, IIb, IIIb). In the direct versions, the I(2)-null is tested against an unspecified alternative since both $\pi_1 = 0$ (first-order integration) and $\pi_1 < 0$ (non-integration) are possible under the respective regression-specification. In the indirect versions, the regression-specification imposes the restriction $\pi_1 = 0$ on both the null and the alternative, so that the I(2)-null is precisely tested against I(1) around zero (case Ib), against I(1) around linear trend (case IIb), or against I(1) around quadratic trend (case IIIb). In all cases the same limiting distributions also apply for higher order DGP's ($d = 2$, $q > 0$), see Hasza/Fuller (1979). The limiting distributions again depend on the underlying DGP and on the regression specification: an intercept in the DGP would change the F-statistic's distribution from $\Phi_1(2)$ to $\frac{1}{2}\chi^2(2)$, whereas an intercept in the regression changes that distribution from $\Phi_1(2)$ to $\Phi_2(2)$.

Case	Restriction	Regressor	Statistic	Distribution (H_0)
Ia	$H_0: \pi_1 = \pi_2 = 0, m_0 = m_1 = 0$ $H_A: \pi_1 \leq 0, \pi_2 \in \mathbb{R}, m_0 = m_1 = 0$	$[x_{tr}]$	$F(\pi_1 = \pi_2 = 0)$	$\Phi_1(2)$ Hasza/Fuller (1979)
Ib	$H_0: \pi_1 = \pi_2 = 0, m_0 = m_1 = 0$ $H_A: \pi_1 = 0, \pi_2 < 0, m_0 = m_1 = 0$	$[x^*_{tr}]$	$t(\pi_2 = 0)$	$\hat{\tau}$ Cheung/Lai (1995a)
IIa	$H_0: \pi_1 = \pi_2 = 0, m_0 = m_1 = 0$ $H_A: \pi_1 \leq 0, \pi_2 \in \mathbb{R}, m_0 \neq 0, m_1 = 0$	$[x_{tr}, 1]$	$F(\pi_1 = \pi_2 = 0)$ $F(H_0)$	$\Phi_2(2)$ Hasza/Fuller (1979) $\Phi_2(3)$ Hasza/Fuller (1979)
IIb	$H_0: \pi_1 = \pi_2 = 0, m_0 = m_1 = 0$ $H_A: \pi_1 = 0, \pi_2 < 0, m_0 \neq 0, m_1 = 0$	$[x^*_{tr}, 1]$	$t(\pi_2 = 0)$ $t(\pi_2 = 0)$	$\hat{\tau}_\mu$ Cheung/Lai (1995a) GLS_μ Cheung/Lai (1995b)
IIIa	$H_0: \pi_1 = \pi_2 = 0, m_0 = m_1 = 0$ $H_A: \pi_1 \leq 0, \pi_2 \in \mathbb{R}, m_0 \neq 0, m_1 \neq 0$	$[x_{tr}, 1, t]$	$F(\pi_1 = \pi_2 = 0)$ $F(H_0)$	$\Phi_3(2)$ Hasza/Fuller (1979) $\Phi_3(4)$ Hasza/Fuller (1979)
IIIb	$H_0: \pi_1 = \pi_2 = 0, m_0 = m_1 = 0$ $H_A: \pi_1 = 0, \pi_2 < 0, m_0 \neq 0, m_1 \neq 0$	$[x^*_{tr}, 1, t]$	$F(H_0)$	Φ_2 Dickey/Fuller (1981)

General Model: $\Delta^2 x_t = \pi_1 x_{t-1} + \pi_2 \Delta x_{t-1} + m_0 + m_1 t + \Sigma_{i=1}^{k-2} g_i \Delta^2 x_{t-i} + e_t$

ADF-Regression: $\Delta^2 x_t$ *on* $x_{tr} \equiv [x_{t-1}, \Delta x_{t-1}; \Delta^2 x_{t-1}, ..., \Delta^2 x_{t-k+2}]$

or $x^*_{tr} \equiv [\Delta x_{t-1}; \Delta^2 x_{t-1}, ..., \Delta^2 x_{t-k+2}]$

Table 3.2. Tests for Integration of Order $d = 2$.

Testing an I(d) Null: A hypothesis of higher-order integration I($d \geq 2$) can be tested directly by specifying a regression corresponding to (3.11) and restricting the coefficients $\pi_1, ..., \pi_d$ jointly to zero. An example for this approach are cases Ia, IIa, IIIa in table 3.2. An alternative approach is to test an I($d \geq 2$)-hypothesis indirectly as a sequence of I(1)-hypotheses. This leads to a sequential testing procedure suggested by Dickey/Pantula (1987) and Pantula (1989). To implement this procedure, denote by $\mathcal{H}(j)$ the hypothesis that a given scalar sequence $\{x_t\}$ is integrated of order j. To test this hypothesis, consider a regression of $\Delta^j x_t$ on $x_{tr}^* \equiv [\Delta^{j-1}x_{t-1}\,;\, \Delta^j x_{t-1}, ..., \Delta^j x_{t-p+j}]$, and define $t(\pi_j=0)$ as the t-statistic restricting the coefficient on the first regressor to zero. Since the regression-specification places, in terms of (3.11), an overall zero restriction on the coefficients $\pi_1, ..., \pi_{j-1}$, this t-statistic tests the null $\mathcal{H}(j)$ against the well defined alternative $\mathcal{H}(j\text{-}1)$. Moreover, since the regression-specification resembles, in terms of table 3.1, an I(1)-test applied to a sequence of (j-1)-th differences, this t-statistic obeys an asymptotic $\hat{\tau}$-distribution under its null (Pantula 1989, Theorem 1). These properties suggest the following 'top-down' testing procedure:

If at most $d_{\max}$ unit roots are possible a-priori, then the true order of integration $0 \le d \le d_{\max}$ can be determined with controlled size α by sequentially testing $\mathcal{H}(j)$ against $\mathcal{H}(j\text{-}1)$ in the order $j = d_{\max}, d_{\max}-1, ..., 2, 1$. At each stage, the respective null $\mathcal{H}(j)$ is rejected in favour of its alternative $\mathcal{H}(j\text{-}1)$ if the statistic $t(\pi_j=0)$ exceeds the lower α-quantile of the $\hat{\tau}$-distribution. The procedure stops at the first non-rejected null hypothesis, whose index j is then adopted as an estimator $\hat{d}$ for d. Of course, the initial regressors can be extended to $[x_{tr}^*, 1]$ or $[x_{tr}^*, 1, t]$, in which case the resulting t-statistics obey an asymptotic $\hat{\tau}_\mu$- or $\hat{\tau}_\tau$-distribution, respectively. An application of this testing procedure is actually contained in table 3.2: the cases Ib, IIb, IIIb constitute the first step in a sequential procedure starting at $d_{\max} = 2$.

Summary: Macroeconomic data series typically feature strong intertemporal dependencies, among them in particular some sort of trending behaviour. A suitable modelling device is the scalar autoregressive model (3.1), which offers combinations of stochastic and deterministic trends to account for such nonstationarities. This convenient variety of modelling alternatives involves, unfortunately, an inconvenient variety of distinct inference procedures. Specifically, the familiar world of textbook inference does usually not apply in the case of stochastic trends (or 'integration') caused by unit roots in the characteristic polynomial of (3.1).

Stochastic trends, however, constitute a useful modelling device to characterize the intrinsic unforecastability of many macroeconomic time series over the long-run. Moreover, stochastic trends allow to model yet another typical feature of (some) macroeconomic time series, namely a discernible tendency to 'trend together' in the long run. The role of common stochastic trends (or 'cointegration') in modelling the dynamics of multivariate time series is one of the topics discussed in the next section.

3.2 Vector Sequences

The general vector autoregressive model, denoted VAR(k), is given by a p-dimensional stochastic sequence $\{x_t\,;\ x \in \mathbb{R}^p\,,\ t \in \mathbb{Z}\}$ satisfying the system of difference equations

$$x_t \;=\; A_1\, x_{t-1} + \ldots + A_k\, x_{t-k} + e_t + d_t \quad , \tag{3.15}$$

where A_i are real $p \times p$ parameter matrices. The autoregressive sequence is driven by a stochastic sequence $\{e_t\,;\ t \in \mathbb{Z}\}$ of vector white noise[35] $e_t \sim wn(0, \Omega)$, and by a deterministic sequence $\{d_t\,;\ t \in \mathbb{Z}\}$ generated as a polynomial in time. In a VAR, each component variable x_{it} depends on its own history and on the history of all other variables included in x_t; there are no exogenous variables except d_t and e_t. The general VAR(k) model is conveniently manipulated by defining and expanding a k-th order polynomial matrix $A(z)$ in an argument $z \in \mathbb{C}$ as follows (see appendix A.1):[36]

$$\begin{aligned} A(z) \;\equiv\; I - \textstyle\sum_{i=1}^{k} A_i\, z^i \;&=\; A(1) \;-\; (1\text{-}z)\, A^*(z) \\ &=\; A(1) \;-\; (1\text{-}z)\, A^*(1) \;+\; (1\text{-}z)^2\, A^{**}(z)\,. \end{aligned} \tag{3.16}$$

The determinant of $A(z)$ is a scalar polynomial of order pk. The system's characteristic equation, $\det A(z) = 0$, therefore has pk solutions l_j called *(latent) roots* of $A(z)$. Roots outside the (complex) unit circle, $|l_j| > 1$, are called *stable*. Roots inside the unit circle, $|l_j| < 1$, are called *explosive*. Roots on the unit circle, $|l_j| = 1$, and notably *unit roots* $l_j = 1$, are again of particular interest. The latent roots of $A(z)$ can be obtained as the reciprocals of the eigenvalues of its companion matrix (see appendix A.1). Using the lag-operator as argument in (3.16) the model (3.15) is written compactly as

$$A(L)\, x_t \;=\; e_t \;+\; d_t \quad , \qquad e_t \sim wn(0, \Omega) \quad , \qquad \forall\ t \in \mathbb{Z}\ . \tag{3.17}$$

This model is general enough to generate, as special cases, a fairly wide range of vector sequences with distinct statistical properties. Several interesting special cases are discussed in the following subsections.

---

[35] Here Ω is a symmetric positive-definite matrix of covariances. If Ω is diagonal, there are no contemporaneously correlated shocks. If Ω is singular, some VAR-equations are nonstochastic, e.g. accounting identities.

[36] A k-th order polynomial matrix $P(z)$ is a $p \times p$ matrix with k-th order scalar polynomials $p_{ij}(z)$ as elements. Rearrangement shows that $P(z)$ is also a k-th order polynomial in z with $p{\times}p$ matrices as parameters. For more on polynomial matrices see for example Frazer/Duncan/Collar (1965) or Barnett/Storey (1970). The scalar polynomials are here identified by $p_{ij}(0) = \delta_{ij}$ (Kronecker's Delta), so that $P(0) = I$ as in (3.16).

3.2.1 Stationary VAR Model

A vector stochastic process is stationary if its components $x_{1t}, ..., x_{pt}$ are individually and jointly stationary. Consider for example the p-dimensional infinite moving-average

$$x_t = \sum_{s=0}^{\infty} C_s \, e_{t-s} \ . \tag{3.18}$$

If the real sequence of parameter matrices is square summable, a limiting random vector x_t is existent and the sequence $\{x_t\}$ weakly stationary.[37] A stochastic sequence with members generated according to (3.18) is called a *vector linear process* if its parameter matrices are square summable and satisfy $0 < |C(1)| < \infty$. The additional condition precludes poles at unity in all elements $c_{ij}(z)$, ensuring finiteness of $C(z)$ for all $|z| \leq 1$, and roots at unity in at least some elements $c_{ij}(z)$, allowing $C(1)$ to be of possibly reduced but not zero rank. Thus no component of a vector linear process is underdifferenced although some components may be overdifferenced.

Sequences of the form (3.18) are conveniently manipulated by defining and expanding the infinite order polynomial matrix (cf appendix A.1)

$$C(z) \equiv \sum_{s=0}^{\infty} C_s \, z^s = C(1) + (1-z)\, C^*(z) \ , \tag{3.19}$$

in analogy to (3.5). The expansion (3.19) will be useful below for isolating stationary components in integrated vector sequences.

Stationarity conditions for the present general VAR(k) model are derived by inverting the polynomial matrix (3.16). An inverse matrix $C(z)$ is obtained by multiplying out the defining relation $C(z)\,A(z) = I$ and collecting terms of equal power in z. Representing the inverse by a power series (3.19) this gives parameter matrices evolving as

$$C_0 = I_{p \times p} \ , \qquad C_s = \sum_{i=1}^{\min(s,k)} C_{s-i}\, A_i \ , \quad s = 1, 2, ..., \infty \ . \tag{3.20}$$

If this system is dynamically stable, that is, if $\det A(z) \neq 0$ for $|z| \leq 1$, then the parameter matrices C_s converge to zero exponentially. In this case the sequence $\{C_s\}$ is l-summable (cf Barnett/Storey 1970, Brillinger 1975). A lag-operator matrix $A(L)$ with all latent roots outside the unit circle is called a stable VAR-operator. Its inverse $C(L)$ is well defined in that its parameters satisfy the restrictions for a vector linear process. Such an inverse is called a

[37] Square summability for a matrix sequence requires each element $c_{ij}(z)$ of the polynomial matrix $C(z)$ to be square summable. This condition is expressed as $\sum_{s=0}^{\infty} \|C_s\|^2 = \sum_{i=1}^{p} \sum_{j=1}^{p} \left(\sum_{s=0}^{\infty} c_{ij,s}^2\right) < \infty$, where $\|C\| \equiv (trace\, C\, C')^{0.5}$ defines a L_2-norm on the space $\mathbb{R}^{p \times p}$. Under square-summability the right-hand-side of (3.18) converges in mean-square to a limiting random vector x_t; see Gihman/Skorohod (1974, p.202).

backward or *causal* MA-operator. Premultiplying this inverse in (3.17) allows to express the autoregressive sequence as an infinite convergently-weighted sum of the driving sequences:

$$x_t \;=\; \sum_{i=1}^{k} A_i\, x_{t-i} + e_t + d_t \;=\; \sum_{s=0}^{\infty} C_s\,(e_{t-s} + d_{t-s}) \quad . \tag{3.21}$$

From this moving-average representation the unconditional moments are conveniently calculated as

$$E[x_t] \;=\; \sum_{s=0}^{\infty} C_s\, d_{t-s} \quad , \quad Cov[x_t, x_{t-\tau}] \;=\; \sum_{s=0}^{\infty} C_{\tau+s}\, \Omega\, C_s' \;<\infty\, .$$

Thus, the VAR-sequence (3.15) is weakly stationary with a causal moving-average representation (3.21) if and only if the polynomial matrix (3.16) has only stable latent roots and the driving deterministic sequence is time-invariant.

3.2.2 Nonstationary VAR Model

Stochastic trends in a VAR arise from latent roots equal to unity. The order of integration, however, depends not only on the number of unit roots (as in the scalar case), but also on their location among the elements of $A(z)$. Unit roots in on-diagonal elements $a_{ii}(z)$ obviously generate integration in x_{it} via this component's own dynamics. Unit roots in off-diagonal elements $a_{ij}(z)$, in contrast, pass a component x_{jt} through a difference filter $(1-L)$ before feeding it into the dynamics of x_{it}, and thus generate long-run independence between the two components. Conversely, elements $a_{ij}(z)$ with only stable roots feed a component x_{jt} directly into the dynamics of x_{it} and thus generate long-run comovement, or *co-integration*, between the two components. The present interest in such types of nonstationarity is expressed in the following assumption:

Assumption 2 *The polynomial matrix (3.16) has $d_0 \geq 0$ latent roots equal to* 1 *(unit roots) and all remaining roots outside the complex unit circle (stable roots).*

An otherwise stable VAR(k)-operator $A(L)$ containing one or more latent unit roots can not be inverted anymore. However, assuming d_0 latent unit roots, its determinant and adjoint can be factored as

$$\det A(L) \;=\; (1-L)^{d_0}\, h(L) \quad , \quad \operatorname{adj} A(L) \;=\; (1-L)^{d_1}\, H(L) \;, \tag{3.22}$$

where $h(L)$ is a stable scalar polynomial and $H(L)$ is a finite-order matrix polynomial which is nonzero and finite at unity, that is, neither overdifferenced nor underdifferenced. The filter $(1-L)^{d_0}$ is the greatest unit-root factor in the determinant. The filter $(1-L)^{d_1}$ is the greatest unit-root factor shared by all elements of the adjoint. Since the adjoint comprises the first minors of the matrix $A(L)$ it holds that $d_0 \geq d_1 \geq 0$ and consequently

$d_0 - d_1 \equiv d \geq 0$. Premultiplying the adjoint in (3.17) and using that generally adj $A(L) \cdot A(L) = \det A(L) \cdot I$ therefore yields a causal MA(∞)-representation, now for the sequence of d-th differences:[38]

$$(1-L)^d x_t \quad = \quad h(L)^{-1} H(L)\,(e_t + d_t) \quad \equiv \quad C(L)\,(e_t + d_t) \ , \tag{3.23}$$

where $C(L)$ is a rational infinite order polynomial matrix satisfying the above restrictions for a vector linear process. The underlying vector autoregressive sequence (3.15) is then called *integrated of order* d, denoted $x_t \sim I(d)$. Moreover, using (3.22) each scalar component x_{it} in x_t can individually be represented as a scalar ARIMA sequence integrated of order $d_i \leq d$ (see Maravall/Mathis 1994). Thus, a vector sequence is $I(d)$ if at least one of its scalar components is $I(d_i = d)$ and any remaining components have smaller orders of integration. Setting $d = 0$ includes, as a special baseline case, also the stationary VAR into the definition of integratedness.

The I(1) Model: Using the expansion in (3.16), which isolates terms of different order of integration, the autoregressive representation (3.17) can be rewritten such that latent unit roots appear explicitly as testable parameter restrictions. A suitable form for the I(1)-case is (cf appendix A.1)

$$G(L)\,\Delta x_t \quad = \quad \Pi_1\, x_{t-1} \ + \ e_t \ + \ d_t \ , \tag{3.24}$$

where $\Pi_1 \equiv -A(1)$ isolates the long-run behaviour of the sequence, and $G(L) \equiv A(1) - A^*(L)$ is some VAR(k-1) operator with $G(0) = I$. Restrictions controlling the number and location of unit roots in $A(z)$ can now be expressed as rank restrictions on the matrix $\Pi_1 \equiv -A(1)$. For the VAR to be integrated of order one it is necessary that the following rank restriction is satisfied:

$$\mathrm{rk}\, A(1) \ = r \ < \ p \qquad \Leftrightarrow \qquad \Pi_1 \ = \ \alpha\,\beta' \ . \tag{3.25}$$

The restriction is restated on the right-hand side using that any $p \times p$ matrix Π_1 of rank r can be factorized into some $p \times r$ matrices α and β of full column rank $r < p$. Full rank of $A(1)$ implies $\det A(1) \neq 0$ or absence of latent unit roots in $A(z)$. Under this restriction all components of x_t are I(0). In contrast, zero rank of $A(1)$ implies $\Pi_1 = 0$, or unit roots in all on- and off-diagonal elements of $A(z)$, so that (3.24) becomes a VAR(k-1) in first differences. Under this restriction all components of x_t are I(1) and independent of each other's levels. Of interest here is the intermediate case: reduced rank of $A(1)$ implies $\det A(1) = 0$, or presence of unit roots in $A(z)$. This reduced rank restriction can be translated into the shown factorization, where the columns of β span the r-dimensional right range space of $A(1)$. Under this restriction the components of x_t are individually I(1), but linked to each other via β'. This leads to the concept of cointegration.

[38] Differencing in a multivariate context still involves multiplication by the scalar $(1-L)$, so that in a vector each component series is differenced individually.

A VAR-sequence integrated of order one is called *stochastically cointegrated* (of rank $r < p$) if the linear combination $\beta' x_t$ is integrated of order zero, and called *deterministically cointegrated* if $\beta' x_t$ is weakly stationary. The columns of β comprise r linearly independent *cointegrating vectors.* This definition differs slightly from the original in Engle/Granger (1987): due to the deterministic term d_t in the present setup the (frequently ignored) distinction between 'I(0)' and 'stationary' becomes relevant and leads to the distinction of stochastic and deterministic cointegration in the spirit of Perron/Campbell (1993).

Before illustrating the concept of cointegration, note first that for any $p \times r$ matrix β of full column rank there exist an orthogonal complement $\beta_\perp$ ($p \times p\text{-}r$) and a generalized or Moore-Penrose inverse $\bar{\beta}$ ($p \times r$), both of full column rank, such that[39]

$$\beta' \beta_\perp = 0_{r \times p-r} \quad , \quad \beta' \bar{\beta} = I_{r \times r} \quad , \quad \bar{\beta}\beta' + \bar{\beta}_\perp \beta'_\perp = I_{p \times p} \; . \qquad (3.26)$$

The complement and generalized inverse of the matrix α are defined analogously. Note further that the factorization of Π_1 in (3.25) is not unique: the product of $(\alpha\xi^{-1})$ and $(\beta\xi')'$ gives the same result for any nonsingular $r \times r$ matrix ξ. Rather, the columns of β provide *some* basis for Π_1's right range space, and the columns of $\beta_\perp$ provide *some* basis for Π_1's right null space.

A statistical illustration of cointegration is now obtained from the moving-average representation of (3.24). As shown in Johansen's (1991) version of Granger's representation theorem, a VAR is (under assumption 2) integrated of order 1 and stochastically cointegrated of rank r if in addition to (3.25) also the the rank condition $\mathrm{rk}\,\Gamma = p - r$ holds. The new $p\text{-}r \times p\text{-}r$ matrix $\Gamma \equiv \alpha'_\perp A^*(1)\,\beta_\perp = -\alpha'_\perp G(1)\,\beta_\perp$ controls unit roots in the first differences of the sequence. The VAR then admits a causal MA(∞)-representation (3.23) with $d = 1$ and impact matrix (see appendix A.2)

$$C(1) \;=\; \beta_\perp(-\Gamma)^{-1}\alpha'_\perp \qquad \text{with} \qquad \mathrm{rk}\,C(1) \;=\; p - r < p \; . \qquad (3.27)$$

Moreover, using the decomposition (3.19), the causal MA(∞)-representation admits a multivariate Beveridge/Nelson decomposition which separates, in analogy to (3.12), a stationary linear process and a non-stationary stochastic trend within the entire VAR-process:[40]

$$x_t \;=\; \tilde{x}_0 \;+\; C^*(L)\,(e_t + d_t) \;+\; C(1)\textstyle\sum_{j=1}^{t}(e_j + d_j) \; , \qquad (3.28)$$

$$\beta' x_t \;=\; \beta'\,\tilde{x}_0 \;+\; \beta' C^*(L)\,(e_t + d_t) \; . \qquad (3.29)$$

[39] Explicit definitions are $\bar{\beta} = \beta(\beta'\beta)^{-1}$ and $\beta_\perp = s_\perp - s(\beta' s)^{-1}\beta' s_\perp$, using selection matrices $s' = [I_r, 0]$ and $s'_\perp = [0, I_{p-r}]$. Note that these definitions imply a symmetry $\bar{\beta}\beta' = \beta\bar{\beta}'$ and similarly $\bar{\beta}_\perp\beta'_\perp = \beta_\perp\bar{\beta}'_\perp$.

[40] Note that $x_t = x_0 + \Sigma_{j=1}^{t} \Delta x_j$. Replacing Δx_j by its moving average representation (3.23), with $d = 1$, and applying the expansion (3.19) gives (3.28). Note that $\tilde{x}_0 \equiv x_0 - C^*(L)\,(e_0 + d_0)$.

The last term in (3.28) shows that each component in x_t is driven by a stochastic trend arising from a linear combination of p random walks via the rows of the matrix $C(1)$. This explains integration. The stochastic trends need not be linearly independent of each other: if the matrix $C(1)$ has reduced rank, as in (3.27), then the p stochastic trends can be reproduced from a basis of $p-r$ *common trends* (Stock/Watson 1988). The effects are seen in (3.29): A linear combination of integrated variables is, usually, likewise integrated. If, however, the variables are combined by a $p \times 1$ vector β_i from the left null space of $C(1)$, so that $\beta_i' C(1) = 0$, then the stochastic trends in individual components cancel out, and the linear combination of I(1) variables becomes I(0). According to the rank deficiency of $C(1)$ there exist r such cointegrating vectors, namely the columns of β. This explains (stochastic) cointegration as shown in (3.29). In summary, $\operatorname{rk} A(1) = r$ linearly independent cointegrating relations correspond to $\operatorname{rk} C(1) = p{-}r$ linearly independent common trends.[41] As borderline cases, full rank of $A(1)$ implies $C(1) = 0$ (absence of common trends), and full rank of $C(1)$ implies $A(1) = 0$ (absence of cointegration). The r-dimensional left null space of $C(1)$ corresponds to the right range space of $A(1)$. It contains all $p \times 1$ cointegrating vectors β_i and is called the *cointegration space*.

A behavioural illustration of cointegration is obtained from the following error-correction representation of (3.24). Precisely, inserting the factorization $\Pi_1 = \alpha\beta'$ into (3.24), and using the identity $\alpha\bar{\alpha}' + \bar{\alpha}_\perp \alpha_\perp' = I_{p \times p}$ to decompose the deterministic sequence, gives a reduced-form error-correction (ECM) representation

$$\Delta x_t = \alpha\,(\beta' x_{t-1} + \bar{\alpha}' d_t) + \textstyle\sum_{i=1}^{k-1} G_i\, \Delta x_{t-i} + \bar{\alpha}_\perp \alpha_\perp' d_t + e_t \quad . \qquad (3.30)$$

The label *error-correction* refers to a simple 'economic' interpretation for the statistical property of cointegration: A relation like $\beta' x = c$ describes a system of r static equilibrium relationships. Therefore, if indeed $\beta' x_t \sim I(0)$ and $\bar{\alpha}' d_t = c$, then the bracketed term in (3.30) is stationary, reverting to its zero mean, and can be interpreted as an equilibrium error inherited from the previous period. A certain proportion of this error, measured by α, is then corrected in the current period as agents try to establish equilibrium, and this (Granger-) causes changes in the variables. If these changes have stable own dynamics, i.e., if $[\alpha_\perp' G(1)\, \beta_\perp]$ is of full rank, then the system embarks on some sort of balanced growth path. It must be stressed, however, that (3.30) is a statistical model which can be given different (observationally equivalent) theoretical interpretations with possibly different policy implications. This problem is addressed in detail in chapter 4.

[41] The trends are not necessarily stochastically independent. Since $e_j \sim N(0, \Omega)$ the p random walks $\Sigma_{j=1}^t e_j$ are correlated. Defining the vector $v_j \equiv \Omega^{-0.5} e_j$ produces uncorrelated random walks $\Sigma_{j=1}^t v_j$.

The I(2) Model: The general VAR model is, of course, also capable of generating higher order integration. Using the expansion (3.16), an interim multiplier representation suitable for the I(2)-case is given by (see appendix A.1)

$$G(L)\,\Delta^2 x_t \;=\; \Pi_1\, x_{t-1} \;+\; \Pi_2 \Delta x_{t-1} \;+\; e_t \;+\; d_t \quad , \tag{3.31}$$

where $\Pi_1 \equiv -A(1)$, $\Pi_2 \equiv A^*(1) - A(1)$, and $G(L)$ is now some VAR(k-2) operator with $G(0) = I$. For the VAR to be integrated of order two it is necessary that the following two rank restrictions are satisfied:

$$\begin{array}{lclcrcl} \operatorname{rk} A(1) & = & r < p & \Leftrightarrow & \Pi_1 & = & \alpha\,\beta' \;, \\ \operatorname{rk}[\alpha'_\perp A^*(1)\,\beta_\perp] & = & s < p-r & \Leftrightarrow & \alpha'_\perp \Pi_2\,\beta_\perp & = & \gamma\,\delta' \;. \end{array} \tag{3.32}$$

The rank restrictions are again restated on the right-hand side as statistically convenient factorizations, where α, β are $p \times r$ matrices of full column rank $r < p$, and γ, δ are $p{-}r \times s$ matrices of full column rank $s < p{-}r$. Obviously, if the $p{-}r{\times}p{-}r$ matrix $\Gamma \equiv \alpha'_\perp A^*(1)\,\beta_\perp = \alpha'_\perp \Pi_2\,\beta_\perp$ has full rank this model collapses into the above I(1) model. Under the reduced-rank restrictions (3.32), however, the underlying VAR admits a causal moving-average representation (3.23) with $d = 2$ (see Johansen 1992c or Paruolo 1996). The corresponding multivariate Beveridge/Nelson decomposition shows the system to be driven by $p - r$ linearly independent stochastic trends, of whom s are I(1) and the remaining $p{-}r{-}s$ are I(2). In an autoregressive representation, the reduced-rank restrictions (3.32) imply two types of linear combinations. First, in s directions a combination $\delta'\beta'_\perp\, x_t$ of levels cointegrates down to I(1). Second, in r directions a combination of levels $\beta' x_t$ and differences $\delta'_\perp \beta'_\perp\, \Delta x_t$ cointegrates down to I(0), which is known as *polynomial cointegration.* It follows that in general $\beta' x_t \sim I(1)$, so that the familiar cointegration vectors do not describe a long run equilibrium solution anymore. Rather, the system simultaneously contains two different types of equilibrium behaviour. A general overview is given by Haldrup (1998). Various representations and interpretations of an I(2)-system are derived by Haldrup/Salmon (1998) using the Smith-McMillan form of the matrix $A(z)$.

Deterministics: The specification of the deterministic regressor d_t controls, together with the system's unit roots, the shape of the deterministic component $C(L)\,d_t$. A sufficiently general specification is $d_t = m_0 + m_1 t$ with some $p \times 1$ parameter vectors m. For the I(1) case, the expressions (3.28) and (3.29) then give the following unconditional expectations:[42]

$$\begin{aligned} E[x_t] &= [C^*(1)m_0 + C^{**}(1)m_1] \;+ \\ &\quad\; [C(1)m_0 + \tfrac{1}{2}C(1)m_1 + C^*(1)m_1]\cdot t \;+\; [\tfrac{1}{2}C(1)m_1]\cdot t^2 \;, \\ E[\beta' x_t] &= \beta'[C^*(1)m_0 + C^{**}(1)m_1] \;+\; \beta'[C^*(1)\,m_1]\cdot t \;, \\ E[\Delta x_t] &= [C(1)m_0 + C^*(1)m_1] \;+\; [C(1)m_1]\cdot t \;. \end{aligned}$$

[42] Recall that $C^*(1) = -\sum_{s=1}^{\infty} s\, c_s$ and $C^{**}(1) = \frac{1}{2}\sum_{s=2}^{\infty} s(s\text{-}1)\, c_s$ denote the first and second derivative of $C(z)$ at $z = 1$ (see also appendix A.1).

This shows how unit roots operate upon, say, an intercept m_0: partly m_0 is funnelled via $C^*(1)$ into a constant $\alpha' m_0$ in the cointegration space, and partly it is integrated via $C(1)$ into a $p-r$ dimensional linear trend $\alpha'_\perp m_0\, t$. Therefore a linear trend in the deterministic component of an I(1) model is ruled out by $m_1 = 0$ plus the requirement that m_0 be proportional to α, expressed as $m_0 = \alpha\, n_0$ for some $r \times 1$ vector n_0. The statistical property of difference-stationarity is consequently modelled by the restrictions $\operatorname{rk} A(1) < p$ and $m_1 = 0$, $\alpha'_\perp m_0 = 0$. The statistical property of trend-stationarity, in contrast, is modelled by the restrictions $\operatorname{rk} A(1) = p$ and $m_0, m_1 \neq 0$. The second expression also shows the concept of deterministic cointegration: the linear combinations $\beta' x_t$ are integrated of order zero but not necessarily stationary. Rather, while stochastic cointegration only requires $\beta' C(1) = 0$, deterministic cointegration in addition requires $\beta' C^*(1) = 0$. These arguments highlight the importance of including a linear trend as a regressor into a VAR: Without such a term, the general model is neither able to distinguish difference- and trend-stationarity, nor able to distinguish stochastic and deterministic cointegration.

For the I(2) case similar arguments apply. The once integrated part of the intercept, namely $\alpha'_\perp m_0\, t$, is partly absorbed by γ and partly again integrated into a $p-r-s$ dimensional quadratic trend $\gamma'_\perp \alpha'_\perp m_0\, t^2$. Therefore a quadratic trend in the deterministic component of an I(2) model is ruled out by the requirement of $\alpha'_\perp m_0$ being proportional to γ, expressed as $\alpha'_\perp m_0 = \gamma\, n_0$ for some $s \times 1$ vector n_0.

Model		Parameter Restrictions				Trend	
$\mathcal{M}_m$		$\operatorname{rk} \Pi_1 \leq p$		$m_1 \in \mathbb{R}$	$m_0 \in \mathbb{R}$	x_t	$\beta' x_t$
$I(0)$	$\mathcal{M}(2)$	$\operatorname{rk} \Pi_1 = p$	$\operatorname{rk} \Gamma = 0$	$m_1 \neq 0$	$m_0 \in \mathbb{R}$	t	
	$\mathcal{M}(1)$	$\operatorname{rk} \Pi_1 = p$	$\operatorname{rk} \Gamma = 0$	$m_1 = 0$	$m_0 \in \mathbb{R}$	1	
	$\mathcal{M}(0)$	$\operatorname{rk} \Pi_1 = p$	$\operatorname{rk} \Gamma = 0$	$m_1 = 0$	$m_0 = 0$		
$I(1)$	$\mathcal{M}(r,2)$	$\operatorname{rk} \Pi_1 < p$	$\operatorname{rk} \Gamma = p\text{-}r$	$m_1 \neq \alpha n_1$	$m_0 \in \mathbb{R}$	t^2	t
	$\mathcal{M}(r,2^*)$	$\operatorname{rk} \Pi_1 < p$	$\operatorname{rk} \Gamma = p\text{-}r$	$m_1 = \alpha n_1$	$m_0 \in \mathbb{R}$	t	t
	$\mathcal{M}(r,1)$	$\operatorname{rk} \Pi_1 < p$	$\operatorname{rk} \Gamma = p\text{-}r$	$m_1 = 0$	$m_0 \neq \alpha n_0$	t	1
	$\mathcal{M}(r,1^*)$	$\operatorname{rk} \Pi_1 < p$	$\operatorname{rk} \Gamma = p\text{-}r$	$m_1 = 0$	$m_0 = \alpha n_0$	1	1
	$\mathcal{M}(r,0)$	$\operatorname{rk} \Pi_1 < p$	$\operatorname{rk} \Gamma = p\text{-}r$	$m_1 = 0$	$m_0 = 0$		
$I(2)$	$\mathcal{M}(r,1;\, s,1)$	$\operatorname{rk} \Pi_1 < p$	$\operatorname{rk} \Gamma < p\text{-}r$	$m_1 = 0$	$\alpha'_\perp m_0 \neq \gamma n_0$	t^2	
	$\mathcal{M}(r,1;\, s,1^*)$	$\operatorname{rk} \Pi_1 < p$	$\operatorname{rk} \Gamma < p\text{-}r$	$m_1 = 0$	$\alpha'_\perp m_0 = \gamma n_0$	t	
	$\mathcal{M}(r,1^*;\, s,0)$	$\operatorname{rk} \Pi_1 < p$	$\operatorname{rk} \Gamma < p\text{-}r$	$m_1 = 0$	$\alpha'_\perp m_0 = 0$	1	

Parameter matrices $\Pi_1 \equiv -A(1)$ *and* $\Gamma \equiv \alpha'_\perp A^*(1)\, \beta_\perp$ *as defined in* (3.32).

Table 3.3. Submodels of the General VAR Model.

The preceding discussion revealed a somewhat bewildering array of possible combinations of stochastic and deterministic trends. To distinguish these combinations a particular notation is adopted here. The trends making up the deterministic component of a stochastic sequence are collectively referred to as *deterministics*. Being some polynomial in time the deterministics are characterized by their *degree*. This degree arises from restrictions simultaneously placed on the matrix $A(z)$ and the deterministic regressor d_t. In analogy to Osterwald-Lenum (1992), the restrictions on d_t are here defined by indices i, j ranging over $0, 1^*, 1, 2^*, 2$. In these indices, the digits refer to zero restrictions and the stars to proportionality restrictions. For example, the case $(i) = (2^*)$ indicates no zero restriction on m_0 or m_1 plus a proportionality restriction on m_1. The case $(i, j) = (1, 1^*)$ indicates a zero restriction on m_1 plus a proportionality restriction on $\alpha_{\perp}' m_0$. The possible cases are for convenience summarized in table 3.3.

Summary: The general VAR model contains several mutually exclusive submodels which are characterized by distinctive statistical properties: the order of integration, the rank of cointegration, and the degree of deterministics. These statistical properties are brought about by certain restrictions on the parameters of the maintained general model (3.15), denoted $\mathcal{M}_m$. Several submodels which have appeared in the previous sections are summarized in table 3.3. The submodels integrated of order one are denoted by $\mathcal{M}(r, i)$, those integrated of order two by $\mathcal{M}(r, i\,; s, j)$. The table's last two columns describe the deterministic component of the respective submodel. For example, the submodel $\mathcal{M}(r, 1)$ is integrated of order one with a linear trend in the levels x_t and a constant in the cointegration relations $\beta' x_t$.

3.2.3 Estimation and Testing

The general VAR model with deterministic regressor $d_t = m_0 + m_1 t$ and Gaussian shocks $e_t \sim i.i.n(0, \Omega)$ is denoted by $\mathcal{M}_m$, the maintained model. Let $\{x_t\}$ be generated by some unknown parameter point within $\mathcal{M}_m$. The problem now is to narrow down this general assertion to a more informative one, namely that the DGP is a parameter point within one of the submodels in table 3.3. Statistical inference is therefore mainly concerned with the determination of the order of integration (d), the cointegration rank (r), and the deterministic degree $(0, 1^*, 1, 2^*, 2)$. Several tests for cointegration exist, and comparisons are available in Reimers (1992), Gonzalo (1994), Hargreaves (1994), or Haug (1996). The present framework suggests an application of the maximum-likelihood procedure developed by Johansen (1988,1991,1994) and Johansen/Juselius (1990,1992). This maximum-likelihood procedure is outlined in the present subsection. The exposition concentrates first on the I(1)-model (3.24)-(3.25) and then proceeds to the I(2)-model (3.31)-(3.32).

Estimation in the I(1)-model: Estimation in the I(1)-model proceeds from the interim multiplier representation (3.24). An available sample of p time series observed at dates $t = -k+1, ..., -1, 0, 1, ..., T$ is therefore arranged into matrices of lagged levels, first differences, and lagged first differences plus deterministic regressor as follows:

$$\underset{p\times T}{X_l} \equiv [x_0, \cdots, x_{T-1}] \qquad \underset{p\times T}{X_d} \equiv [\Delta x_1, \cdots, \Delta x_T] \qquad \underset{[p(k-1)+2]\times T}{X} \equiv \begin{bmatrix} \Delta x_0 & \cdots & \Delta x_{T-1} \\ \vdots & \ddots & \vdots \\ \Delta x_{-k+2} & \cdots & \Delta x_{T-k+1} \\ 1 & \cdots & 1 \\ 1 & t & T \end{bmatrix}$$

Using these data matrices, the assertion of $\{x_t\}$ being generated by some unknown parameter point within $\mathcal{M}_m$ is formulated as a probability model

$$\begin{aligned} l(\Pi_1, G, \Omega) &= -pT/2\ \ln(2\pi) - T/2\ \ln|\Omega| - 1/2\,\mathrm{tr}\,[e'\,\Omega^{-1}e] \\ X_d &= \Pi_1 X_l + GX + e \ , \end{aligned} \tag{3.33}$$

where $G \equiv [G_1, ..., G_{k-1}, m_0, m_1]$, and $e \equiv [e_1, ..., e_T]$ is a $p \times T$ matrix of Gaussian shocks. This framework allows to estimate Π_1 by a statistical technique known as reduced rank regression.

If no restrictions are placed on G and Ω, both matrices can be concentrated out of the log-likelihood function (3.33). Setting the respective first derivatives of $l(\cdot)$ simultaneously equal to zero yields the following estimators (see appendix A.3)

$$\hat{\Omega}(\Pi_1) = \frac{1}{T}\,(X_d - \Pi_1 X_l)\,P\,(X_d - \Pi_1 X_l)' \tag{3.34}$$

$$\hat{G}(\Pi_1) = (X_d - \Pi_1 X_l)\,X'(X\,X')^{-1} \ , \tag{3.35}$$

where $P \equiv I - X'(X\,X')^{-1}X$ is a symmetric idempotent $T \times T$ projection matrix. Postmultiplying X_d and X_l by P produces series of first differences and lagged levels each corrected for the deterministics and the entire short-run dynamics. The concentrated model obtained by inserting the above estimators into (3.33) relates these two new series

$$\begin{aligned} l(\Pi_1) &= \text{constant} - T/2\ \ln|\,\hat{\Omega}(\Pi_1)\,| \\ X_d P &= \Pi_1\, X_l P + e \ . \end{aligned} \tag{3.36}$$

Maximizing the likelihood thus amounts to minimizing the determinant of (3.34). The maintained model is now expressed as the hypothesis (cf table 3.3)

$$\mathcal{H}_m : \qquad \mathrm{rk}\,\Pi_1 \le p, \quad m_1 \in \mathbb{R}, \quad m_0 \in \mathbb{R} \ .$$

Under this hypothesis (3.36) becomes a simple linear regression between series of corrected first differences and corrected lagged levels. The ML-estimator is given by

$$\hat{\Pi}_1 \;=\; S_{dl} S_{ll}^{-1} \;, \tag{3.37}$$

where $S_{ij} \equiv \frac{1}{T} X_i P X_j'$ are $p \times p$ sample moment matrices $(i, j = l, d)$. Insertion into (3.35) and (3.34) gives the complete ML-estimators for these parameters. The whole procedure amounts to OLS applied to (3.24) equation by equation. The probability model has the form of a SURE-system with equal regressors, so that OLS is consistent and efficient despite the cross-equation covariances contained in Ω. The maintained hypothesis provides a benchmark against which restrictions concerning the stochastic and structural properties of the data density can be tested. This is done in the following hypotheses.

First, based on the rank condition (3.25), the restriction "DGP not I(0)" can be expressed as the statistical hypothesis

$$\mathcal{H}(\hat{r}, 2): \qquad \mathrm{rk}\, \Pi_1 \leq \hat{r} < p \;, \quad m_1 \in \mathbb{R} \,, \;\; m_0 \in \mathbb{R} \tag{3.38}$$

or equivalently $\Pi_1 = \hat{\alpha}\,\hat{\beta}'$, where the matrix $\hat{\alpha}$ is $p \times \hat{r}$ with *some* column rank and the matrix $\hat{\beta}$ is $p \times \hat{r}$ with *full* column rank. In this case (3.36) becomes a reduced rank regression. This type of regression is treated in Tso (1981) and applied to cointegrated VAR's by Johansen (1988). Note that the matrix $\hat{\alpha}$ is not restricted by the hypothesis. This is statistically convenient since the likelihood can now be further concentrated with respect to this matrix. The flip-side of this convenience is that the factorization $\hat{\alpha}\hat{\beta}'$ now sets but an upper limit for the rank of Π_1, compare (3.38) and (3.25). This seemingly innocuous alteration is in fact the reason behind the sequential cointegration testing procedure outlined below. Here, regressing $(X_d P)$ on $(\hat{\beta}' X_l P)$ gives an estimator

$$\hat{\alpha}(\hat{\beta}) \;=\; S_{dl}\, \hat{\beta}\, (\hat{\beta}' S_{ll}\, \hat{\beta})^{-1} \quad . \tag{3.39}$$

Insertion of this estimator into (3.36) gives a likelihood $l(\hat{\beta})$ which depends solely on the final unknown parameter:

$$\begin{aligned} l\,(\hat{\beta}) \;&=\; \mathit{constant} \;-\; T/2 \,\ln\, \{\, |S_{dd} - S_{dl}\hat{\beta}\, (\hat{\beta}' S_{ll} \hat{\beta})^{-1} \hat{\beta}' S_{dl}|\, \} \qquad (3.40) \\ &=\; \mathit{constant} \;-\; T/2 \,\ln\, \{\, |S_{dd}| \cdot |\hat{\beta}'(S_{ll} - S_{ld} S_{dd}^{-1} S_{dl})\hat{\beta}| \;/\; |\hat{\beta}' S_{ll} \hat{\beta}|\, \} \\ &=\; \mathit{constant} \;-\; T/2 \,\ln\, \{\, |S_{dd}| \cdot |v'(I - \Lambda)\, v| \;/\; |v'v|\, \} \;. \end{aligned}$$

The second line in this expression is obtained by comparing expressions for the determinant of partitioned matrices.[43] The third line incorporates the a-priori restrictions ensuring statistical identification of Π_1 and thus a unique maximum of the likelihood function (compare section 2.1.1). In particular, $\hat{\beta}$

[43] Provided that S_{dd} and $\hat{\beta}' S_{ll}\, \hat{\beta}$ are both nonsingular (cf Anderson 1984, p.594).

is here a-priori required to satisfy $\hat{\beta} = BE\,v$, for a $p \times \hat{r}$ selection-matrix v and for nonsingular $p \times p$ matrices B and E defined by[44]

$$B' S_{ll} B \;=\; I_{p\times p} \quad , \qquad E'\,(B' S_{ld} S_{dd}^{-1} S_{dl} B)\, E \;=\; \Lambda_{p\times p} \quad . \tag{3.41}$$

The matrix $\Lambda = \mathrm{diag}(\lambda_1 > \lambda_2 > \cdots > \lambda_p)$ here contains the eigenvalues of the symmetric matrix $B' S_{ld} S_{dd}^{-1} S_{dl} B$, and the columns of E contain the corresponding orthonormal eigenvectors. Thus, $\hat{\beta}$ is here (just-)identified by the restriction $\hat{\beta}' S_{ll} \hat{\beta} = I_{\hat{r}\times\hat{r}}$ which in effect imposes a unit variance and zero covariance on the disequilibria of the concentrated series.

The log-likelihood $l\,(\hat{\beta})$ can now be maximized over all selection matrices v. Since the eigenvalues in Λ are arranged in descending order the minimum of the determinant is achieved at $v = [I_{\hat{r}\times\hat{r}}, 0]'$. Thus the final estimator and the maximum of the likelihood function, under the restriction that $\hat{\beta}$ be a $p \times \hat{r}$ matrix, are given by[45]

$$\hat{\beta} \;=\; B\,E\;[I_{\hat{r}\times\hat{r}},\,0]' \tag{3.42}$$

$$l_{\max}(\hat{r},2) \;=\; \text{constant} \;-\; T/2\;\ln\left\{\,|S_{dd}|\;\prod_{i=1}^{\hat{r}}(1-\lambda_i)\,\right\} \;. \tag{3.43}$$

Inserting (3.42) into (3.39) gives $\hat{\alpha} = S_{dl}\,\hat{\beta}$. From the orthogonality of the eigenvectors follows $\hat{\beta}_\perp = S_{ll} BE\,[0, I_{p-\hat{r}}]'$ and $\hat{a}_\perp = S_{dd}^{-1} S_{dl} BE\,[0, I_{p-\hat{r}}]'$. An estimator $\hat{C}$ for the moving-average impact matrix $C(1)$ is then easily assembled. The columns of $\hat{\beta}$ contain the eigenvectors associated to the $\hat{r}$ largest eigenvalues of $S_{ld} S_{dd}^{-1} S_{dl}$ in the metric of S_{ll}. These eigenvalues λ_i in turn are the square of the i-th canonical correlation coefficient between the series $X_d P$ and the series $X_l P$; see Tso (1981, p.187). The reduced rank regression thus looks for those linear combinations of $I(d)$-variables which maximize correlation with the $I(d$-$1)$-part of the process. If present, cointegrating vectors dominate all other linear combinations in this respect.

Moving one step further down in table 3.3, the restriction "DGP not I(0) nor $\mathcal{M}(r,2)$" is expressed as the hypothesis

$$\mathcal{H}(\hat{r},2^*): \qquad \mathrm{rk}\,\Pi_1 \,\le\, \hat{r} \,<\, p \;, \quad m_1 = \hat{\alpha}\, n_1 \,, \;\; m_0 \in \mathbb{R} \;\;.$$

To implement the hypothesis define $G = [G_1, ..., G_{k-1}, m_0]$ and $\Pi_1 = \hat{\alpha}[\hat{\beta}', n_1]$. That is, Π_1 is augmented by a $\hat{r} \times 1$ parameter vector n_1 capturing the linear trend in the cointegration space. After conformably defining the data matrices

[44] The matrix B is obtained by setting $B = (T')^{-1}$ in the Choleski decomposition $S_{ll} = TT'$ with T lower triangular, or by setting $B = TD^{-1/2}$ in the singular-value decomposition $S_{ll} = TDT'$ with D containing the nonzero eigenvalues of S_{ll} as diagonal, and T the corresponding orthonormal eigenvectors as columns.

[45] For $\hat{r}$=0 the maximized likelihood becomes $l_{\max}(0,2) = \text{constant} - T/2\,\ln\,|S_{dd}|$.

X^* (as X without regressor t) and X_l^* (as X_l plus regressor t) estimation now proceeds as above. Concentration of the likelihood relates series of first differences and lagged levels corrected for the constant and the short-run dynamics:

$$X_d\, P^* \;=\; \Pi_1\, X_l^*\, P^* \;+\; e\;. \tag{3.44}$$

Under the present restriction on Π_1 this is a reduced rank regression similar to (3.36). Note that the matrix S_{dd}^* is $p\times p$, the matrices $S_{dl}^* = S_{ld}^{*\prime}$ are $p\times p{+}1$, and the matrices S_{ll}^*, B, E, Λ are $p{+}1\times p{+}1$. However, the last eigenvalue λ_{p+1}^* in Λ is identically zero since the matrices Π_1 and $B' S_{ld}^* S_{dd}^{*\,-1} S_{dl}^* B$ have at most rank p. The final estimator and the maximized log-likelihood function under the present restriction are given by[46]

$$\hat\beta^* \;=\; B\,E\,[I_{\hat r\times\hat r},\,0]' \tag{3.45}$$

$$l_{\max}(\hat r, 2^*) \;=\; \text{constant} \;-\; T/2\,\ln\{\,|S_{dd}^*|\,\textstyle\prod_{i=1}^{\hat r}(1-\lambda_i^*)\,\}\;. \tag{3.46}$$

Finally, the two restrictions $\mathcal{H}(\hat r,1)$ and $\mathcal{H}(\hat r,0)$ are formulated and implemented in analogy to $\mathcal{H}(\hat r,2)$, whereas the restriction $\mathcal{H}(\hat r,1^*)$, postulating the constant to be non-integrating, is implemented in analogy to $\mathcal{H}(\hat r,2^*)$.

Estimation in the I(2)-model: Estimation in the I(2)-model proceeds from the interim multiplier representation (3.31). In this representation, the deterministic regressor is specified as $d_t \equiv m_0$ to avoid cubic trends. To set up a likelihood function define the $p\times T$ matrices X_{dd}, X_l, X_{dl} of second differences, lagged levels, and lagged first differences, respectively. Let the matrix X mop up the various lagged second differences, and let $\mathbf{1}$ denote a $1\times T$ vector of ones. In this notation the general probability model (3.33) with $m_1 = 0$ is expressed as

$$l\,(\Pi_1,\Pi_2,G,\Omega) \;=\; -pT/2\,\ln(2\pi) \;-\; T/2\,\ln|\Omega| \;-\; 1/2\,\mathrm{tr}\,[\,e'\,\Omega^{-1}e\,]$$

$$X_{dd} \;=\; \Pi_1 X_l \;+\; \Pi_2\, X_{dl} \;+\; G\,X \;+\; m_0\mathbf{1} \;+\; e\;.$$

Using the redefined projection matrix $P \equiv I - X'(XX')^{-1}X$ the unrestricted parameters G are again concentrated out by

$$X_{dd}P \;=\; \Pi_1 X_l P \;+\; \Pi_2 X_{dl} P \;+\; m_0\mathbf{1}P \;+\; e\;. \tag{3.47}$$

Based on the rank condition (3.32), the restriction "DGP not I(0) nor I(1)" can now be expressed as the statistical hypothesis (cf table 3.3)

$$\mathcal{H}(\hat r,1;\hat s,1):\quad \mathrm{rk}\,\Pi_1 \le \hat r < p\,,\;\; \mathrm{rk}\,\Gamma \le \hat s < p-\hat r\,,\;\; m_1 = 0\,,\;\; \alpha_\perp' m_0 \in \mathbb{R}\,,$$

where $\Gamma = \alpha_\perp'\,\Pi_2\,\beta_\perp$. Estimation under this hypothesis follows a two-stage procedure: In a first stage, (3.47) is estimated under the restriction $\Pi_1 = \hat\alpha\,\hat\beta'$

[46] Note that $\hat\beta^*$ is a $p{+}1\times\hat r$ matrix: its last row contains the estimator $\hat n_1'$.

for unrestricted Π_2 and m_0. This is equivalent to estimation of (3.36) under hypothesis $\mathcal{H}(\hat{r}, 1)$. Treating the resulting estimates as population values, the second stage then continues with a p-r dimensional subsystem of (3.47). Precisely, premultiplying $\alpha'_\perp$ in (3.47) and using the last identity from (3.26) gives $\alpha'_\perp \Pi_1 = 0$ and $\alpha'_\perp \Pi_2 (\beta_\perp \bar{\beta}'_\perp + \bar{\beta}\beta')$, and therefore the subsystem

$$\alpha'_\perp X_{dd}P = \Gamma(\bar{\beta}'_\perp X_{dl}P) + \alpha'_\perp \Pi_2 \bar{\beta}(\beta' X_{dl}P) + \alpha'_\perp m_0(\mathbf{1}P) + \alpha'_\perp e .$$

Since the parameters of $(\beta' X_{dl}P)$ are unrestricted this term can be concentrated out. Defining the $(p\text{-}r) \times T$ matrices $Z_d \equiv \alpha'_\perp X_{dd}$ and $Z_l \equiv \bar{\beta}'_\perp X_{dl}$ the concentrated subsystem is described by

$$Z_d QP = \Gamma Z_l QP + \alpha'_\perp m_0 \mathbf{1} QP + \alpha'_\perp e , \tag{3.48}$$

where $Q \equiv I - PX'_{dl}\beta(\beta' X_{dl} P X'_{dl}\beta)^{-1}\beta' X_{dl}$ is a $T \times T$ projection matrix. Under present hypothesis $\mathcal{H}(\hat{r}, 1; \hat{s}, 1)$ the constant in this equation is also unrestricted. Concentrating it out finally produces

$$Z_d RQP = \Gamma Z_l RQP + \alpha'_\perp e , \tag{3.49}$$

where $R \equiv I - QP\mathbf{1}'(\mathbf{1}QP\mathbf{1}')^{-1}\mathbf{1}$ is a projection matrix. Under the present hypothesis, this equation becomes a reduced rank regression with $\Gamma = \hat{\gamma}\hat{\delta}'$, where $\hat{\gamma}$ is $p\text{-}\hat{r} \times \hat{s}$ with some column rank and $\hat{\delta}$ is $p\text{-}\hat{r} \times \hat{s}$ with full column rank. The reduced rank regression (3.49) can now be estimated in analogy to (3.36), defining the conditional[47] sample moment matrices $S_{ij.r} \equiv \frac{1}{T} Z_i RQPZ_j$ (for subscripts $i, j = l, d$). The resulting maximized log-likelihood of the subsystem contains p-$\hat{r}$ ordered eigenvalues ρ_i which are used for the construction of test statistics in the next subsection.

Moving yet another step further down in table 3.3, the restriction "DGP not I(0) nor I(1) nor $\mathcal{M}(r, 1;\ s, 1)$" is finally expressed as the hypothesis

$$\mathcal{H}(\hat{r}, 1; \hat{s}, 1^*) : \quad \operatorname{rk} \Pi_1 \leq \hat{r} < p, \ \operatorname{rk} \Gamma \leq \hat{s} < p - r, \ m_1 = 0, \ \alpha'_\perp m_0 = \hat{\gamma} n_0 ,$$

or $\Gamma = \hat{\gamma}[\hat{\delta}', n_0]$, so that the once integrated intercept is fully absorbed on the I(1)-level and a quadratic trend does not arise. Estimation under this hypothesis proceeds as above until equation (3.48). Then, defining the regressor matrix $Z_l^* \equiv [Z'_l, \mathbf{1}']'$ the reduced rank regression is

$$Z_d QP = \Gamma Z_l^* QP + \alpha'_\perp e ,$$

which can be estimated in analogy to $\mathcal{H}(\hat{r}, 2^*)$. In a similar fashion the restriction $\mathcal{H}(\hat{r}, 1^*; \hat{s}, 0)$ is formulated and estimated: The first stage of the estimation procedure is in this case equivalent to estimation of (3.36) under $\mathcal{H}(\hat{r}, 1^*)$. The second stage reduced rank regression then corresponds to (3.48) with $\alpha'_\perp m_0 = 0$.

---

[47] Conditional on the rank r and hence on the dimension of the subsystem.

Test-Statistics: The likelihood-ratio $\ln Q = l_{max}[\mathcal{H}_0] - l_{max}[\mathcal{H}_A]$ suggests itself for hypothesis testing in the present framework. Two such likelihood ratios concerning the rank of Π_1, labelled the *trace statistic* (TR) and the *maximal eigenvalue statistic* (ME) by Johansen/Juselius (1990), are easily constructed from the maximized log-likelihoods of the I(1)-model: [48]

$$\begin{aligned} TR\,(\hat{r},i) &\equiv -2\ln Q\ [\mathcal{H}(\hat{r},i) \mid \mathcal{H}(p,i)] &&= -T\textstyle\sum_{i=\hat{r}+1}^{p} \ln(1-\lambda_i) \\ ME\,(\hat{r},i) &\equiv -2\ln Q\ [\mathcal{H}(\hat{r},i) \mid \mathcal{H}(\hat{r}+1,i)] &&= -T\ln(1-\lambda_{\hat{r}+1})\ , \end{aligned}$$

where the λ denote sample eigenvalues calculated from a reduced rank regression like (3.36) under the respective restriction $i = 0, 1^*, 1, 2^*, 2$ on the deterministics. The null hypothesis is in both cases $\mathcal{H}(\hat{r},i)$, which postulates $p-\hat{r} > 0$ common I(d)-trends for some order of integration $d \geq 1$. The two statistics test this null against the unrestricted alternative $\mathcal{H}(p,i)$ or against the less restricted alternative $\mathcal{H}(\hat{r}+1,i)$, respectively.

Two other trace statistics, one about the rank of Γ alone and one about the rank of both Γ and Π_1, are constructed in Johansen (1995a) and Paruolo (1996) from the maximized log-likelihoods of the I(2)-model:

$$\begin{aligned} TR(\hat{s},j \mid \hat{r},i) &\equiv -2\ln Q\ [\mathcal{H}(\hat{r},i;\ \hat{s},j) \mid \mathcal{H}(\hat{r},i)] &&= -T\textstyle\sum_{i=\hat{s}+1}^{p-\hat{r}} \ln(1-\rho_i) \\ TR(\hat{r},i;\ \hat{s},j) &\equiv -2\ln Q\ [\mathcal{H}(\hat{r},i;\ \hat{s},j) \mid \mathcal{H}(p,i)] &&= TR(\hat{s},j \mid \hat{r},i) + TR\,(\hat{r},i) \end{aligned}$$

where the ρ denote sample eigenvalues calculated from a reduced rank regression like (3.49) under the respective restriction $j = 0, 1^*, 1$ on the deterministics. The null hypothesis is in both cases $\mathcal{H}(\hat{r},i;\ \hat{s},j)$, which postulates $p-\hat{r}-\hat{s} > 0$ common I(d)-trends and $\hat{s}$ common I(d–1) trends for some $d \geq 2$. The two statistics test this null against the less restricted alternative $\mathcal{H}(\hat{r},i)$ or against the unrestricted alternative $\mathcal{H}(p,i)$, respectively.

Properties of Estimators and Statistics: The asymptotic properties of estimators under the various I(1)-models $\mathcal{M}(r,i)$ are studied in Johansen (1991), Lütkepohl/Reimers (1992) and Paruolo (1997). Since the matrices Π_1 and $C(1)$ are unique (invariant to the choice of the basis of the cointegration space), their estimators are consistent: the deviations $[\hat{G}_i - G_i]$, $[\hat{\Omega} - \Omega]$, $[\hat{\Pi}_1 - \Pi_1]$, and $[\hat{C} - C(1)]$ all converge to some zero-mean normal distribution if scaled by $\sqrt{T}$. However, the matrices α and β are not unique and their estimators hence lack proper population values. Some statistically identifying a-priori restrictions are necessary for consistent estimation. The maximum likelihood procedure adopts $\hat{\beta}' S_{11} \hat{\beta} = I$. An alternative normalization

[48] Here $l_{max}[\mathcal{H}_0]$ is given by (3.43), whereas $l_{max}[\mathcal{H}_A]$ is given by (3.43) with summation limit $\hat{r}+1$ (ME-statistic) or summation limit p (TR-statistic). In the latter case the rank of Π_1 is not restricted at all. Inserting these expressions gives $\ln Q = [-\frac{T}{2}\Sigma_{i=1}^{\hat{r}} \ln(1-\lambda_i)] - [-\frac{T}{2}\Sigma_{i=1}^{p} \ln(1-\lambda_i)] = \frac{T}{2}\Sigma_{i=\hat{r}+1}^{p} \ln(1-\lambda_i)$. Multiplying through with -2 then gives the TR-statistic.

is $\hat{\beta}_c = \hat{\beta}(c'\hat{\beta})^{-1}$, for some known $p \times \hat{r}$ matrix c of full column rank, which is also invariant to the choice of the basis of the cointegration space. For $\hat{r} = r$ the deviation $[\hat{\beta}_c - \beta_c]$ converges to a zero-mean mixed normal distribution if scaled by T (superconsistency), whereas the corresponding deviations $[\hat{\alpha}_c - \alpha_c]$ converge to a zero-mean normal distribution if scaled by $\sqrt{T}$.

The asymptotic properties of the statistics $TR(\hat{r}, i)$ and $ME(\hat{r}, i)$ under various I(1)-models $\mathcal{M}(r, i)$ are studied in Johansen (1988, 1991, 1994): The sample eigenvalues $\lambda_1, ..., \lambda_r$ converge in probability to their nonzero population counterparts, and the sample eigenvalues $\lambda_{r+1}, ..., \lambda_p$ converge to zero, at rate T^{-1}. Consequently the scaled eigenvalues $T\lambda_1, ..., T\lambda_r$ diverge, whereas the scaled eigenvalues $T\lambda_{r+1}, ..., T\lambda_p$ converge in distribution to the eigenvalues of a $p\text{-}r \times p\text{-}r$ stochastic matrix.[49] The sum $T\,\Sigma\lambda_{r+i}$ hence converges to the trace of this matrix (TR-distribution), and $T\lambda_{r+1}$ alone converges to the maximal eigenvalue of this matrix (ME-distribution). The corresponding test statistics obey the same limiting distributions since $-T\ \ln(1{-}\lambda) = T\lambda + o_p(1)$. The limiting distributions are nonstandard and depend on the true deterministic degree. Asymptotic quantiles over a range of common trends are tabulated by simulation for the cases $i = 0, 1^*, 1, 2^*, 2$ in Osterwald-Lenum (1992) and MacKinnon/Haug/Michelis (1996).[50] Approximations using the Gamma distribution are provided by Doornik (1998). Several cases of misspecification are also treated: The limiting distribution of $TR(\hat{r}, 2)$ under model $\mathcal{M}(r, 2^*)$, which is the multivariate version of Dickey/Fuller's $\hat{\tau}_\tau$-distribution, is tabulated in Perron/Campbell (1993, Table 1). The limiting distribution of $TR(\hat{r}, 1)$ under model $\mathcal{M}(r, 1^*)$, which is the multivariate version of Dickey/Fuller's $\hat{\tau}_\mu$-distribution, is tabulated in Johansen/Juselius (1990, Table A2). The distribution of $TR(\hat{r}, 0)$ under model $\mathcal{M}(r, 0;\ s, 0)$ is tabulated in Johansen (1995a, Table 2).

The asymptotic properties of the statistics $TR(\hat{s}, j|\hat{r}, i)$ and $TR(\hat{r}, i; \hat{s}, j)$ under the various I(2)-models $\mathcal{M}(r, i; s, j)$ are similar and hence but shortly summarized. The limiting distribution of $TR(\hat{s}, j|\hat{r}, 1)$ is given by a TR-

[49] Precisely, the scaled sample eigenvalues converge to the $p - r$ eigenvalues ρ obtained as solutions of

$$\left| \rho I_{p-r} - \int dB\, F' \left(\int FF'du \right)^{-1} \int F\, dB' \right| = 0 ,$$

where B is a $p - r$ dimensional standard Brownian motion on the unit interval, and F depends on B and on the true polynomial degree of the deterministic component; see Johansen (1994, Theorem 1).

[50] The first paper simulates the expressions for the asymptotic distributions. The second paper simulates the models $\mathcal{M}(r, i)$ and calculates the statistics for a number of finite sample sizes. Response surface regressions are then used to estimate the asymptotic quantiles.

distribution of dimension $p - r - s$ and case $j = 1, 1^*, 0$ deterministics; see Johansen (1994, 1995a). The limiting distribution of $TR(\hat{r}, i; \hat{s}, j)$ is derived and tabulated by simulation for case $(i, j) = (0, 0)$ in Johansen (1995a, Table 3), and for the cases $(i, j) = (1^*, 0)$, $(1, 1^*)$, $(1, 1)$ in Paruolo (1996, Tables 5,6,13). Unsurprisingly, for $\hat{s} = p - \hat{r}$ all these distributions collapse into the corresponding TR-distribution.

Testing (co-)integration: The true rank r of the matrix Π_1 is of course unknown and so is its factorization into two full column-rank matrices. The hypothetical factorization $\Pi_1 = \hat{\alpha}\hat{\beta}'$ corresponds to the statistical hypothesis $\mathcal{H}(\hat{r}, \cdot) : \operatorname{rk} \Pi_1 \leq \hat{r} < p$ and leads to the reduced rank regression (3.36). Since the matrix G is unrestrictedly concentrated out, this hypothesis merely rules out an I(0)-model. Thus $\mathcal{H}(\hat{r}, \cdot)$ is really a *composite null*: it postulates $p - \hat{r}$ common trends integrated of any order $d \geq 1$. Consequently, the limiting distribution of a statistic calculated under this null is indeterminate without further information.[51] This information can be generated by a sequential testing procedure proposed by Pantula (1989) for scalar time series. It stipulates, basically, that a null be tested only after all other hypotheses nested therein have been rejected before, either by test or by a-priori assumption. These rejections leave but a single hypothesis in the composite null and thus uniquely determine the applicable limiting distribution. This principle of sequential testing is extensively applied in the following cointegration tests.

The first problem is to determine the rank r for some fixed deterministics, with I($d \geq 2$)-models ruled out a-priori. The behaviour of the test statistics then depends on the true (r) and the conjectured ($\hat{r}$) cointegration rank. Let $TR(\hat{r}, i)$ denote the trace statistic[52] calculated from a sample generated by model $\mathcal{M}(r, i)$. As critical value, let $q(\alpha; \hat{r}, i)$ denote the tabulated $(1 - \alpha)$ quantile of the TR-distribution for a number $p - \hat{r}$ of common trends and case i deterministics. Now, under $r > \hat{r}$ the sample eigenvalues $\lambda_{\hat{r}+1}, ..., \lambda_r$ converge to their nonzero population counterparts, so that $T\lambda_{\hat{r}+1}, ..., T\lambda_r$ and hence the trace-statistic itself diverge to infinity. Therefore asymptotically $P\left[TR(\hat{r}, i) > q(\alpha; \hat{r}, i)\right] = 1$; the trace statistic has well defined power. Under $r = \hat{r}$ the sum of scaled sample eigenvalues $T\lambda_{\hat{r}+1}, ..., T\lambda_p$ and hence the trace statistic itself converge to the trace of a $p\text{-}\hat{r} \times p\text{-}\hat{r}$ stochastic matrix, the TR-distribution, so that $P\left[TR(\hat{r}, i) > q(\alpha; \hat{r}, i)\right] = \alpha$. Finally, under $r < \hat{r}$ the trace statistic also converges, but to the sum of the $p - \hat{r}$ smallest eigenvalues of a $p\text{-}r \times p\text{-}r$ stochastic matrix rather than the proper TR-distribution. To remedy this problem Johansen (1992a, Theorem 2) proposes a sequential test procedure: testing the hypotheses successively in the order $\hat{r} = 0, 1, ..., p\text{-}1$

[51] Consider for example the two limiting distributions available for the trace statistic $TR(\hat{r}, 0)$, one under model $\mathcal{M}(r, 0)$ and one under model $\mathcal{M}(r, 0;\ s, 0)$. Both models could represent the DGP under the restriction $\mathcal{H}(\hat{r}, 0)$.

[52] The arguments apply, mutatis mutandis, also to the maximal eigenvalue statistic.

rules out the undesirable case $r < \hat{r}$ in each single test. Rejection of $\mathcal{H}(\hat{r}\text{-}1, i)$ and acceptance of $\mathcal{H}(\hat{r}, i)$ then allow to infer a true cointegration rank $r = \hat{r}$ with controlled size α.

The second problem is to determine the ranks r and s for some fixed deterministics, with I($d \geq 3$)-models ruled out a-priori. One sequential procedure, proposed by Johansen (1995a, Theorem 9), determines r and s successively: First the hypotheses $\mathcal{H}(\hat{r}, i)$ are tested as above in the order $\hat{r} = 0, 1, ..., p\text{-}1$ using the statistics $TR(\hat{r}, i)$ against the TR-distribution. Then, for the first non-rejected $\hat{r}$, the hypotheses $\mathcal{H}(\hat{r}, i;\ \hat{s}, j)$ are tested in the order $\hat{s} = 0, 1, ..., p\text{-}\hat{r}\text{-}1$ using the statistics $TR(\hat{s}, j|\ \hat{r}, i)$ against the TR-distribution. This procedure has well defined power. Its size however, being the joint size of two tests, is not equal to α and tabulated in Johansen (1995a, Table 4). Another sequential procedure, proposed by Johansen (1995a, Theorem 8) and Paruolo (1996, Theorem 4.2), determines r and s simultaneously: The hypotheses $\mathcal{H}(\hat{r}, i;\ \hat{s}, j)$ are tested for given $\hat{r}$ in the order $\hat{s} = 0, 1, ..., p\text{-}\hat{r}$ using the statistics $TR(\hat{r}, i;\ \hat{s}, j)$ against their appropriate distributions. This is repeated in the order $\hat{r} = 0, 1, ..., p\text{-}1$ and stops at the first non-rejected hypothesis. It is noted that the I(2)-hypotheses $\mathcal{H}(\hat{r}, i; \hat{s}, j)$ and the I(1)-hypotheses $\mathcal{H}(\hat{r}, i)$ are both tested in the course of this simultaneous procedure: the former in each instance $\hat{s} < p\text{–}\hat{r}$ and the latter in each instance $\hat{s} = p\text{–}\hat{r}$. The procedure has well defined power and controlled size α.

The third problem is to simultaneously determine the true rank r and the true deterministic degree, with I($d \geq 2$)-models ruled out a-priori. In this case the set of hypotheses is nested in two directions: First $\mathcal{H}(\hat{r}\text{-}1, i) \subset \mathcal{H}(\hat{r}, i)$ and second $\mathcal{H}(\hat{r}, i\text{-}1) \subset \mathcal{H}(\hat{r}, i)$. A sequential test procedure is proposed by Johansen (1992a, Theorem 3): For a fixed $\hat{r}$ the hypotheses $\mathcal{H}(\hat{r}, i)$ are tested successively in the order $i = 0, 1^*, 1, 2^*, 2$ using the statistics $TR(\hat{r}, i)$ or $ME(\hat{r}, i)$ against their respective TR- or ME-distributions. This is repeated in the order $\hat{r} = 0, 1, ..., p\text{-}1$ and stops at the first non-rejected hypothesis. The procedure has well defined power and controlled size.

Testing Deterministics: A related problem is to determine the unknown true deterministic degree for a given cointegration rank. Consider the proportionality restriction $m_1 = \hat{\alpha} n_1$. Setting $\hat{r} = p$ produces $\hat{\alpha} = I_{p \times p}$, rendering m_1 effectively unrestricted. Therefore $\mathcal{H}(p, 2) = \mathcal{H}(p, 2^*)$. Conversely, setting $\hat{r} = 0$ produces $\hat{\alpha} = 0_{p \times p}$, rendering m_1 effectively zero. Therefore $\mathcal{H}(0, 2^*) = \mathcal{H}(0, 1)$. The associated log-likelihoods are identical in both cases. This fact is exploited in the following expansions:

$$\begin{aligned} l(r, 2^*) - l(r, 2) &= \{l(r, 2^*) - l(p, 2^*)\} - \{l(r, 2) - l(p, 2)\} \\ l(r, 1) - l(r, 2^*) &= \{l(r, 1) - l(0, 1)\} - \{l(r, 2^*) - l(0, 2^*)\} \ . \end{aligned}$$

Inserting into these expansions the respective expressions for the maximized likelihoods, for example (3.46) and (3.43), allows to construct two likelihood ratios testing the proportionality-restriction $m_1 = \hat{\alpha}\, n_1$ and the zero-restriction $m_1 = 0$, respectively:

$$
\begin{aligned}
q(r, 2^*) &\equiv -2 \ln Q\left[\mathcal{H}(r, 2^*) | \mathcal{H}(r, 2)\right] &= -T \textstyle\sum_{i=r+1}^{p} \ln\{(1-\lambda_i^*) / (1-\lambda_i)\} \\
q(r, 1) &\equiv -2 \ln Q\left[\mathcal{H}(r, 1) | \mathcal{H}(r, 2^*)\right] &= T \textstyle\sum_{i=1}^{r} \ln\{(1-\lambda_i^\circ) / (1-\lambda_i^*)\}\,.
\end{aligned}
$$

Johansen (1994) shows the statistic $q(r, 2^*)$ and the analog statistic $q(r, 1^*)$ to be asymptotically distributed as $\chi^2(p-r)$ under their respective nulls. Likewise, the statistic $q(r, 1)$ and the analog statistic $q(r, 0)$ are shown to be asymptotically distributed as $\chi^2(r)$ under their respective nulls. The tests $q(r, 1)$ and $q(r, 0)$ are equivalent to testing a zero restriction on the last row of the estimator $\hat{\beta}^*$ obtained under hypothesis $\mathcal{H}(r, 2^*)$ or $\mathcal{H}(r, 1^*)$, respectively.

Summary: The preceding section 3.2 discussed several attractive aspects of the vector autoregressive model. To begin with, the general model (3.15) can be reparameterized in order to separate an (interesting) long-run behaviour from some (uninteresting) transitory dynamics. The long-run concerns the behaviour of the underlying stochastic sequence at zero frequency, and is controlled by the number and the allocation of unit roots in the characteristic equation of the system. Here this behaviour is isolated in the interim multiplier representations (3.24) and (3.31), and controlled by the rank restrictions (3.25) and (3.32), respectively. The many possible constellations of unit roots, and their interaction with the deterministic regressor, then induce a rich variety of submodels which are summarized in table 3.3.

This variety, however, also considerably complicates the estimation methods and testing procedures for a VAR model which are outlined in subsection 3.2.3. These procedures attempt to determine the order of integration (d), the cointegration rank (r), and the deterministic degree $(0, 1^*, 1, 2^*, 2)$. Since the hypotheses $\mathcal{H}(\hat{r}, i)$ and $\mathcal{H}(\hat{r}, i; \hat{s}, j)$ used to implement the unit root restrictions (3.25) and (3.32) are in fact composite hypotheses, these statistical features have to be established within a carefully tailored sequential testing procedure involving a variety of non-standard limiting distributions.

Despite these complications, the truly attractive aspect from a methodological point of view is that the VAR model allows to detect interesting long-run 'equilibrium' relations by means of a purely statistical criterion, namely that linear combinations of I(d)-variables be I(d-1). This in turn relieves economic theory from proving the existence of these relations to the more adequate task of their economic interpretation, which is one of the topics addressed in the following chapter.

4 Structural ECM Models

In chapter 2 the process of econometric modelling was divided into two stages (compare table 2.1). The first stage covers the transition from sample to population. The relevant statistical theory, namely the cointegrated VAR model, was detailed in chapter 3. The second stage covers the transition from population to structure. The corresponding entrance of economic theory into the statistical model is detailed in the present chapter. To this end, the cointegrated VAR model is first factorized into a conditional and a marginal VAR. The conditional VAR is then subjected to suitable just-identifying restrictions producing an economically meaningful structural ECM, and to certain over-identifying restrictions producing useful exogeneity- and causality properties for the conditional model.

A distinctive feature of the general VAR model is its indiscriminate and joint treatment of all individual variables included in the vector x_t. The statistical properties delineated within this model - notably integration and cointegration - accordingly pertain systemwide to all variables in the VAR. This profligacy is reduced in the present section, which delineates statistical properties characterizing only subsets of variables. These properties - namely stability, exogeneity, causality - allow to isolate meaningful and more informative submodels within a cointegrated VAR by means of simple, testable parameter restrictions. Unfortunately, this reduction in dimensionality involves a complication in terms of notation since subsets of variables and subsets of cointegration relations have to be distinguished. To introduce the necessary definitions, the cointegrated VAR model with Gaussian shocks is replicated in its reduced-form error correction representation (3.30):

$$\Delta x_t = \alpha\beta' x_{t-1} + \textstyle\sum_{i=1}^{k-1} G_i \, \Delta x_{t-i} + d_t + e_t \ , \quad e_t \sim i.i.n(0, \Omega) \ . \qquad (4.1)$$

This model forms the basis of the present chapter. It is, in particular, assumed that a certain cointegration rank $0 < r < p$ and a certain specification for the deterministic regressor d_t have been established before.

Proceeding from (4.1), the model's variables and its cointegration relations are now suitably classified to establish a taxonomy for the subsequent structural analysis.

Classification of Variables: To distinguish subsets of variables, the p components in the vector x_t are classified into g conditioned and q marginalized components. Using selection matrices H_y and H_z these are expressed as[53]

$$\underset{g\times 1}{y_t} \;\equiv\; \underset{g\times p}{H_y'}\; \underset{p\times 1}{x_t} \qquad \textit{Conditioned Variables } (g)$$

$$\underset{q\times 1}{z_t} \;\equiv\; \underset{q\times p}{H_z'}\; \underset{p\times 1}{x_t} \qquad \textit{Marginalized Variables } (q)$$

where of course $g + q = p$. For the errors in (4.1) this classification produces a similar partition $e_{yt} \sim i.i.n(0, \Omega_{yy})$ and $e_{zt} \sim i.i.n(0, \Omega_{zz})$ with covariance matrix Ω_{zy}, using $\Omega_{ij} \equiv H_i'\Omega H_j$ in obvious notation.

The classification into conditioned and marginalized variables motivates a corresponding split of the general VAR model into two likelihood-independent submodels. To this end, the general model's parameters are conformably partitioned: as $G_{y.i} \equiv H_y'G_i$ or $G_{yz.i} \equiv H_y'G_iH_z$ for the short-run parameters, for example, and as $\alpha_z \equiv H_z'\alpha$ or $\beta_y \equiv H_y'\beta$ for the long-run parameters. Moreover, a new error sequence $e_{ct} \equiv e_{yt} - \omega e_{zt}$ and a new deterministic sequence $d_{ct} \equiv d_{yt} - \omega d_{zt}$ are defined, using $\omega \equiv \Omega_{yz}\Omega_{zz}^{-1}$ to account for contemporaneous covariances among the VAR-shocks. The general model is then split by premultiplying to (4.1) the transformation matrix

$$\underset{p\times p}{\mathrm{T}} \;\equiv\; \begin{bmatrix} I_{g\times g} & -\omega \\ 0 & I_{q\times q} \end{bmatrix} \begin{bmatrix} H_y' \\ H_z' \end{bmatrix} .$$

Since T is of full rank this operation does not change the joint probability density of the VAR, the original sequence and the transformed sequence are observationally equivalent (compare section 2.2.1). The transformed sequence is now represented by the two submodels

$$\begin{aligned} \Delta y_t \;=\; & (\alpha_y - \omega\alpha_z)\,\beta' x_{t-1} \;+\; \omega\,\Delta z_t \;+\; d_{ct} \;+\; e_{ct} \\ & \qquad\qquad + \;\textstyle\sum_{i=1}^{k-1} (G_{y.i} - \omega G_{z.i})\,\Delta x_{t-i} \end{aligned} \tag{4.2}$$

$$\begin{aligned} \Delta z_t \;=\; & \alpha_z\,\beta' x_{t-1} \;+\; d_{zt} \;+\; e_{zt} \\ & \qquad\qquad + \;\textstyle\sum_{i=1}^{k-1} G_{z.i}\,\Delta x_{t-i} \;, \end{aligned} \tag{4.3}$$

whose errors e_{ct} and e_{zt} are uncorrelated by construction. In terms of the SGM concept mentioned in section 2.1, the conditional errors e_{ct} constitute an innovation against the information $\mathcal{I}_t = \sigma(z_t, X_{t-k}^{t-1})$. In fact, the whole split amounts to a factorization of the joint density $f(x_t|X_{t-k}^{t-1})$ implied by model (4.1) into a conditional density $f_c(y_t|z_t, X_{t-k}^{t-1})$ implied by submodel

[53] In principle H_y and H_z could be any known matrices of full column rank satisfying $H_y'H_z = 0_{g\times q}$ (no double-selection) and $[H_y, H_z]\,[H_y, H_z]' = I_{p\times p}$.

(4.2) and a marginal density $f_m(z_t|X_{t-k}^{t-1})$ implied by submodel (4.3). Since the joint density is Gaussian the parameters of the two submodels are indeed variation free (see footnote 16). The factorization serves two purposes: under weak exogeneity and non-causality the marginal model (4.3) can be neglected for estimation or forecasting (cf Engle/Hendry/Richard 1983), and under stability the conditional model (4.2) can be developed into a structural ECM. For this discussion it is useful to classify also the x-variables on the right-hand side of (4.2)-(4.3) into subsets y and z. The cointegrated VAR is then:

$$\begin{aligned}\Delta y_t = {} & (\alpha_y - \omega\alpha_z)\,\beta_y'\, y_{t-1} + (\alpha_y - \omega\alpha_z)\,\beta_z'\, z_{t-1} + \omega\Delta z_t + d_{ct} + e_{ct} \qquad (4.4)\\ & + \textstyle\sum_{i=1}^{k-1}(G_{yy.i} - \omega G_{zy.i})\,\Delta y_{t-i} + \sum_{i=1}^{k-1}(G_{yz.i} - \omega G_{zz.i})\,\Delta z_{t-i}\end{aligned}$$

$$\begin{aligned}\Delta z_t = {} & \alpha_z\beta_y'\, y_{t-1} + \alpha_z\beta_z'\, z_{t-1} + d_{zt} + e_{zt} \qquad (4.5)\\ & + \textstyle\sum_{i=1}^{k-1} G_{zy.i}\Delta y_{t-i} + \sum_{i=1}^{k-1} G_{zz.i}\Delta z_{t-i} \; .\end{aligned}$$

In the sequel, interest concentrates on the conditional VAR model given by (4.2) or (4.4), abbreviated CVAR. For expositional convenience its lagged differences will sometimes be suppressed ($k = 1$) without loss of generality.

Classification of Cointegration Relations: To distinguish subsets of cointegration relations, the $r \times p$ matrix β' is partitioned into submatrices β_1' $(r_1 \times p)$ and β_2' $(r_2 \times p)$, where of course $r_1 + r_2 = r$. The adjustment matrix α is similarly partitioned into $[\alpha_1; \alpha_2]$. Combining this partition with the above classification of variables, the two matrices α and β are partitioned column-wise into dimensions r_1 and r_2, and row-wise into dimensions g and q. The cointegration relations are now classified into r_1 relations holding across the whole system and r_2 relations holding only among marginalized variables:

$$\underset{r_1\times p}{\beta_1'}\;\underset{p\times 1}{x_t} = \underset{r_1\times g}{\beta_{y1}'}\;\underset{g\times 1}{y_t} + \underset{r_1\times q}{\beta_{z1}'}\;\underset{q\times 1}{z_t} \qquad \textit{Systemwide Relations } (r_1)$$

$$\underset{r_2\times p}{\beta_2'}\;\underset{p\times 1}{x_t} = \underset{r_2\times q}{\beta_{z2}'}\;\underset{q\times 1}{z_t} \qquad \textit{Marginal Relations } (r_2)$$

This classification obviously implies $r_2 \leq q$. In the borderline case $r_2 = q$ the matrix β_{z2} becomes invertible, so that any linear combination of marginalized variables is cointegrating, implying $z_t \sim I(0)$. Moreover, the classification also involves a restriction on the cointegration space, namely $\beta_{y2}' = 0$. However, this restriction is binding only for $r_1 < g$. In the borderline case $r_1 = g$ the matrix β_{y1} becomes invertible, so that all y-variables can be excluded from r_2 cointegration relations by simply rotating the cointegration space.[54] Both borderline cases reappear in the discussion of stability and causality below.

[54] If β_{y1} is invertible, a $r \times r$ matrix ξ can be defined which is identity except for a $r_2 \times r_1$ term $-\beta_{y2}'(\beta_{y1}')^{-1}$ in its lower left corner. The matrix $\xi\beta'$ then has r_2 rows not involving any y-variable. Since $\alpha\beta' = \alpha\xi^{-1}\xi\beta'$ this operation merely rotates the cointegration space.

4.1 Just-Identification

Under dynamic stability the conditional VAR model (4.2) or (4.4) can be further transformed via just-identifying restrictions. These restrictions insert economic content into the statistical model. The result is a structural error-correction model (SECM). The transition from CVAR to SECM is the topic of the present section.

4.1.1 Dynamic Stability

A conditional model is dynamically stable if, following a shock, its conditioned variables eventually revert to their equilibrium values. This type of stability is closely related to cointegration. The two concepts however differ in that cointegration is a property of a (vector) stochastic sequence, whereas stability is a property of a (conditional) model and may thus depend on a certain choice of conditioned variables. For a formal definition of stability, the CVAR (4.4) is expressed as a multivariate autoregressive-distributed lag (ADL) model:

$$B(L)\, y_t \;=\; D(L)\, z_t \;+\; d_{ct} \;+\; e_{ct} \;, \tag{4.6}$$

where $B(L)$ and $D(L)$ are k-th order polynomial matrices of dimension $g \times g$ and $g \times q$, respectively. The long-run matrices of the ADL-model (4.6) and the CVAR-model (4.4) are obviously linked by

$$\underset{g\times g}{B(1)} \;=\; -\underset{g\times r}{(\alpha_y - \omega\alpha_z)}\,\underset{r\times g}{\beta_y'} \;=\; -\underset{g\times r_1}{(\alpha_{y1} - \omega\alpha_{z1})}\,\underset{r_1\times g}{\beta_{y1}'}$$

$$\underset{g\times q}{D(1)} \;=\; \underset{g\times r}{(\alpha_y - \omega\alpha_z)}\,\underset{r\times q}{\beta_z'} \;=\; \underset{g\times r_1}{(\alpha_{y1} - \omega\alpha_{z1})}\,\underset{r_1\times q}{\beta_{z1}'} \;+\; \underset{g\times r_2}{(\alpha_{y2} - \omega\alpha_{z2})}\,\underset{r_2\times q}{\beta_{z2}'} \;.$$

The CVAR represented by (4.6) is called *stable* if all latent roots of $B(L)$ lie outside the complex unit circle.[55] Under assumption 2 in section 3.2.2, a sufficient condition for stability is full rank of $B(1)$ such that the own dynamics of the y-variables do not contain unit roots.[56] If the own dynamics of certain variables in an integrated VAR are stable, then these variables are still integrated, but endogenous in that they acquire this property solely by reacting to other, marginalized variables. Stability therefore neatly squares with the idea of cointegration arising from the adjustment of actual variables y_t towards equilibrium values y_t^*. The equilibrium values can be thought of as being provided by underlying economic *target relations* representing goals of agents in terms of integrated marginalized variables. Following Davidson/Hall

[55] Stability is here unrelated to the property of time-invariance, for which the label 'constancy' is employed.

[56] Full rank of $B(1)$ precludes unit roots. Assumption 2 in section 3.2.2 precludes explosive roots. Together these two conditions leave but stable roots in $B(L)$. This in turn implies $\det B(1) > 0$ (see appendix A.1).

(1991), some g target relations are assumed hidden in $B(1)\, y_t^* = D(1)\, z_t$, the long-run solution of (4.6). Under stability the matrix $B(1)$ can be inverted and the system has a unique solution for the targets y_t^*. From the above expressions for $B(1)$ and $D(1)$, the corresponding disequilibrium $y_t - y_t^*$ can be decomposed into two partial disequilibria. The first comprises cointegration residuals $u_t \equiv y_t + (\beta_{y1}')^{-1}\beta_{z1}' z_t$ and describes the disequilibrium driving the conditioned variables given a certain state of marginalized variables. The second comprises cointegration residuals $\beta_{z2}' z_t$ and describes the deviation of these marginalized variables from their own equilibrium values.[57] This decomposition allows to rewrite the CVAR (4.4). Under stability (and k=1) this model becomes

$$\Delta y_t = -B(1)\, u_{t-1} + (\alpha_{y2} - \omega\alpha_{z2})\beta_{z2}'\, z_{t-1} + d_{ct} + e_{ct} + \omega\Delta z_t\,, \qquad (4.7)$$

$$\Delta u_t = -B(1)\, u_{t-1} + (\alpha_{y2} - \omega\alpha_{z2})\beta_{z2}'\, z_{t-1} + d_{ct} + e_{ct} + \left(\omega + (\beta_{y1}')^{-1}\beta_{z1}'\right) \Delta z_t \qquad (4.8)$$

Both equations are equivalent. The first shows the endogenous variables as adjusting according to both partial disequilibria of the previous period, whereas the second shows the dynamic properties of the partial disequilibrium u_t. The matrix $B(1)$ governs stability in both equations. Its full rank ensures $I(0)$-ness and hence mean reversion of the g-dimensional VAR sequence $\{u_t\}$. This property is clearly essential to sustain an interpretation as a disequilibrium error.

The notion of stability is frequently associated with two other, intuitively plausible stability measures. In the tradition of stochastic macroeconomic models, an autonomous partial disequilibrium is introduced by simply adding an exogenous error term u_t to a static long-run relation. The relation's stability is then measured by the unconditional variance $var(u_t)$, both absolutely (finite variance) and relatively (low variance). A classic example for this approach is Poole (1970), who shows the relative size of error variances in the IS-/LM equations to be crucial for an optimal choice of monetary policy instruments. The second measure of stability arose with the appearance of buffer stock models in economics and error-correction models in econometrics. These models endogenize a partial disequilibrium by specifying a dynamic adjustment equation besides the static long-run relation. The stability of the latter is then measured by the adjustment speed in the former, both absolutely (nonzero speed) and relatively (high speed).

[57] For example, one disequilibrium ($r_1 = 1$) could describe the deviation of actual money from the level desired for given values of nominal output and interest rates. Two other disequilibria not involving money ($r_2 = 2$) could then describe the deviations of nominal output and interest rates from their respective equilibrium values.

The representations (4.7) and (4.8) now show that these two notions are in fact equivalent interpretations of the present definition of stability: In (4.7) the matrix $B(1)$ has a direct interpretation as a set of scalar adjustment coefficients, and the stability condition $\det B(1) > 0$ associates large latent roots with a high overall adjustment speed. In (4.8) the matrix $B(1)$ governs the autoregressive part of the disequilibrium sequence. As shown in section 3.2.1, the unconditional variance of a stationary vector sequence depends on the inverse of its VAR operator. The parameter matrices of this inverse converge to zero at a rate dictated by the latent roots of the VAR operator. Large latent roots thus correspond to a low unconditional variance.

As an example, consider a single-equation conditional model ($r = g = 1$). The matrix $B(1)$ then reduces to a scalar $b(1)$, and the necessary stability condition $\det B(1) > 0$ collapses into the familiar requirement that the overall reaction in (4.7) or (4.8) be negative. Combining the remaining terms on the right-hand-side of (4.8) into a stationary sequence $\{\eta_t\}$, the disequilibria form an AR(1) sequence $u_t = [1 - b(1)]\, u_{t-1} + \eta_t$ with characteristic root $\lambda_1 = [1-b(1)]^{-1}$. If this root is stable, if $|\lambda_1| < 1$ or equivalently $0 < b(1) < 2$, then the sequence of disequilibria is stationary and mean-reverting with finite unconditional variance $var(u_t) = var(\eta_t) \,/\, \left(1 - [1-b(1)]^2\right)$, cf section 3.1.1. This constitutes a simple formulation of Granger's representation theorem linking error correction ($0 < b(1) < 2$) to cointegration ($0 < var(u_t) < \infty$). Moreover, the larger the root of the AR-operator ($[1\text{-}b(1)]^{-1} \rightarrow \infty$), the higher the adjustment speed ($b(1) \rightarrow 1$) and the lower the disequilibrium variance ($var(u_t) \rightarrow var(\eta_t)$), that is, the more 'stable' the conditional model. The instable case $b(1) = 0$ corresponds to the absence of cointegration. This case serves as a null hypothesis in standard cointegration tests: the single-step procedure in Banerjee/Dolado/Mestre (1998) relies on the t-ratio of $b(1)$ from (4.7), whereas the two-step procedure in Engle/Granger (1987) relies on the t-ratio of $b(1)$ from (4.8).

In summary, stability of the conditional model (4.6) requires a full rank $\operatorname{rk} B(1) = r_1 = g$. Under stability the target relations effective in (4.6) have a unique solution $y_t^* = B(1)^{-1} D(1)\, z_t$. The actual variables y_t then adjust towards these targets and thereby acquire the property of integration from the marginalized variables z_t. Stability thus implies systemwide cointegration in the sense defined before. The converse is not true. Several cases of instability occurring together with systemwide cointegration are delineated by Davidson/Hall (1991). First, a case called *insufficient targets* arises if $\operatorname{rk} B(1) = r_1 = r < g$. The target relations then have multiple solutions for y_t^* since only r relations are linearly independent. Thus, the target relations determine an insufficient number of targets since only $r < g$ targets are independently attainable in the sense that their equilibrium error is an I(0)-sequence. Second, a case called *inconsistent targets* arises if $\operatorname{rk} B(1) = r_1 < r = g$. The target relations then have no solution for y_t^* since $r_2 > 0$ relations do not involve any of the conditioned variables. Thus, although in this case the target relations determine a sufficient number of $r = g$ independently attainable targets, these targets are inconsistent with the chosen conditional model since r_2 of them concern marginalized variables. Third, instability also arises from a reduced rank of the adjustment matrix, $\text{rk}\,(\alpha_y - \omega\alpha_z) < r_1 = g$. The target relations may then have a unique solution, but not all of them effectively enter the conditional model so that the conditioned variables can not adjust towards all existing targets. Thus, the failure of some CVAR to show cointegration may well be due to a wrong choice of conditioned variables leading to instability rather than outright lack of an underlying equilibrium relation.

4.1.2 Structural ECM

The conditional VAR model preserves a clear distinction between the long-run and the short-run properties of an underlying autoregressive sequence. This section discusses the separate identification of first the long-run and then the short-run parameters, which allows to reparameterize a stable conditional VAR into a system of simultaneous ECM equations in structural form. A-priori information taken from economic theory enters at two points: First in the identification of the long-run parameter β, which is an instance of statistical identification discussed in section 2.1. Second in the identification of the short-run parameters, which is an instance of structural identification discussed in section 2.2. Both cases are now treated in turn.

Identification of Long-Run: From section 3.2.2 recall the factorization $\Pi_1 = \alpha\beta'$ of the long-run matrix in a VAR model. This factorization is not unique, i.e., any set of cointegration vectors b_i comprising the columns of β spans but one basis of the r-dimensional cointegration space. A unique factorization can be achieved by requiring the set of cointegration vectors to satisfy a suitable set of homogenous linear restrictions. Suppose $p - s_i$ such restrictions are available for the i-th cointegration vector. Collecting them as columns of a $p \times (p - s_i)$ full rank matrix R_i spans a space for the restricted parameters in this vector. The $p \times s_i$ orthogonal complement $H_i \equiv R_{i\perp}$ spans the space for the remaining freely varying parameters. An individual cointegration vector b_i is then identified by requiring

$$R_i' b_i = 0 \qquad \Leftrightarrow \qquad b_i = H_i \varphi_i \tag{4.9}$$

for some given restrictions R_i and some free $s_i \times 1$ vector φ_i. Examples for R_i and H_i are given in appendix A.5. A cointegration vector b_i is now uniquely characterized by some restrictions R_i (up to an arbitrary normalization) if it can not be reproduced by any linear combination of the remaining vectors, so that b_i is distinguished as the only vector from the cointegration space satisfying (4.9). To be in this sense suitable for all cointegration vectors the entire set of restrictions $R_1, ..., R_r$ should meet the classical rank condition

$$\mathrm{rk}\,(R_i' b) \;=\; r-1 \quad , \quad i=1,...,r \ . \tag{4.10}$$

If each matrix R_i implements exactly $p - s_i = r - 1$ restrictions and (4.10) holds, then the set of restrictions merely rotates the base of the cointegration space without restricting the space itself, i.e., without changing Π_1. In this case the set of cointegration vectors (namely b) is called *just-identified.* If, however, any single R_i imposes $p-s_i > r-1$ restrictions and (4.10) holds, then the cointegration space is genuinely restricted and the matrix Π_1 changes. In this case b is called *over-identified.* Succinctly, imposing 1 normalization and $r-1$ other restrictions satisfying (4.10) on each cointegration relation leaves the likelihood (3.43) unchanged. Imposing more restrictions changes the likelihood, and only this over-identification leads to statistically testable hypotheses (cf section 4.2).

The classical rank condition (4.10) is, unfortunately, not quite operational since usually but the restrictions R_i are known from economic theory, whereas for b only a random variable $\hat{b}$ is available as an estimate. However, substituting $b = [H_1\varphi_1, ..., H_r\varphi_r]$ in (4.10) leads to an alternative, operational condition on the (row-)rank of the restriction matrices, namely

$$\mathrm{rk}\,(R_i' H_{j_1}, ..., R_i' H_{j_n}) \;\geq\; n \quad , \quad n=1,...,r-1 \tag{4.11}$$

for each possible set $(j_1, ..., j_n)$ of indices not matching index i. This 'generic' identification condition involves no particular estimates. Rather, as shown by Johansen (1995b), it is necessary and sufficient for the just-identification of 'almost all' cointegration vectors. An example for such generically identifying matrices H_i is also given in appendix A.5.

The calculation of a cointegration vector subject to a set of just-identifying restrictions is accomplished via an eigenvalue problem. Let β contain the vectors obtained under Johansen's maximum likelihood procedure, i.e., under the nonlinear restriction $\beta' S_{11} \beta = I_{r \times r}$ implemented via (3.41). These likewise just-identifying restrictions impose unit variances and zero covariances on the disequilibria of concentrated levels. To replace them by alternative, perhaps economically more interesting linear restrictions (4.9), a recombination of β lying in the space spanned by the H_i must be found. For the i-th cointegration vector this amounts to solving

$$B'\beta'\beta B \;=\; I_{r\times r} \quad , \quad E_i' \, (B'\beta' H_i (H_i' H_i)^{-1} H_i' \beta B) E_i \;=\; \Lambda_i \tag{4.12}$$

for a matrix E_i of eigenvectors and a diagonal matrix Λ_i of eigenvalues, in analogy to (3.41). The just-identified cointegration vector is then given by $\beta B e_i$, where e_i denotes the column from E_i corresponding to the largest eigenvalue. Solving the eigenvalue problem for each individual design matrix H_i gives a nonsingular transformation matrix $N_1 \equiv B[e_1, ..., e_r]$. This allows to calculate a matrix $\bar{b} = \beta N_1$ of just-identified cointegration vectors with a default normalization $\bar{b}'\bar{b} = I_{r\times r}$.

To sustain an interpretation as a proper economic equilibrium relation the preliminary vectors in $\bar{b}$ have to be renormalized on the conditioned variables. This is simply achieved by collecting the inverse elements along the diagonal of $\bar{b}_y \equiv H_y'\bar{b}$ in a (diagonal) normalization matrix N_2. Defining $N \equiv N_1 N_2$ then gives a final matrix of structural cointegration vectors

$$b_{p\times r} = \beta N \qquad \text{with} \qquad b_{y.ii} = 1 \ , \tag{4.13}$$

where the $b_{y.ii}$ are the diagonal elements of $b_y \equiv H_y'b$. The normalization on the conditioned variables ($b_{y.ii} = 1$) does not materially change the overall identification scheme. Nevertheless, it involves the obvious condition that the cointegration rank matches the number of conditioned variables ($r = g$), and that none of these variables is actually excluded from every just-identified cointegration vector ($r = r_1$). This condenses into the single condition that the original CVAR matrix β_y be square and nonsingular. The adjustment coefficients corresponding to (4.13) are of course given by $\alpha(N')^{-1}$. This matrix is, however, merely adapted to a changed β and not identified in its own right. The identification of adjustment dynamics is the next topic.

Identification of Short-Run: Following the discussion in section 2.2.1, the probability model (4.2) is viewed as the reduced form of some observationally equivalent structural model. In the present linear case, following (2.4) and (2.5), a structural model is obtained by premultiplying some nonsingular $g \times g$ matrix M to the conditional VAR model (4.2). This linear reparameterization does not change the likelihood, and does also not change the separately identified cointegration vectors. The resulting structural model is just-identified in that no other structure also satisfies the defining restrictions imposed by the chosen matrix M.

The precise design of the short-run identification matrix M and the long-run identification matrices R_i is determined by some a-priori theory. Economic theory is often informative about the long-run but usually silent about the short-run. One possible economic restriction on the short-run of an entire system could be a Walras-restriction, requiring that the system's disequilibria sum to zero in each period. This restriction is however extremely difficult to implement statistically. Therefore the design of M is here determined by practical considerations. Specifically, following Boswijk (1994, 1995) the identification matrix M is chosen such that the adjustment matrix in the prospective SECM becomes diagonal:

$$a_{g\times r} = M(\alpha_y - \omega\alpha_z)(N')^{-1} \stackrel{!}{=} \operatorname{diag}(a_{ii}) \ . \tag{4.14}$$

The choice of a diagonal adjustment matrix has the advantage that only one structural disequilibrium $b_i' x_{t-1}$ enters the i-th equation of the SECM. As an additional advantage, each adjustment coefficient a_{ii} is actually independent of the non-corresponding long-run identification schemes $R_{j\neq i}$. Thus, given a suitable identification of the i-th cointegration vector (as money demand for example), the i-th SECM equation can be interpreted as the corresponding structural adjustment equation irrespective of the particular identification chosen for the remaining equations. The price for this convenience is, however, an additional condition, namely the requirement that the CVAR adjustment matrix $(\alpha_y - \omega\alpha_z)$ be square and nonsingular.

Under this condition the diagonalization in (4.14) can be achieved by a simple projection. Define $\alpha_c \equiv (\alpha_y - \omega\alpha_z)(N')^{-1}$ as the adjustment matrix to be diagonalized by premultiplication of M. Moreover, let $s_\perp$ denote a $g \times 1$ selection vector picking the i-th column of a given matrix, and let s denote the corresponding $g \times (g-1)$ selection matrix picking all remaining columns. The elements of the diagonal structural adjustment matrix (4.14) are then given by

$$a_{ii} \;=\; M_{ii}\; s'_\perp\, \alpha_c \left[I - s\,(s'\alpha_c\, s)^{-1}\, s'\alpha_c\right]\; s_\perp \;. \tag{4.15}$$

This projection determines a uniquely up to an arbitrary normalization of M. An obvious normalization is $M_{ii} = 1$. Once a is determined the remaining elements of M are obtained by inverting the defining relationship (4.14).

Recall that the above diagonalization of a and normalization of b relied upon the nonsingularity of the matrices $\alpha_y - \omega\alpha_z$ and β_y, respectively, in the CVAR model (4.2). These requirements condense into the single stability condition that $B(1)$ be square ($r_1 = g$) and of full rank. After a short summary of the whole identification procedure some tests assessing the validity of this condition are discussed.

Structural ECM: Combining the above long-run and short-run identification schemes, the conditional VAR model (4.2) produces a structural error-correction model (SECM) given by[58]

$$\begin{aligned} M\Delta y_t \;=\; & M\omega\Delta z_t \;+\; a\,b'x_{t-1} \;+\; Md_{ct} \;+\; Me_{ct} \qquad\qquad (4.16)\\ & +\; \textstyle\sum_{i=1}^{k-1} M\,(G_{y.i} - \omega G_{z.i})\;\Delta x_{t-i} \;, \end{aligned}$$

with $M_{ii} = 1$, and b and a defined by (4.13) and (4.14), respectively. Here the identification of a and the normalization of b require that the underlying CVAR be stable as defined in subsection 4.1.1. Since the adjustment matrix a is diagonal, the SECM-equation explaining the dynamic movement of the i-th conditioned variable ($\Delta y_{i.t}$) includes, by construction, only the i-th structural cointegration relation ($b'_i\, x_{t-1}$), normalized on the same variable. The influence of the remaining cointegration relations is nevertheless preserved through the additional contemporaneous changes $\Delta y_{j\neq i.t}$ feeding through M

[58] Note, however, that the label 'SECM' is not generally a trademark confined to the present definition (4.16). Examples for other likewise 'structural' conditional models are given by Ericsson (1995).

into each SECM-equation. Thus a SECM still constitutes a simultaneous system of error-correction equations. In contrast to a CVAR, however, a SECM allows to confront empirical data with economic theory by isolating the reaction of a conditioned variable to one specific, suitably specified economic long-run relation of interest. For example, one cointegration relation could be identified to resemble a theoretical static money demand function. Through the corresponding adjustment coefficient a_{ii} a SECM would then isolate the empirical reaction of any selected conditioned variable (money or prices) to the implied money market disequilibrium, irrespective of the identification of other disequilibria. The significance of the structural adjustment coefficients can be tested by a Wald-statistic, derived in section 4.2.4 below.

4.2 Over-Identification

The conditional VAR model (4.2), and therefore also the SECM (4.16), are not necessarily independent of the marginal model (4.3). Rather, only under well defined restrictions the marginal model can be neglected for estimation and forecasting, namely under weak exogeneity and Granger-noncausality. These two concepts thus capture important qualitative properties of a useful econometric model. Another interesting property is that of time-invariance, or constancy, of the cointegration space. All three concepts can be formulated as testable over-identifying restrictions within the Johansen maximum-likelihood procedure.

Cointegration vectors provide long-run relations between components of x_t as a statistical benchmark. Structural hypotheses on the matrix β are therefore tested against the statistical hypothesis $\mathcal{H}(r,i)$ formulated in section 3.2.3. Given non-uniqueness of the factorization $\Pi_1 = \alpha\beta'$ these structural hypotheses have to be formulated as restrictions on the whole cointegration space, as over-identifying restrictions on β. Johansen (1991, Theorem C.1) shows that for a known cointegration rank any likelihood ratio testing n over-identifying restrictions is asymptotically distributed as chi-square with n degrees of freedom. Two generic types of over-identifying hypotheses are here sufficient for the formulation of subsequent tests.

A first generic type of over-identifying hypothesis imposes the same $(p-s) < (p-r)$ restrictions on each column of β, and hence on the entire cointegration space, via

$$\mathcal{H}_1(r,i) : \qquad \beta = H\phi \ , \tag{4.17}$$

where H is some $p\times s$ matrix of full column rank implementing the restriction, and maximization of the likelihood is over all $s \times r$ matrices ϕ. An example for the design matrix H is given in appendix A.5. The hypothesis is tested by inserting $\beta = H\phi = HBEv$ into the log-likelihood (3.40). Estimation then proceeds as in section 3.2.3, using the $s \times s$ matrices B, E, Λ defined by $B'(H'S_{ll}H)B = I$ and $E'(B'H'S_{ld}S_{dd}^{-1}S_{dl}H\,B)\,E = \Lambda$. The resulting maximized likelihood $l^1_{\max}(r,i)$ contains the determinant of S_{dd} and the r largest eigenvalues λ_{1j} from Λ. Comparison with $l_{\max}(r,i)$ from (3.43) then allows to construct a $\chi^2\,(rp{-}rs)$ distributed likelihood ratio[59]

$$-2\ln Q\,\left[(\mathcal{H}_1(r,i) \mid \mathcal{H}(r,i)\right] \;=\; T\sum_{j=1}^{r}\ln\{(1{-}\lambda_{1j})\,/\,(1{-}\lambda_j)\}\,. \qquad (4.18)$$

This ratio tests the over-identifying restriction (4.17) against the corresponding just-identified I(1)-model with same deterministic degree.

A second generic type of over-identifying hypothesis imposes r_k out of the r cointegrating vectors in β as known. This restriction is formulated as

$$\mathcal{H}_2(r,i):\qquad \beta \;=\; [\beta_k\,;\,\beta_u]\;, \qquad (4.19)$$

where β_k is some $p \times r_k$ matrix containing the known cointegrating vectors, and maximization of the likelihood function is now over all unknown $p \times r_u$ matrices β_u. Under the hypothesis, $\beta_k' X_l P$ is an I(0)-series and therefore concentrated out of the likelihood (3.33) like short-run dynamics. Partitioning also $\alpha = [\alpha_k; \alpha_u]$ then leads to a reduced rank regression (see appendix A.3)

$$X_d Q P \;=\; \alpha_u \beta_u'\, X_l Q P \,+\, e\;, \qquad (4.20)$$

where $Q \equiv I - \frac{1}{T} P X_l'\,\beta_k(\beta_k' S_{ll}\beta_k)^{-1}\beta_k' X_l$ defines a $T \times T$ projection matrix concentrating out the known cointegration relations. Using the $p \times p$ sample moment matrices $S_{ij.u} \equiv \frac{1}{T} X_i\,QP\,X_j'$ estimation of α_u and β_u then proceeds as in section 3.2.3, with but one exception: the matrix $S_{ll.u}$ is of reduced rank $p - r_k$ such that only its singular-value decomposition is feasible (see appendix A.3). This rank deficiency reduces the dimension of the matrices responsible for the just-identification of the unrestricted cointegration relations: the matrix B is now $p \times p{-}r_k$, and the matrices E and Λ are $p{-}r_k \times p{-}r_k$. The matrix Λ contains the ordered $p{-}r_k$ eigenvalues of the matrix $(B' S_{ld.u} S_{dd.u}^{-1} S_{dl.u} B)$ as diagonal. The matrix E contains the associated eigenvectors as columns. The final estimator is again $\hat{\beta}_u = BE\,[I_{r_u \times r_u}, 0]'$. The resulting maximized likelihood $l^2_{\max}(r_u, i)$ contains the determinant of $S_{dd.u}$ and the r_u largest eigenvalues λ_{2j}. Again, comparison with $l_{\max}(r,i)$ from (3.43) allows to construct a $\chi^2(r_k p - r_k r)$ distributed likelihood ratio[60]

[59] Under hypothesis $\mathcal{H}(r,i)$, or shortly $\mathcal{H}$ hereafter, the matrix β has $pr - r^2$ free parameters since r^2 parameters are used to normalize the cointegration space. Under hypothesis $\mathcal{H}_1$ the matrix β has $sr{-}r^2$ free parameters via ϕ. Subtracting the latter from the former gives a total of $(p{-}s)\,r$ over-identifying restrictions.

[60] The matrix β_k has no free parameters by hypothesis. The matrix β_u must be chosen from a space orthogonal to β_k. This is expressed as $\beta_u = \beta_{k\perp}\,\phi$, where the matrix ϕ provides $(p{-}r_k)\,r_u - r_u^2$ free parameters. Subtracting this number from the free parameters under $\mathcal{H}$ gives a total of $[pr{-}r^2] - [(p{-}r_k)\,r_u - r_u^2] = (p{-}r)r_k$ over-identifying restrictions.

$$-2\ln Q\;[\mathcal{H}_2(r,i)\mid\mathcal{H}(r,i)] \;=\; T\left\{\ln|S_{dd.u}| - \ln|S_{dd}| + \textstyle\sum_{j=1}^{r_u}\ln(1-\lambda_{2j}) - \sum_{j=1}^{r}\ln(1-\lambda_j)\right\}\;.$$

This generic hypothesis $\mathcal{H}_2$ will prove useful for the test on noncausality in section 4.2.3 below. The slightly simpler generic hypothesis $\mathcal{H}_1$ provides a useful framework for the tests on constancy and on weak exogeneity, which are presented now.

4.2.1 Constancy

The restriction formulated in (4.17) allows a simple recursive test for the constancy of a cointegration space. To implement recursive estimation let $S = [I_{t\times t}\,,\,0_{t\times(T-t)}]'$ denote a $T\times t$ selection matrix. The concentrated model (3.36) over any sub-period $(-k+1,...,-1,0,1,...,t)$ is then expressed as

$$X_dPS \;=\; \Pi_1\,X_lPS \;+\; eS\;\;, \tag{4.21}$$

where the $T\times T$ projection matrix P concentrating out the short-run is now given either by $P_{(R)} \equiv S(I - S'X'(XSS'X')^{-1}XS)S'$ or by the original $P_{(F)} \equiv I - X'(XX')^{-1}X$. Defining the sample moment matrices $S_{ij.t} \equiv \frac{1}{t}X_iPS\,S'P'X_j'$ estimation of (4.21) then proceeds as in section 3.2.3, giving an unrestricted estimate $\hat\beta_t$. The two versions of the projection matrix allow two different approaches to recursive testing (Hansen/Johansen 1993): In the first version (matrix $P_{(R)}$) the entire model is re-estimated as if only observations up to time t were available. In the second version (matrix $P_{(F)}$) only the long-run matrix Π_1 is re-estimated, whereas the short-run and the deterministic regressor are kept fixed at their full sample values. This modification eliminates the influence of short-run fluctuations which otherwise would contaminate the test in finite samples, and moreover reduces the dependency on varying degrees of freedom.

To implement the hypothesis of constancy, let b denote some known $p\times r$ matrix whose columns are hypothesized to span the cointegration space. Setting $H = b$ in (4.17) and estimating $\mathcal{H}_1(r,i)$ with the moment matrices $S_{ij.t}$ then produces a likelihood ratio similar to (4.18). This ratio tests the space spanned by the columns of $\hat\beta_t$ for equality with the one spanned by the columns of b, or succinctly $sp(\hat\beta_t) = sp(b)$. Repeating this procedure sequentially over $t = T_0,...,T$ gives a sequence of likelihood ratios. If none of them exceeds its $\chi^2(pr-r^2)$ critical value, then the hypothesis of a time-invariant cointegration space is not rejected. The only remaining question is how to chose the reference matrix b. One possibility is the full sample estimate $\hat\beta_T$, which exhibits the smallest variance among all estimates $\hat\beta_t$. Another possibility is a somewhat earlier estimate $\hat\beta_{T-n}$, which produces more 'balance' in the test.

4.2.2 Weak Exogeneity

Marginalized variables z are called *weakly exogenous* for some parameter of interest if (i) this parameter is a function of only the conditional model's parameters, and (ii) the parameters in the conditional and marginal model are variation free (Engle/Hendry/Richard 1983). The second condition is satisfied for (4.2) and (4.3) by virtue of Gaussianity (cf footnote 16). Therefore the z-variables are weakly exogenous for the parameters α_y and β of interest if $\alpha_z = 0$, that is, if present z-variables do not react to past disequilibria $\beta' x_{t-1}$. Under this restriction the system (4.2)-(4.3) becomes

$$\begin{aligned} \Delta y_t &= \omega\, \Delta z_t + \alpha_y \beta' x_{t-1} + d_{ct} + e_{ct} \\ \Delta z_t &= d_{zt} + e_{zt} \quad , \end{aligned} \tag{4.22}$$

where k=1 for convenience. The weak exogeneity restriction is easily testable within Johansen's maximum likelihood procedure. Precisely, weak exogeneity involves restricting $q \le p - r$ rows of α to zero such that $\alpha_z = 0$. This restriction can be translated into the following equivalent though statistically more convenient form[61]

$$\mathcal{H}_3(r,i) : \qquad \alpha = H_y \, \psi \ . \tag{4.23}$$

Maximization of the concentrated likelihood is then over all $g \times r$ matrices ψ and all $p \times r$ matrices β. Since under the hypothesis these parameters can be recovered from the conditional density alone, estimation here proceeds from a g-dimensional reduced rank regression obtained by premultiplying $(H_y' {-} \omega H_z')$ to the concentrated model (3.36). This regression is given by [62]

$$H_y' X_d Q P = H_y' H_y \, \psi \, \beta' X_l Q P + e_c \ , \tag{4.24}$$

where $Q \equiv I - \frac{1}{T} P X_d' H_z \, (H_z' S_{dd} H_z)^{-1} H_z' X_d$ defines a $T \times T$ projection matrix concentrating the marginal submodel out of (4.22). Using $p{\times}p$ sample moment matrices $S_{ij.z} \equiv \frac{1}{T} X_i \, Q P X_j'$ estimation of ψ and β from the remaining conditional submodel then proceeds as in section 3.2.3. In particular:

$$\psi(\beta) = (H_y' H_y)^{-1} H_y' \, S_{dl.z} \, \beta (\beta' S_{ll.z} \beta)^{-1}$$

$$B' S_{ll.z} B = I_{p \times p} \quad , \quad E' \, B' S_{ld.z} H_y (H_y' S_{dd.z} H_y)^{-1} H_y' S_{dl.z} B \, E = \Lambda_{p \times p} \, .$$

Since $S_{dd.z}$ has reduced rank g the diagonal matrix Λ contains at most g nonzero eigenvalues λ_{3j}. The maximized likelihood of the whole model is the product of those of the conditional and the marginal submodel. It contains

---

[61] Recall that $H_z' H_y = 0$ (cf footnote 53) so that $\alpha_z \equiv H_z' \alpha = H_z'(H_y \psi) = 0$.

[62] Inserting estimator (3.34) into the definition $\omega = H_y' \Omega H_z \, (H_z' \Omega H_z)^{-1}$ produces, under hypothesis $\mathcal{H}_3$, the expression $\omega = H_y' (S_{dd} {-} \alpha \beta' S_{ld}) \, H_z (H_z' S_{dd} H_z)^{-1}$. Note that ω is zero if $H_y' \Omega H_z = 0$, i.e. if Ω is block-diagonal.

the determinant of S_{dd} and the r largest eigenvalues λ_{3j}. Comparison with $l_{\max}(r,i)$ allows to construct the $\chi^2(qr)$ distributed likelihood ratio[63]

$$-2\ln Q\;[(\mathcal{H}_3(r,i)\mid \mathcal{H}(r,i)] \;=\; T\textstyle\sum_{j=1}^{r}\ln\{(1-\lambda_{3j})\,/\,(1-\lambda_j)\}\;. \qquad (4.25)$$

This likelihood ratio tests the weak exogeneity restriction within the closed cointegrated VAR model (4.1). Intuitively, the restriction $\mathcal{H}_3(r,i)$ attempts to cut unwanted links between the (interesting) conditional model (4.2) and the (uninteresting) marginal model (4.3) in order to 'open up' the previously closed model. Another restriction pursuing this task is the following slightly more general noncausality restriction.

4.2.3 Granger-Noncausality

Marginalized variables z are called *not Granger-caused* by some conditioned variables y if for the marginal density holds $f_m(z_t\mid X^{t-1}) = f_m(z_t\mid Z^{t-1})$; see also footnotes 17 and 18. Inspection of (4.5) immediately shows that in a VAR model this property holds if the restrictions $\alpha_z\beta_y' = 0$ and $G_{zy.i} = 0$ (at all lags i) are satisfied, that is, if present z-variables do not react to any past y-variables. Following Granger/Lin (1995), the variables z are called *in the long-run not Granger-caused* by y if only the first restriction is satisfied, that is, if present z-variables do not react to past y-levels. This concept of noncausality pertaining but to the long-run is particularly well suited for macroeconometric applications where, for example, the quantity of money could be assumed endogenous in the short-run, but exogenously controllable by the central bank in the long-run (cf section 1.1).

An equivalent formulation of long-run Granger-noncausality (GNC) under the present classification of cointegration relations is $\alpha_{z1} = 0,\ \beta_{y2} = 0$.[64] Under this restriction the system (4.4)-(4.5) becomes

$$\begin{aligned}\Delta y_t &= \omega\Delta z_t + \alpha_{y1}\beta_1'\,x_{t-1} + (\alpha_{y2}-\omega\alpha_{z2})\beta_{z2}'\,z_{t-1} + d_{ct} + e_{ct}\\ \Delta z_t &= \alpha_{z2}\,\beta_{z2}'\,z_{t-1} + d_{zt} + e_{zt}\,,\end{aligned}\qquad (4.26)$$

where again k=1 for convenience. Thus, in the long run $\{z_t\}$ is a self-causal subsequence within $\{x_t\}$. Its statistical properties at zero frequency are hence determined in exact analogy to the general VAR, namely by the rank r_2 of

[63] Under hypothesis $\mathcal{H}$ the matrix α has pr free parameters. Under hypothesis $\mathcal{H}_3$ the matrix α has gr free parameters via ψ. Subtracting the latter from the former gives a total of qr over-identifying restrictions.

[64] The restriction can be written as $\alpha_z\beta_y' = [\alpha_{z1}\beta_{y1}' + \alpha_{z2}\beta_{y2}'] = 0$. The above classification prescribes $\beta_{y2}' = 0$ (no conditioned variables in the r_2-relations) and $\beta_{y1}' \neq 0$ (at least one systemwide cointegration relation). Therefore in the present setup $\alpha_{z1} = 0,\ \beta_{y2} = 0$ is the only allowable parameter constellation achieving GNC.

the $q \times q$ matrix $\alpha_{z2}\,\beta'_{z2}$: full rank ($r_2 = q$) implies $z_t \sim I(0)$, whereas reduced rank ($r_2 < q$) implies $z_t \sim I(1)$. Note that the GNC restriction implies weak exogeneity of z for the long-run parameters α_{y1} and β_1 in the conditional model. For $r_2 = 0$ the GNC restriction obviously collapses into the above weak exogeneity restriction.

The restrictions imposing long-run Granger-noncausality are testable within Johansen's maximum likelihood procedure, as a combination of the hypotheses $\mathcal{H}_1$, $\mathcal{H}_2$, $\mathcal{H}_3$. Precisely, GNC involves restricting $q \leq p - r_1$ rows of α_1 to zero such that $\alpha_{z1} = 0$, and restricting $g \leq p - r_2$ rows of β_2 to zero such that $\beta_{y2} = 0$. This joint restriction can be translated into the following equivalent though statistically more convenient form[65]

$$\mathcal{H}_4(r,i): \qquad \alpha = [H_y\psi,\, \alpha_2] \quad , \quad \beta = [\beta_1,\, H_z\phi] \quad . \tag{4.27}$$

Maximization of the concentrated likelihood is then over all $g \times r_1$ matrices ψ, all $p \times r_2$ matrices α_2, all $p \times r_1$ matrices β_1, and all $q \times r_2$ matrices ϕ. This maximization does not easily reduce to an eigenvalue problem. Instead a switching algorithm similar to Johansen/Juselius (1992) can be applied.

In step one, the values for α_1 and β_1 are fixed (at some initial values or at estimates from step two) and analog to $\mathcal{H}_2$ a reduced rank regression $(X_d - \alpha_1\beta'_1X_l)P = \alpha_2\beta'_2X_lP + e$ is solved for α_2 and β_2, implementing the restriction on the latter as in $\mathcal{H}_1$. This returns $r_2 \leq q$ nonzero eigenvalues. In step two, the values for α_2 and β_2 are fixed (at estimates from step one) and analog to $\mathcal{H}_2$ a reduced rank regression $(X_d - \alpha_2\beta'_2X_l)P = \alpha_1\beta'_1X_lP + e$ is solved for α_1 and β_1, implementing the restriction on the former as in $\mathcal{H}_3$. This returns $r_1 \leq g$ nonzero eigenvalues. Both steps then repeat until convergence. The likelihood ratio testing $\mathcal{H}_4(r,i)$ against $\mathcal{H}(r,i)$ is asymptotically $\chi^2(qr_1 + gr_2 - r_1r_2)$ distributed.[66] In the borderline case $g = r_1$ the restriction $\beta_{y2} = 0$ is not binding since all y-variables could be excluded from r_2 cointegration relations by simply rotating the cointegration space. The hypothesis $\mathcal{H}_4(r,i)$ then collapses into a $\chi^2(qr_1)$ statistic testing $\alpha_{z1} = 0$ similar to $\mathcal{H}_3(r,i)$.

65 Note that $\alpha_z\beta'_y = H'_z\alpha\beta'H_y = H'_z\,[\alpha_1\beta'_1 + \alpha_2\beta'_2]\,H_y$. Due to the orthogonality of the selection matrices (cf footnote 53) the restriction $H'_z\alpha_1 = 0$ is equivalent to $\alpha_1 = H_y\psi$ in analogy to $\mathcal{H}_3$, and the restriction $\beta'_2H_y = 0$ is equivalent to $\beta_2 = H_z\phi$ in analogy to $\mathcal{H}_1$.

66 The matrix β_2 has $qr_2 - r_2^2$ free parameters via ϕ. The matrix β_1, chosen from a space orthogonal to β_2 such that $\beta_1 = \beta_{2\perp}\theta$, has $(p\text{-}r_2)\,r_1 - r_1^2$ free parameters via θ. Subtracting the free parameters under $\mathcal{H}_4$ from those under $\mathcal{H}$ gives a total of $[pr - r^2] - [qr_2 - r_2^2 + (p\text{-}r_2)\,r_1 - r_1^2] = gr_2 - r_1r_2$ over-identifying restrictions on β. The matrix α_2 has pr_2 free parameters, while α_1 has gr_1 free parameters via ψ. Subtracting the free parameters under $\mathcal{H}_4$ from those under $\mathcal{H}$ gives a total of $[pr] - [gr_1 + pr_2] = qr_1$ over-identifying restrictions on α.

4.2.4 Instability

A conditional VAR model is stable if the $g \times g$ matrix $B(1) \equiv (\alpha_y - \omega\alpha_z)\beta_y'$ arising from this particular choice of conditioned variables in (4.4) is nonsingular. The stability of a CVAR is crucial for its reformulation as a structural ECM. A failure of stability should therefore yield testable implications in an empirically formulated SECM. A failure of stability may arise for several reasons. Instability from insufficient targets arises if the chosen number of conditioned variables exceeds the true number of cointegration relations ($g > r$). In this case some of the modelled disequilibria $b'x_{t-1}$ in (4.16) are actually not mean reverting, so that the corresponding adjustment coefficients should be empirically negligible. Instability from inconsistent targets arises if the conditioned variables do actually not occur in $r_2 > 0$ cointegration relations, so that the normalization in (4.13) is invalid. In this case some of the modelled disequilibria $b'x_{t-1}$ in (4.16) do actually not represent deviations of a conditioned variable from its own structural equilibrium value, so that again the corresponding adjustment coefficients should be empirically negligible. Finally, instability from an inadequate choice of conditioned variables arises if the conditional model fails to include all cointegration relations, so that the matrix $(\alpha_y - \omega\alpha_z)$ is actually of reduced rank. In this case the diagonalization (4.14) is invalid, rendering the corresponding adjustment coefficients again empirically negligible. In summary, if a SECM is formulated over an actually instable CVAR, then some of the adjustment coefficients a_{ii} in the SECM (4.16) should be 'close' to zero.

The restriction $a_{ii} = 0$ cannot be implemented into the present likelihood ratio testing framework since the formulation of a SECM is not possible under the null of instability. However, a SECM can always be formulated for an unrestricted stability matrix $B(1)$. An unrestricted likelihood suffices for the construction of a Wald test. For this test, the SECM (4.16) over some given sample size T is rewritten using the notation introduced in section 3.2.3. Specifically, let again X_l denote the $p \times T$ matrix of lagged levels, and X the matrix of lagged first differences plus constant and time trend. Moreover, let $\Delta Z \equiv [\Delta z_1, ..., \Delta z_T]$ denote the $q \times T$ matrix of differenced marginalized variables, let $\Delta y_i \equiv [\Delta y_{i,1}, ..., \Delta y_{i,T}]$ denote the $1 \times T$ vector of differences in the i-th conditioned variable, and let finally ΔY_j denote the (g-1) $\times T$ matrix of differences in all remaining conditioned variables. Then the i-th equation of the SECM (4.16) produces the probability model

$$\Delta y_i \;=\; a_{ii}\, b_i'\, X_l \;+\; G_i\, [\Delta Y_j \,,\, \Delta Z \,,\, X']' \;+\; e_i \quad , \tag{4.28}$$

where G_i denotes a vector of appropriate dimension containing all unrestricted parameters. The vector of restricted parameters is here given by $a_{ii}\, b_i' = a_{ii}\, \varphi_i' H_i' \equiv \delta_i'\, H_i'$, incorporating the identifying a-priori information for b_i via (4.9). Since the short-run is just-identified, this model can be estimated by two-stage OLS (see Spanos 1986, pp.626). In the first stage, fitted values $\Delta\hat{Y}_j$ are obtained from an OLS regression of ΔY_j on $[X_l, \Delta Z, X']'$. In the second stage, these fitted values are inserted into (4.28), so that the matrix of regressors with unrestricted parameters now reads as $W \equiv [\Delta\hat{Y}_j, \Delta Z, X']'$. This allows to concentrate the model to

$$\Delta y_i P = \delta_i' H_i' X_l P + e_i \quad , \tag{4.29}$$

where δ_i is of dimension $s_i \times 1$, and $P \equiv I - W'(WW')^{-1}W$ as usually defines a $T \times T$ projection matrix. The instability hypothesis now translates into $\delta_i = 0$ for the concentrated model. Testing this restriction by a Wald-statistic requires an unrestricted estimator $\hat{\delta}_i$ plus an estimator $\hat{V}(\hat{\delta}_i)$ for the covariance matrix of this estimator. Applying OLS to (4.29) yields:

$$\hat{\delta}_i = (H_i' X_l P X_l' H_i)^{-1} H_i' X_l P \, \Delta y_i' \quad ,$$

$$\hat{V}(\hat{\delta}_i) = \hat{\sigma}^2 \, (H_i' X_l P X_l' H_i)^{-1} \quad ,$$

where $\hat{\sigma}^2 = (T-m)^{-1} \, \hat{e}_i \, \hat{e}_i'$ is the regressions residual variance corrected for the number m of regressors in (4.28). The Wald statistic testing $\delta_i = 0$ is then given, as usual, by

$$W(\hat{\delta}_i) \equiv \underset{1\times s_i}{\hat{\delta}_i'} \, \hat{V}(\hat{\delta}_i)^{-1} \underset{s_i\times 1}{\hat{\delta}_i} \quad . \tag{4.30}$$

Note that, in its construction, the Wald statistic resembles the square of an ordinary t-ratio. From the estimate $\hat{\delta}_i$ the long-run in (4.28) is estimated as a $p \times 1$ vector $\hat{a}_{ii} \, \hat{b}_i = H_i \, \hat{\delta}_i$ using the respective design matrix from (4.9). Consequently, the structural adjustment coefficient $\hat{a}_{ii}$ is given by the i-th element of the $g \times 1$ vector $H_y'(H_i \hat{\delta}_i)$, and the corresponding structural cointegration vector normalized on the i-th conditioned variable is given by $\hat{b}_i = H_i \hat{\delta}_i \,/\, \hat{a}_{ii}$. Being derived from a conditional model in a Gaussian framework, these two estimators could also have been obtained from limited-information maximum likelihood estimation of the VAR, that is, from (4.24) with subsequent application of (4.13) and (4.14).

The asymptotic distribution of the Wald statistic $W(\hat{\delta}_i)$ is derived and tabulated by Boswijk (1994) under the a-priori assumption that $\alpha_z = 0$. Since this assumption allows only instability due to insufficient targets, the Wald test in this case constitutes but an alternative cointegration test whose outcome might at best corroborate the results of the Johansen procedure. However, as long as instability due to inconsistent targets can be ruled out, the test remains consistent with somewhat smaller critical values. Moreover, given that the estimator $\hat{a}_{ii}$ is but a random variable, the Wald statistic provides a useful standardization for the comparison of adjustment coefficients across equations or across models, and it will be used also for this purpose in chapter 6 below.

Summary: The complete VAR model (4.1), integrated of order one, can be split into a conditional and a marginal model by premultiplying a certain transformation matrix T. For the VAR's long-run this operation gives

$$\mathrm{T}\,\Pi_1\,x_{t-1} \;=\; \mathrm{T}\,\alpha\beta' x_{t-1} \;=\; \begin{bmatrix} (\alpha_y - \omega\alpha_z)\beta_y' & (\alpha_y - \omega\alpha_z)\beta_z' \\ \alpha_z\beta_y' & \alpha_z\beta_z' \end{bmatrix} \begin{bmatrix} y_{t-1} \\ z_{t-1} \end{bmatrix}.$$

Given a cointegration rank r, the long-run matrix $\Pi_1 = -A(1)$ isolates the $p - r$ latent unit roots of the VAR operator (3.16). The over-identifying restrictions considered in this chapter essentially concern the allocation of these latent unit roots within Π_1, or $\mathrm{T}\Pi_1$ for that matter. Specifically, the weak exogeneity restriction allocates q unit roots in the own dynamics of all z-variables (zero rank of $\alpha_z\beta_z'$). In contrast, the stability restriction prohibits any unit roots in the own dynamics of all y-variables (full rank of $(\alpha_y - \omega\alpha_z)\beta_y'$). The two restrictions therefore imply each other under $g = r$. Finally, the noncausality restriction and the weak exogeneity restriction both prevent stationary links from y to z variables (zero rank of $\alpha_z\beta_y'$). Loosely, these over-identifying restrictions attempt to establish statistical properties of a subset of variables by isolating an interesting conditional VAR model within the whole system.

The conditional VAR model can be just-identified into a structural ECM model. This allows to confront actual data and economic theory within a statistically valid framework. Specifically, the structural ECM produces an adjustment coefficient isolating the reaction of a conditioned variable to disequilibria implied by some specified economic long-run relation of interest. This adjustment coefficient, or its standardization as a Wald-statistic, can be used to assess the stability of this economic relation, both absolutely (nonzero adjustment speed) and relatively (high adjustment speed). An alternative stability measure is the disequilibrium variance of the specified economic relation. Although intuitively likewise appealing, this measure has two statistical drawbacks: First, any design for the covariance matrix of disequilibria (e.g., diagonalization) involves nonlinear restrictions for which the generic identification condition (4.11) does not hold (cf Johansen 1995b). Second, the case of instability implies an infinite disequilibrium variance, which is a rather unoperational restriction in a statistical model. Therefore the focus in the present chapter has been on the adjustment coefficients appearing in a structural ECM.

The disequilibrium variance as a measure of stability is nevertheless not completely discarded. Rather, it occupies a prominent role in aggregation theory, i.e., in the investigation of effects arising from cross-sectional aggregation of static economic relations. In the next chapter these effects are discussed in detail, and shown to appear simultaneously in both measures of stability.

5 Aggregation

The logical implications of aggregation and, hence, some accessory properties expected in a European money demand function are explored by aggregation theory. This theory is well developed for the case of un-weighted linear aggregation of static linear relations between stationary variables. One popular result states that parameter equality across countries is a condition for 'safe' aggregation. However, this conventional strand of aggregation theory does not really match the peculiarities encountered in the case of European money demand functions.

The formulation and estimation of a European money demand function involves three peculiarities. First, all European aggregates are inevitably derived from scaled national variables: national stocks and flows (e.g., money or output) are converted by some exchange rate into a common denomination, and national prices (e.g., deflator or interest rate) are weighted by some share of a country in the overall market. Second, the European aggregates are derived from original national variables whereas the European model is formulated in terms of logged variables. This leads to the concept of quasilinear aggregation. Third, the European static relation is embedded as a long-run equilibrium into a dynamic error-correction model. The stability of this ECM - measured by the strength of cointegration (test statistic τ), the size of disequilibrium (variance σ^2), and the speed of adjustment (loading α) - could be distorted by aggregation effects.

The present chapter therefore explores to what extent the results of conventional aggregation theory carry over to quasilinear aggregation and to cointegration, and what behaviour can be expected from aggregate European models under these circumstances. Another problem dealt with in this chapter is the actual construction of aggregate European variables. It is shown that the popular procedure of forming weighted sums of national variables is theoretically justified from index number theory. Moreover, the role of alternative exchange rates in the construction of European aggregates is discussed.

5.1 Aggregation of Relations

In this section some basic concepts of aggregation theory are reviewed, in the spirit of Green (1964), Ijiri (1971) or Chipman (1975). The purpose of aggregation theory is to study relationships between models formulated on a micro level and a macro level, respectively. Here the two levels are described by open models resembling the identified long-run of a structural SECM (4.16) as presented in chapter 4.

Precisely, the micro level consists of $n = 1, ..., N$ components (countries). Each component is described by a single dependent variable y_n and by several explanatory variables z_{qn} which are indexed by $q = 1, ..., Q$ and collected in a $Q \times 1$ micro vector $\mathbf{z}_n = [z_{1n} \cdots z_{qn} \cdots z_{Qn}]'$. The macro level (Europe) is similarly described by a single aggregate y and several aggregates z_q collected in a $Q \times 1$ macro vector $\mathbf{z} = [z_1 \cdots z_q \cdots z_Q]'$. Each constellation of micro- and macrovariables represents a point $x \in \mathcal{X}$ in a real product space of dimension $Q{+}1{\times}N{+}1$. Over these variables an *aggregation structure* is defined as follows:

$$
\begin{aligned}
y_n &= f_n(z_{1n}, \cdots, z_{Qn}), \quad n = 1, ..., N && \textit{Micro Functions} \\
y &= h\,(y_1, \cdots, y_N) && \textit{Aggregation Rule (passive)} \\
z_q &= k_q(z_{q1}, \cdots, z_{qN}), \quad q = 1, ..., Q && \textit{Aggregation Rules (active)} \\
y &= f\,(z_1, \cdots, z_Q) && \textit{Macro Function}
\end{aligned}
$$

This setup is (so far) deterministic and only national variables enter the n-th micro function. An aggregation structure implies two functions linking the dependent macro variable y to the explanatory micro variables z_{qn}. These two functions are

$$
\begin{aligned}
y_p &\equiv h\{\, f_1(\cdot), \cdots, f_N(\cdot)\,\} && \textit{Principal Function} \\
y_s &\equiv f\{\, k_1(\cdot), \cdots, k_Q(\cdot)\,\} && \textit{Surrogate Function}
\end{aligned}
$$

Internal consistency of the aggregation structure clearly requires equivalence of the two functions, so that much effort in aggregation theory is devoted to solving the functional equation $y_p(\cdot) = y_s(\cdot)$. A mathematical overview is given by Pokropp (1978). If at least one constellation of functions f_n, h, k_q, f exists such that equivalence obtains over all points $x \in \mathcal{X}$ (all $x \in \mathcal{X}_0 \subset \mathcal{X}$), then the aggregation structure is called *globally (locally) consistent.*[67] Under consistency a change in any of the explanatory micro variables z_{qn} has a same effect on the dependent macro variable y via either route, so that the respective gradients are equal:

[67] The popular labels of *perfect* or *exact* aggregation apply to both global and local consistency. Of course 'consistency' here denotes a logical and not a statistical property.

$$\frac{\partial h}{\partial y_n}\frac{\partial f_n}{\partial z_{qn}} = \frac{\partial f}{\partial z_q}\frac{\partial k_q}{\partial z_{qn}} \qquad \forall\ q, n\ . \tag{5.1}$$

If this consistency condition is not met, micro theory (principal function) and macro theory (surrogate function) may generate contradictory results.[68] These contradictions are captured in the notion of an *aggregation error.*

A macro function is frequently interpreted as describing the behaviour of some fictitious representative agent. Following VanDaal/Merkies (1988) an aggregation structure is called *representative* or *analog* if the mathematical properties of all micro functions and the macro function coincide for some aspect of interest. Interesting aspects could be the functional form, the signing of derivatives, the degree of homogeneity, or even the whole mathematical background in a certain optimization procedure. Analogy and consistency are separate notions which may but need not coincide.

To reconcile the above aggregation structure with the stochastic cointegration framework in chapter 4, the micro- and macro functions appearing in the structure are subsequently interpreted as conditional expectation operators. That is, the micro functions $f_n(\cdot)$ map an explanatory random vector $\mathbf{z}_n$ not exactly into y_n, but into a dependent random variable $E[y_n|\mathbf{z}_n]$ which is an approximation of y_n in the sense of an optimal prediction.[69] The macro function $f(\cdot)$ similarly maps an explanatory random vector $\mathbf{z}$ into $E[y|\mathbf{z}]$. The aggregation rules remain deterministic, they are interpreted as Borel functions transforming random variables y_n, z_{qn} into random variables y, z_q. In this framework, a principal prediction $\hat{y}_p(\cdot)$ is obtained by conditioning on marginalized microvariables and subsequent passive aggregation of micro expectations. Conversely, a surrogate prediction $\hat{y}_s(\cdot)$ is obtained by actively aggregating marginalized microvariables and subsequent conditioning on the resulting explanatory macrovariable.

The modifications have one serious consequence. In the deterministic case a unique macro variable $y = y_p = y_s$ exists only under consistency. In the stochastic case, however, a unique macro variable $y = y_p$ exists via the passive aggregation rule without further restrictions. This necessitates a different

68 Consider two micro functions $y_n = \mu_n + g_n z_n$ explaining money demand through nominal income. Assume aggregation by simple summation. Upon a change $+\Delta z_1 = -\Delta z_2$ in the income distribution, the principal function ('micro theory') then implies a change $\Delta y = (g_1 - g_2)\Delta z_1$ in aggregate money demand, while the surrogate function ('macro theory') implies $\Delta y = 0$ since aggregate income is unchanged. Unless the micro parameters are equal the two implications contradict each other, rendering the aggregation structure inconsistent.

69 The term 'prediction' is used for approximations of a (random) variable x_t from some contemporaneous information $\mathcal{I}_t$. The term 'forecast' is used for approximations of x_t from some past information $\mathcal{I}_{t-1}$.

definition of consistency. A stochastic aggregation structure is therefore here called consistent if the two prediction errors $u_p \equiv y - \hat{y}_p$ and $u_s \equiv y - \hat{y}_s$ coincide, or equivalently if the aggregation error $\xi \equiv \hat{y}_p - \hat{y}_s = u_s - u_p$ is zero almost surely.[70] The precision of the approximations $\hat{y}_p$ and $\hat{y}_s$ is measured by the variances of the respective prediction errors. Under consistency these variances are equal. Under inconsistency, however, an *aggregation loss* occurs, defined as $var(u_s) - var(u_p) > 0$.

The appearance of an aggregation loss can be traced to an information loss. Let therefore $\mathcal{G}_p$ denote the σ-field generated by all national vectors $\mathbf{z}_n$ in the underlying probability space, and $\mathcal{G}_s$ the σ-field generated by the aggregate vector $\mathbf{z}$. If these vectors are linked by a Borel function $k(\cdot)$ such that $\mathbf{z} = k(\mathbf{z}_1, ..., \mathbf{z}_N)$, then it holds that $\mathcal{G}_s \subseteq \mathcal{G}_p$. For equality to hold it is necessary that $k(\cdot)$ is one-to-one (injective). Usually aggregation rules are not injective, i.e., knowledge of the aggregate $\mathbf{z}$ and of the aggregation rule $k(\cdot)$ is not enough to recover the national vectors $\mathbf{z}_n$. Thus there is a loss of information involved in the operation of aggregation, expressed as $\mathcal{G}_s \subset \mathcal{G}_p$. This inequality in turn implies $var(u_s) > var(u_p)$, compare Davidson (1994, p.147,156). The argument becomes obvious if the functions h and f_n are linear. In this case, using the law of iterated expectations and the linearity of conditional expectations, the surrogate prediction can be expressed as

$$
\begin{aligned}
E[y \,|\, \mathcal{G}_s] &= E[\, h\{f_1(\mathbf{z}_1), ..., f_N(\mathbf{z}_N)\} \mid \mathcal{G}_s \,] \\
&= h\{\, E[\, f_1(\mathbf{z}_1), ..., f_N(\mathbf{z}_N) \,|\, \mathcal{G}_s \,] \,\} \\
&= h\{\, f_1(E[\mathbf{z}_1|\mathcal{G}_s]), ..., f_N(E[\mathbf{z}_N|\mathcal{G}_s]) \,\} \\
&\neq h\{\, f_1(\mathbf{z}_1), ..., f_N(\mathbf{z}_N) \,\} \ .
\end{aligned} \tag{5.2}
$$

If the two information sets were equal ($\mathcal{G}_s = \mathcal{G}_p$), then $E[\mathbf{z}_n|\mathcal{G}_s] = \mathbf{z}_n$, and the surrogate prediction matched the principal prediction. Usually, however, the information sets are not equal ($\mathcal{G}_s \subset \mathcal{G}_p$) and the inequality in the last line of (5.2) applies. The inferiority of the surrogate prediction can thus be pinned down to an imprecision in approximating $\mathbf{z}_n$ by $E[\mathbf{z}_n|\mathcal{G}_s]$. This imprecision will return below as a projection error in the auxiliary equation (5.4).

The original objective of aggregation theory concerned the aggregation of micro production functions (VanDaal/Merkies 1988) and of micro demand functions (Stoker 1993). However, a-priori an aggregation structure is free in that none of its elements is given or fixed. Thus different approaches of defining 'the' aggregation problem exist. First, for given micro functions and aggregation rules, some macro function can be chosen such that consistency holds.

[70] Two random variables $\hat{y}_p$, $\hat{y}_s : \Omega \mapsto \mathbb{R}$ are equal if $\hat{y}_p(\cdot) = \hat{y}_s(\cdot)$ over all elementary events ω in the underlying probability space $\{\Omega; \mathcal{F}, P(\cdot)\}$, except possibly on P-zero sets.

This leads to random coefficient models, for example in Zellner (1969) or recently Läufer (1992a, 1995). A non-random parameterization of the macro function is, in this approach, only possible under suitable restrictions on the distribution of explanatory microvariables across components, as for example in Stoker (1984) or Lewbel (1989, 1992). Second, for given micro functions and a given macro function, some aggregation rules can be chosen such that consistency holds. This approach is pursued in Klein (1946) or recently in Fagan/Henry (1998). Third, for given micro functions and aggregation rules, a macro function can be chosen which satisfies some analogy requirement, accepting a possibly non-zero aggregation error. This *analogy approach* usually prescribes a same functional form for macro- and micro functions. It dominates the literature on aggregation theory and on European money demand functions.

The following sections apply the analogy approach to static linear relations. This is motivated by the present interest in static long-run equilibrium relations isolated from empirical time series through cointegration analysis. Inevitably, this narrow focus of course skips a considerable body of literature on the aggregation of dynamic linear relations. Forni/Lippi (1997) provide an extensive treatment, with an emphasis on the common and idiosyncratic shocks effective in the Wold representations of micro variables. They show for example that the dynamic shape of a macro relation can, in general, not be interpreted as evidence for intertemporal optimization behaviour on the level of micro components. In fact, they show that even static micro relations can produce dynamic macro relations.

A second caveat concerns the interpretation of the macro level. The macro function describes, justified or not, the behaviour of some representative agent in an 'individual experiment'. The economy as a whole however constitutes a 'market experiment' which possibly deprives the representative agent of its original control variables. This point is forcefully made by Laidler (1982) and in more detail by Lane (1990), who show that partial adjustment in some representative agent's money demand (individual experiment) need not imply partial adjustment for the whole economy (market experiment). In a more abstract framework, Ramsey (1996) similarly challenges the practice of interpreting macro variables as mere aggregates of micro variables, and proposes to treat macro functions 'in their own right' as describing system properties which not necessarily prevail in individual components.

5.1.1 Linear Aggregation of Static Linear Relations

A linear aggregation structure is the basis of conventional aggregation theory, from Theil (1954) to Pesaran/Pierse/Kumar (1989). It is expressed as[71]

$$
\begin{aligned}
y_{nt} &= \mu_n + \gamma_n' \mathbf{z}_{nt} + u_{nt}\,, \quad u_{nt} \sim i.d.(0, \sigma_n^2) && \textit{Micro Functions} \\
y_t &= \textstyle\sum_{n=1}^{N} h_n \, y_{nt} && \textit{Aggregation Rule (passive)} \\
\mathbf{z}_t &= \textstyle\sum_{n=1}^{N} K_n \, \mathbf{z}_{nt} && \textit{Aggregation Rule (active)} \\
y_t &= \mu + \gamma' \mathbf{z}_t + u_t\,, \qquad u_t \sim i.d.(0, \sigma^2) && \textit{Macro Function}
\end{aligned}
$$

where $K_n \equiv diag(k_{1n}, \cdots, k_{Qn})$ is a $Q \times Q$ matrix and the aggregation factors k_{qn}, h_n some real numbers. The variables in this structure may be interpreted as logarithms of some original variables, and the factors as proper weights (values between zero and one, summing to unity). In this case the aggregation structure constitutes a monotonic transformation of an alternative structure comprising geometric averages as aggregation rules and Cobb-Douglas type behavioural equations, a setup used in Klein (1946) and Fagan/Henry (1998). Of course this interpretation is not compulsory, and conventional aggregation theory usually specifies $k_{qn} = h_n = 1$ (simple summation).

According to the analogy approach, the micro functions and aggregation rules are here assumed given, whereas the macro function is undetermined except for the requirement of linearity. The micro functions constitute either textbook regressions ($y_{nt}, \mathbf{z}_{nt} \sim I(0)$, hence $u_{nt} \sim I(0)$) or cointegrating regressions ($y_{nt}, \mathbf{z}_{nt} \sim I(1)$, but $u_{nt} \sim I(0)$). In either case the errors u_{nt} are stationary and ergodic with constant variances σ_n^2, possibly nonzero cross covariances (allowing for SURE effects), and possibly nonzero serial covariances (allowing for partial disequilibrium adjustment in an embedding ECM). The aggregation problem now consists in linking the undetermined macro parameters (μ, γ, σ^2) and the aggregation loss (ξ) somehow to the given micro parameters $(\mu_n, \gamma_n, \sigma_n^2)$ and aggregation factors (h_n, k_{qn}).[72]

The principal prediction is obtained by passively aggregating conditional micro expectations. In a linear aggregation structure the prediction error u_{pt} and its variance σ_p^2 are consequently given by

$$
\begin{aligned}
u_{pt} &= y_t - \textstyle\sum_{n=1}^{N} h_n \, E[y_{nt} | \mathbf{z}_{nt}] = \textstyle\sum_{n=1}^{N} h_n \, u_{nt} \\
\sigma_p^2 &= var(\textstyle\sum_{n=1}^{N} h_n \, u_{nt}) \ .
\end{aligned}
\tag{5.3}
$$

[71] A time index t seems redundant since no dynamic relations appear. It is nevertheless maintained to distinguish random variables from parameters and to provide a reference for the concept of stationarity.

[72] In this formulation the aggregation problem is an identification problem, searching for a unique correspondence between micro- and macro parameters. This motivates Stoker's (1984) concept of *complete* aggregation structures.

The principal variance σ_p^2 thus depends on the factors h_n and on the cross correlations r_{nm} among the micro errors. Suppose the factors h_n are proper weights. In this case the principal variance can be reduced below the weighted average of micro variances (cross correlations below one), or even below the smallest single micro variance (cross correlations below a certain positive value[73]). This effect of variance-reduction is well known from portfolio theory and hence called a *portfolio gain*, in the spirit of Läufer (1992a, 1992b).[74]

To obtain a surrogate prediction the explanatory micro vectors are projected onto their aggregate. This yields the famous auxiliary equations

$$\mathbf{z}_{nt} \;=\; b_n \,+\, B_n\, \mathbf{z}_t \,+\, \mathbf{v}_{nt} \quad , \qquad n = 1, ..., N \; . \tag{5.4}$$

Each auxiliary equation decomposes one micro vector into a projection and an orthogonal zero-mean projection error. Since the explanatory micro vectors necessarily add up to their aggregate, the auxiliary equations' parameters satisfy $\Sigma_{n=1}^N K_n b_n = 0_{Q\times 1}$ and $\Sigma_{n=1}^N K_n B_n = I_{Q\times Q}$. The projection errors satisfy $\Sigma_{n=1}^N K_n \mathbf{v}_{nt} = 0_{Q\times 1}$. This cross-equation restriction precludes their interpretation as a stochastic disturbance or shock. The parameter matrix B_n summarizes the contemporaneous covariances among the explanatory microvariables. Its typical element $b_{*q.n}$ contains the information provided by all other microvariables for the q-th microvariable in country n. The projection resembles a conditional expectation $E[\mathbf{z}_{nt}|\mathbf{z}_t]$, and can be thought of as the generalized inverse of the active aggregation rule (cf Chipman 1975). According to (5.2) the surrogate prediction is therefore given by

$$E[y_t|\mathbf{z}_t] \;=\; \textstyle\sum_{n=1}^N h_n \left(\mu_n + \gamma_n' b_n + \gamma_n' B_n\, \mathbf{z}_t\right) \; . \tag{5.5}$$

The errors of the auxiliary equations and those of the micro functions are orthogonal to each other and to $\mathbf{z}_t$. The surrogate function's prediction error u_t (macro error) and its variance σ^2 (macro variance) are therefore given by

$$\begin{aligned} u_t \;&=\; y_t - E[y_t|\mathbf{z}_t] \;=\; \textstyle\sum_{n=1}^N h_n\, u_{nt} \,+\, \xi_t \\ \sigma^2 \;&=\; \sigma_p^2 \,+\, var(\xi_t) \; , \end{aligned} \tag{5.6}$$

where the random variable $\xi_t \equiv \Sigma_{n=1}^N h_n \gamma_n' \mathbf{v}_{nt}$ just describes the aggregation error. This aggregation error is zero in two situations. First under $h_n \gamma_n' = \gamma' K_n \;\forall\, n$ (micro homogeneity restriction), which renders the micro parameters linearly dependent.[75] This restriction ensures global consistency

[73] For two micro functions with error standard deviations $\sigma_n \leq \sigma_m$ this value is given by $r_{nm} < \sigma_n/\sigma_m$.

[74] Strictly speaking, the portfolio gain derived by Läufer appears under a different condition in the context of quasilinear aggregation as discussed in section 5.1.2. The label is nevertheless also applied in the present context.

[75] For simple sums or averages this amounts to the popular requirement of parameter equality across countries.

and immediately satisfies (5.1). Second under $\mathbf{v}_{nt} = 0$ (compositional stability restriction), which renders the explanatory micro variables linearly dependent. This condition ensures local consistency, and circumvents (5.1) since micro variables can not be varied independently. Apart from these two situations the aggregation error is a nondegenerate random variable with positive variance.

Comparing (5.5) with the macro function gives $\gamma' = \Sigma_{n=1}^{N} h_n \gamma_n' B_n$ for the vector of macroparameters. The deviation of the q-th macroparameter from the average of corresponding microparameters is called the *aggregation bias* of this particular parameter:

$$\gamma' - \sum_{n=1}^{N} h_n \gamma_n' = \sum_{n=1}^{N} h_n \gamma_n' (B_n - I) .$$

This bias concerns representativity: Unless B_n is diagonal, the q-th macroparameter depends both on corresponding (γ_{qn}) and noncorresponding (γ_{*n}) microparameters. The prescription that the macroparameter be constant causes the aggregation error: if rather than constants B_n the random weights $\mathbf{z}_{nt}\, \mathbf{z}_t^{-1}$ were used in the expression for γ, then the aggregation error would be absorbed into a random macroparameter γ_t such that $\gamma_t' \mathbf{z}_t = \gamma' \mathbf{z}_t + \xi_t$. A zero aggregation error is, however, neither necessary nor sufficient for a zero aggregation bias (Ringwald 1980, p.71).

The macro regression of y_t on $\mathbf{z}_t$ constitutes a (correctly specified) model for the surrogate prediction. It can likewise be analyzed in terms of micro- and auxiliary regressions. In fact, the vector $\Sigma_{n=1}^{N} h_n \hat{\gamma}_n' \hat{B}_n$ may even be called the *pseudo true value* of the estimator $\hat{\gamma}$. Estimation and testing conventionally proceed under the assumption of textbook micro-regressions. The macro error is then estimated as a residual from OLS applied to the macro equation, whereas the micro errors are estimated as residuals either from OLS applied separately to each micro equation or from GLS applied jointly to all micro equations within a SURE system. The respective residual variances allow to construct estimators for the aggregation loss, for example $var(\hat{\xi})_{OLS} = \hat{\sigma}^2_{OLS} - \hat{\sigma}^2_{p,OLS}$ following Grunfeld/Griliches (1960).[76] Despite their popularity in applied literature these estimators are not necessarily reliable: Pesaran/Pierse/Kumar (1989) demonstrate a finite-sample bias both in $\hat{\sigma}^2_{p,OLS}$ and in $\hat{\sigma}^2_{p,GLS}$ which possibly tricks an estimator $var(\hat{\xi})$ into wrongly indicating an aggregation gain. They propose an unbiased OLS-based estimator for the principal variance, and a direct test for zero aggregation error. Lee/Pesaran/Pierse (1990) propose a direct test for zero aggregation bias.

[76] Precisely, the popular 'GG-criterion' compares a principal (R_c^2) and a surrogate (R_a^2) coefficient of determination. These are tied to the respective residual variances via $(1 - R_c^2)/(1 - R_a^2) = \hat{\sigma}^2_{p,OLS}/\hat{\sigma}^2_{OLS}$. The decisive drawback of the GG-criterion is however not its construction, but its reliance on OLS.

5.1.2 Quasilinear Aggregation of Static Linear Relations

Theoretical and empirical studies of European money demand show a curious and apparently unrealized discrepancy. Theoretical studies proceed, habitually, from a log-linear micro model and then, plausibly, sum the micro variables to obtain a macro model. Empirical studies in contrast proceed, plausibly, from sums of micro data series and then, habitually, log these aggregates to specify a macro model. These two procedures are *not* equivalent. Rather, speaking in terms of log-variables, the first procedure implies a linear aggregation structure, whereas the second procedure implies the following quasilinear aggregation structure:[77]

$$\begin{aligned} y_{nt} &= \mu_n + \gamma_n' \mathbf{z}_{nt} + u_{nt}\,, \quad u_{nt} \sim i.d.(0,\sigma_n^2) && \textit{Micro Functions} \\ y_t &= \ln\left(\textstyle\sum_{n=1}^N h_n \exp y_{nt}\right) && \textit{Aggregation Rule (passive)} \\ z_{qt} &= \ln\left(\textstyle\sum_{n=1}^N k_{qn} \exp z_{qnt}\right) && \textit{Aggregation Rules (active)} \\ y_t &= \mu + \gamma' \mathbf{z}_t + u_t\,, \quad u_t \sim i.d.(0,\sigma^2) && \textit{Macro Function} \end{aligned}$$

Again, a possible though not compulsory interpretation of this structure assumes the factors h_n, k_{qn} to be proper weights and the variables to be logarithms of some original variables. In this case the quasilinear structure is a monotonic transformation of an alternative aggregation structure comprising arithmetic averages as aggregation rules and Cobb-Douglas type behavioural equations. Consistent aggregation is not possible in either version: a famous result by Nataf (1948) shows additive separability of micro functions *and* aggregation rules to be necessary and sufficient for globally consistent aggregation; see also Green (1964), VanDaal/Merkies (1981) or Lau (1982). The consistency condition (5.1) here becomes

$$h_n\,(Y_{nt}/Y_t)\,\gamma_{qn} \;=\; \gamma_q\,k_{qn}\,(Z_{qnt}/Z_{qt}) \qquad \forall\, q,n\;,$$

where the upper-case variables denote exponentials of the corresponding lower-case variables. Global consistency is clearly not possible if constant macroparameters γ_q are required. However, local consistency is possible if the explanatory variables are suitably restricted such that in original levels all variables move in proportion to their respective arithmetic means. Alternatively expressed, the share of a variable in its aggregate must be independent of that aggregates level. This property is known as *mean scaling* and resembles the compositional stability restriction encountered in the previous section. Augmented by a micro homogeneity restriction it allows for locally consistent quasilinear aggregation, as for example in Lewbel (1989, 1992).

---

[77] A function $h(\cdot)$ is called *quasilinear* if $h(\cdot) = g^{-1}[\,h_1 g(\cdot) + ... + h_N\, g(\cdot)\,]$ for some continuous and strictly monotonic function $g(\cdot)$ with inverse $g^{-1}(\cdot)$ and some real constants $h_1, ..., h_N$ (see Eichhorn 1978, p.142).

The principal prediction is obtained by passively aggregating conditional micro expectations. In a quasilinear aggregation structure the prediction error u_{pt} is therefore given by

$$u_{pt} \;=\; y_t - \ln\left(\sum_{n=1}^{N} h_n \exp E[y_{nt}|\mathbf{z}_{nt}]\right) \;=\; \ln\left(\sum_{n=1}^{N} w_{nt} \exp u_{nt}\right) \;, \qquad (5.7)$$

where $w_{nt} \equiv h_n \exp E[y_{nt}|\mathbf{z}_{nt}] \;/\; \Sigma_{n=1}^{N} h_n \exp E[y_{nt}|\mathbf{z}_{nt}]$ defines the weight of a component prediction in the principal prediction, on the level of original variables. This expression is obviously a quasilinear analogue of the principal prediction (5.3). Using the first-order Taylor approximation $\exp u_{nt} \approx 1+u_{nt}$ one obtains the linearization[78]

$$u_{pt} \;\approx\; \sum_{n=1}^{N} w_{nt}\, u_{nt} \quad , \qquad \sigma_p^2 \;\approx\; var(\sum_{n=1}^{N} w_{nt}\, u_{nt}) \;. \qquad (5.8)$$

The variables w_{nt} are random, but weights by construction. Consequently there is again scope for a portfolio gain to arise in the principal variance, albeit now under the entirely different necessary condition that (5.8) constitute a reasonable approximation. This type of portfolio gain is pointed out by Läufer (1992a, 1995), who employs an expression similar to (5.8) to define the error term of a European money demand function. The properties of the weights w_{nt} depend on the micro parameters (h_n, μ_n, γ_n) and the explanatory micro vectors $(\mathbf{z}_{nt})$. If the parameters or the explanatory variables of the n-th component are large relative to those of the other components, then $w_{nt} \approx 1$ and the principal variance simply mirrors the n-th micro variance. Simulation evidence suggests that for reasonable magnitudes the parameters exert little influence on the weights, whereas the stochastic properties of the explanatory microvariables do matter in small samples.

The surrogate prediction is immediately obtained from the macro function. Due to the information loss involved in aggregation, the surrogate variance can again be expressed as principal variance plus aggregation loss, in analogy to (5.6). Since consistency is not achievable under quasilinear aggregation, the aggregation loss is moreover expected to remain strictly positive. Via its two components the surrogate (or macro) variance σ^2 is exposed to competing influences: a variance-decreasing portfolio gain and a variance-increasing aggregation loss. Which influence eventually dominates depends on the parameter constellation and, crucially, on the stochastic properties of the explanatory microvariables. The simulation experiment conducted in section 5.1.4 below will address this question again.

[78] Suppose the distribution of u_{nt} is normal with expectation zero and variance σ_n^2. The distribution of $\exp u_{nt}$ is then log-normal with expectation $\exp(\sigma_n^2 \,/\, 2)$ and variance $(\exp \sigma_n^2 - 1)\, \exp \sigma_n^2$. Empirical standard deviations in macroeconometrics are usually well below 10 percent (or $\sigma_n^2 < 0.01$). This gives the approximations $E[\exp u_{nt}] \approx 1$ and $var[\exp u_{nt}] \approx \sigma_n^2$.

5.1.3 Aggregation and Cointegration

Suppose the micro functions are cointegration relations, so that the variables y_{nt} and $\mathbf{z}_{nt}$ are individually I(1) and their linear combination u_{nt} is I(0). This section delineates two alternative sufficient conditions for cointegration to carry through from micro to macro level in a linear aggregation structure.

The first case relates to the concept of local consistency. Being linear combinations of integrated micro variables, the aggregates y_t and $\mathbf{z}_t$ are also integrated if the aggregation rules are not, by chance, themselves cointegrating. Therefore the macro function is cointegrating if its error u_t is I(0). Since the micro errors u_{nt} are I(0) by assumption, the issue boils down to whether the aggregation error ξ_t is I(0). The aggregation error is non-trivially I(0) if the auxiliary equations are not spurious projections, that is, if the explanatory micro variables are cointegrating functions of their aggregates so that $\mathbf{v}_{nt} \sim I(0)$ and hence $\xi_t \sim I(0)$. This is a weaker form of the compositional stability restriction encountered in section 5.1.1, where the micro variables are exact linear functions of their aggregates. An equivalent formulation is that in each auxiliary equation the micro vector $\mathbf{z}_{nt}$ is driven by the same stochastic trends as the aggregate $\mathbf{z}_t$. Hence, given cointegrating micro functions the macro function is also cointegrating if the $Q \cdot N$ micro variables z_{qnt} are driven by the same set of $s \leq Q$ common stochastic trends. For example, national prices could all be driven by a single common price trend, or national real output by a single common productivity trend. Insofar a test for cointegration in a European money demand specification constitutes an indirect joint test of purchasing power parity, interest rate parity, and some productivity parity holding across the countries involved.

The second case of cointegration carrying through from micro to macro level relates to the concept of global consistency. Suppose the explanatory micro variables are not cointegrated across countries, so that the auxiliary equations are spurious projections in that $\mathbf{v}_{nt} \sim I(1)$. In this situation the aggregation error is likewise integrated, $\xi_t \sim I(1)$, and its variance, the aggregation loss, diverges at rate t. There is, however, one exception: the aggregation error is by definition zero under global consistency. The aggregation loss is consequently exposed to competing influences. On the one hand, it is driven to infinity via the integrated errors from the auxiliary equations. On the other hand, for certain parameters it remains pinned down to zero via the consistency property. Judged by its residual variance $\hat{\sigma}^2$ the macro function can therefore be expected to show cointegration at (and in the vicinity of) a consistent parameter constellation. This is a another form of the micro homogeneity restriction encountered in section 5.1.1. Its effect is clearly visible in the simulation results depicted in figures 5.2 and 5.4 below. Insofar a test for cointegration in a European money demand specification constitutes an indirect test of parameter-equality holding across the countries involved.

Closed VAR Model: As a generalization, the present framework of an open model in a dependent variable y and several explanatory variables z is briefly replaced by a closed model in a vector variable x. Suppose therefore the n-th micro unit is described by an integrated VAR in a p-dimensional vector $x_{nt} \equiv [x_{1nt}, \cdots, x_{pnt}]$. The notion of $r_n < p$ static linear relations holding between these micro variables is then captured by a $p \times r_n$ matrix β_n of cointegration vectors, so that the micro functions assume the form $\beta_n' x_{nt} = u_{nt}$. Cointegration at the macro level is correspondingly described as $\beta' x_t = u_t \sim I(0)$, for some $p \times r$ matrix β. The local-consistency argument for the existence of cointegration is now conveniently stated in terms of the stochastic trends driving the pN micro variables $[x_{1t}, \cdots, x_{Nt}]$ and thereby the p aggregate variables x_t.

The (assumed) existence of r_n cointegration relations within the VAR describing the n-th micro unit is expressed by the multivariate Beveridge/Nelson decomposition

$$\underset{p\times 1}{x_{nt}} = \underset{p\times s_n}{A_n} \underset{s_n\times 1}{T_{nt}} + \underset{p\times 1}{S_{nt}} , \tag{5.9}$$

where $s_n \equiv p - r_n$. The vector T_{nt} contains the s_n common stochastic trends driving the p micro variables x_{nt} through the rows of the matrix A_n. The vector S_{nt} lumps together the stationary component of the decomposition. The (hypothesized) existence of r cointegration relations within the VAR describing the aggregates is similarly expressed as

$$\underset{p\times 1}{x_t} = \underset{p\times s}{A} \underset{s\times 1}{T_t} + \underset{p\times 1}{S_t} . \tag{5.10}$$

Now, for (5.10) to follow from (5.9) under a linear aggregation rule it is clearly sufficient to reduce the number of stochastic trends effective at the micro level. This is achieved by stipulating that the $\Sigma_{n=1}^{N} s_n$ common trends driving the micro variables are in turn themselves driven by s 'common common trends', expressed as $T_{nt} = G_n T_t$. In order to keep the stochastic trends in T_{nt} linearly independent of each other, the $s_n \times s$ matrices G_n must be of full row rank $s_n \leq s \; \forall n$. Using $B_n \equiv A_n G_n (A'A)^{-1} A'$ this condition can be cast into the form of an 'auxiliary reduced rank regression'

$$x_{nt} = B_n x_t + v_{nt} \qquad \text{with} \qquad \mathrm{rk}\, B_n = s_n \leq s < p , \tag{5.11}$$

where $v_{nt} \sim I(0)$. Thus, if equation (5.11) holds for all micro units, then the macro VAR is cointegrated with rank $r \leq \min(r_n)$.

The global-consistency argument again applies to micro variables which are not cointegrated across countries. Using aggregation by simple summation, Gonzalo (1993) shows that in this case the macro function features cointegration if the intersection of the null spaces of the matrices A_n is non-empty. That is, the existence of a cointegration vector that is equal for all micro units is sufficient for this cointegration relation to carry through to the macro level. Generalized to the present setting the condition simply states that macro cointegration can be expected at (and in the vicinity of) a consistent parameter constellation.

Error-Correction Model: A static cointegration relation is frequently embedded as a long-run solution into a dynamic error correction model. Such a model relates changes in a dependent variable (Δy_t) to deviations from the long-run solution (u_{t-1}) through some adjustment parameter (α). A non-instantaneous adjustment ($\alpha \neq -1$) is often interpreted as the optimal behaviour of a representative agent balancing (myopically or under rational expectations) the costs of adjustment against the costs of being off equilibrium, see for example Wolters/Lütkepohl (1997). This interpretation is, however, theoretically dubious since individual optimization does not imply aggregate rationality (Kirman 1992), and empirically dubious since the sluggish adjustment ($\alpha \to 0$) usually found in empirical models implies incredibly large adjustment costs (Engsted/Haldrup 1997).

A better explanation of non-instantaneous adjustment on a macro level are aggregation effects. An empirical demonstration of sluggish adjustment emerging from aggregation is given by Seitz (1993). The present framework allows for a brief theoretical analysis. An ECM model can be connected to a (linear) aggregation structure by relating the adjustment speed (α) to the size of the disequilibrium (σ^2). To derive this relation, consider a simplified micro ECM with weakly exogenous regressors, similar to (4.22):

$$\begin{aligned} u_{nt} &\equiv y_{nt} - \mu_n - \gamma_n' \mathbf{z}_{nt} && \textit{Static Disequilibrium} \\ \Delta y_{nt} &= \alpha_n\, u_{n.t-1} + e_{cnt} && \textit{Dynamic Adjustment} \\ \Delta \mathbf{z}_{nt} &= \mathbf{e}_{znt} && \textit{Weak Exogeneity} \end{aligned}$$

As indicated by the notation, the error u_{nt} in an ECM always represents an endogenous disequilibrium rather than an exogenous shock. Consequently the micro variance σ_n^2 here depends on the set of micro parameters, namely α_n and γ_n', and on the system's innovations (cf section 4.1.1). In particular:

$$\sigma_n^2 = \left(1 - (1+\alpha_n)^2\right)^{-1} var(e_{cn} - \gamma_n' \mathbf{e}_{zn}) \quad .$$

Obviously a lower micro adjustment speed ($\alpha_n \to 0$) corresponds to a higher micro disequilibrium variance ($\sigma_n^2 \to \infty$).[79] This is a simple consequence of Granger's representation theorem linking error correction ($-2 < \alpha_n < 0$) to cointegration ($0 < \sigma_n^2 < \infty$). The aggregation problem now involves finding expressions for the yet undetermined parameters σ^2 and α in an analog macro

[79] In the extreme case $\alpha_n = 0$ the sequence u_{nt} is not weakly stationary and (hence) the variables y_{nt} and $\mathbf{z}_{nt}$ not cointegrated.

ECM. An expression for σ^2 is easily found from (5.6). An expression for α can be found by means of another auxiliary equation describing the conditional density of a micro error as $u_{nt} = c_n\, u_t + error$. The parameter c_n of this density is given by the covariance $cov(u_{nt}, u_t)$ divided by σ^2. Since the errors of the micro functions and those of the auxiliary equations (5.4) are orthogonal it follows that $cov(u_{nt}, u_t) = cov(u_{nt}, u_{pt})$. Substitution into the aggregate $\Delta y_t = \Sigma\, h_n \Delta y_{nt}$ then produces for the macro adjustment parameter

$$\alpha \;=\; \left(\textstyle\sum_{n=1}^{N} h_n\, \alpha_n\, cov(u_{nt}, u_{pt})\right)\, / \,\sigma^2 \;. \qquad (5.12)$$

Thus, a higher macro disequilibrium variance ($\sigma^2 \to \infty$) again corresponds to a lower macro adjustment speed ($\alpha \to 0$). Judging from (5.6), a higher macro variance σ^2 is produced (ceteris paribus) from an aggregation loss in the static macro relation. This in turn increases the denominator in (5.12) without changing the nominator, and hence induces a downward bias in the macro adjustment parameter α. This theoretical aggregation effect is clearly visible in the simulation results shown in figures 5.2 and 5.4 below.

As a generalization, suppose r static linear micro relations $\beta_n' x_{nt} = u_{nt}$ are embedded as long-run equilibrium into a multivariate micro ECM. From the moving average representation of this ECM follows $u_{nt} = \beta_n' C_n^*(L)\, e_{nt}$ (see section 3.2). In words, the actual r-dimensional disequilibrium comprises the accumulated backlog of incompletely absorbed past and present shocks. The close connection between adjustment speed and disequilibrium variance also surfaces in the Johansen estimation procedure. Suppressing the n-subscripts for convenience, the estimator for the adjustment parameters is given by $\hat{\alpha} = S_{dl}\beta\, (\beta' S_{ll}\beta)^{-1}$. The term in brackets constitutes the sample variance of the equilibrium errors, using series corrected for short run dynamics and deterministics. The estimation procedure now just-identifies the long run parameters such that the disequilibrium variance becomes an $r \times r$ identity matrix, and then determines the matrix of adjustment parameters. Alternative identification schemes are however equally admissible and yield different values for the estimators (see section 4.1). Comparing (say) money demand on micro and macro level may therefore depend on the chosen identification, in particular if the number of cointegration relations differs on both levels.

5.1.4 Simulation Evidence

The aggregation effects outlined in the previous sections are now illustrated in a simulation experiment. In this experiment, the micro-level consists of two countries each described by a pair of cointegrated time series. These series are aggregated according to linear and quasilinear aggregation rules. The properties of an analog macro model formulated over the aggregated series are then investigated for large and for small samples.

Precisely, in the experiment each country ($n = 1, 2$) is described by a simplified micro ECM with weakly exogenous regressors similar to (4.22):

$$\begin{aligned} u_{nt} &\equiv y_{nt} - \gamma_n z_{nt} - \mu_n \\ \Delta y_{nt} &= \omega_n \Delta z_{nt} + \alpha_n u_{n\,t-1} + e_{cnt} \qquad , \quad e_{nct} \sim i.i.n(0, \Omega_{nc}) \\ \Delta z_{nt} &= (a_{1n} - 1)\, z_{n\,t-1} + a_{2n}\, z_{n\,t-2} + e_{znt} \; , \quad e_{nzt} \sim i.i.n(0, \Omega_{nz}) \; , \end{aligned}$$

where the Gaussian innovations e_n are uncorrelated across countries. In the terminology of chapter 4, the first equation constitutes a conditional submodel. For $-2 < \alpha_n < 0$ it generates an y-variable which is error correcting around a stationary disequilibrium (see page 66). The second equation defines this disequilibrium as the deviation from a linear equilibrium relation $y_{nt} = \mu_n + \gamma_n z_{nt}$. The third equation provides the augmenting marginal model. It generates a z-variable which is weakly exogenous for $[\alpha_n, \sigma_n^2]$ and not Granger-caused by the conditioned variable. Moreover, the explanatory micro variables z_{1t} and z_{2t} are also independent of each other, so that local consistency due to compositional stability is ruled out.

From this population, aggregates y_t and z_t are now constructed under linear and quasilinear aggregation rules. The analog conditional macro model for these aggregates is given by

$$\begin{aligned} y_t &= \mu + \gamma z_t + u_t \\ \Delta y_t &= \omega \Delta z_t + \alpha u_{t-1} + e_{ct} \; . \end{aligned} \tag{5.13}$$

The simulation experiment itself consists of 1000 replications. In each replication, one marginal sequence $\{z_{nt}\}$ and one innovation sequence $\{e_{cnt}\}$ is generated for each country over a fixed sample size T. For country 2 a single conditional sequence $\{y_{2t}\}$ is generated under a fixed value γ_2. For country 1, however, a number of conditional sequences $\{y_{1t}\}$ is generated by parametrically varying γ_1 over a certain range of values. Aggregate sequences $\{z_t\}$ and $\{y_t\}$ are then generated for each parameter constellation according to both aggregation rules. This setup allows to portray the effects of linear and quasilinear aggregation against the difference between the two micro long-run parameters, i.e., against the degree of global consistency.

The values for the long-run parameters are set to $\gamma_2 = 2$ and $\gamma_1 \in [0.5\,;\,4]$. The adjustment parameters are set to $\alpha_1 = -0.7$ and $\alpha_2 = -0.4$, so that the micro variables y_{nt} and z_{nt} cointegrate. A contemporaneous impact of the marginal variable in the conditional model is allowed for by $\omega_1 = \omega_2 = 0.3$. The autoregressive parameters are set to $a_{1n} = 0.8$ and $a_{2n} = 0.2$ for both countries so that both sequences $\{z_{nt}\}$ are integrated. The micro innovations e_{nct} and e_{nzt} have the same standard deviation 0.02 and zero covariances. The factors in the aggregation rules are set to unity, implying simple summation of logged variables and original variables, respectively.

From the generated time series, the specified micro model is estimated for each country and the analog macro model (5.13) for each aggregation rule. The OLS-based two-step estimation procedure from Engle/Granger (1987) is applied to obtain estimates $[\hat{\gamma}_n\,, \hat{\sigma}^2_n\,, \hat{\alpha}_n]$ and $[\hat{\gamma}, \hat{\sigma}^2, \hat{\alpha}]$ for the micro- and macro-parameters of interest. The residuals from the static micro regressions are used to calculate principal prediction errors according to (5.3) and (5.7), from which then the exact principal variances $(\hat{\sigma}^2_p)$ are derived. The surrogate variances $(\hat{\sigma}^2)$ are immediately available as residual variance from the static macro regressions. The following figures 5.1 to 5.4 show the average values of these estimates obtained from 1000 replications of the DGP.

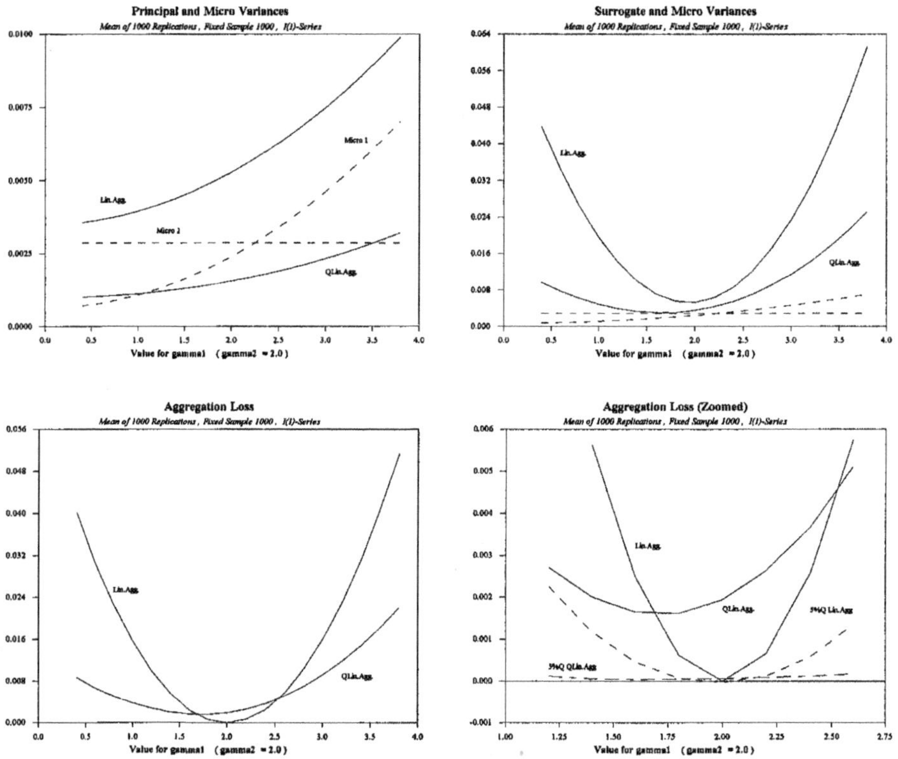

Fig. 5.1. Large Sample Simulation

The results of large sample simulation ($T = 1000$) are shown in figures 5.1 and 5.2. Consider the first quarter of figure 5.1. The micro residual variance $\hat{\sigma}^2_1$ grows with γ_1. This depicts the endogeneity of an ECM-disequilibrium noted in section 5.1.3. The principal variance exceeds both micro variances under linear aggregation. This is not surprising since simple-sum aggregation precludes the type of portfolio gain described in section 5.1.1. Under quasilinear aggregation, however, the principal variance is lower than both micro variances for a large range around γ_2. This depicts the type of portfolio gain described in section 5.1.2, which arises irrespective of whether the aggregation rule is a simple sum or a weighted average. The second quarter of figure 5.1 shows the residual variance of the static macro regression (surrogate variance) under linear and quasilinear aggregation. Both are decidedly larger than any of the micro variances. This implies an aggregation loss, depicted in the third and fourth quarter. Under linear aggregation the loss is zero at $\gamma_1 = 2$ where the micro homogeneity restriction holds. Under quasilinear aggregation the loss is always positive, reflecting the impossibility of consistent aggregation. The empirical 5% quantiles of both losses are above zero.

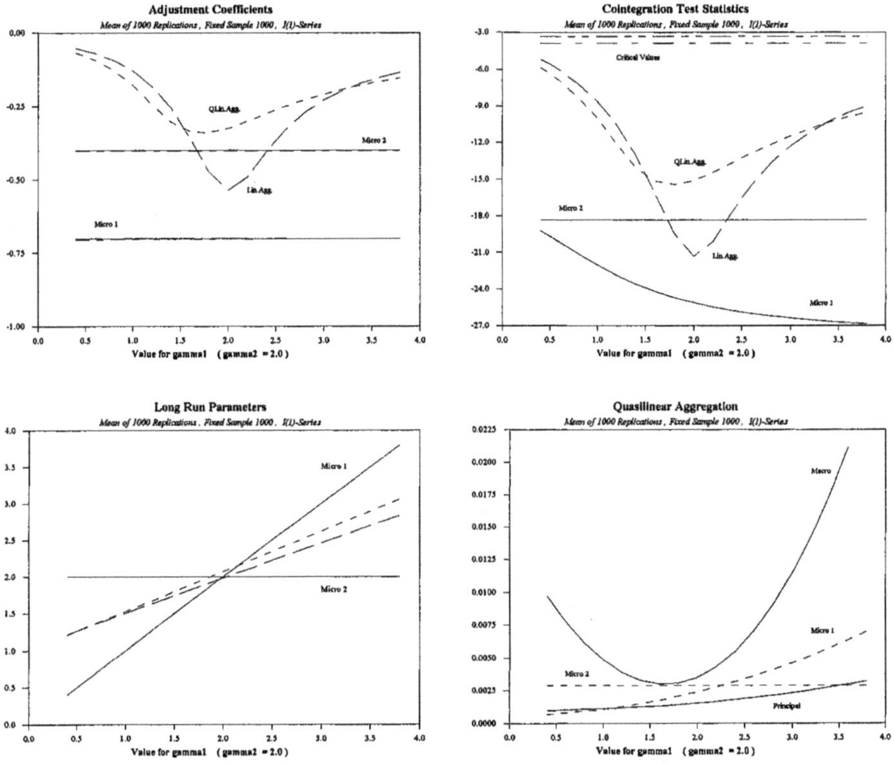

Fig. 5.2. Large Sample Simulation

The first quarter of figure 5.2 shows the estimated adjustment coefficients. Under both aggregation methods the macro adjustment parameter is at its maximum if the aggregation loss is at its minimum. Under linear aggregation it then roughly corresponds to a weighted average of micro adjustments. Under quasilinear aggregation, however, it remains biased below the smallest micro adjustment, reflecting a strictly positive aggregation loss. If the aggregation loss increases, the variance of u_{t-1} likewise increases relative to that of Δy_t, and the ECM regressions 'see' an ever slower reaction. As a result both macro adjustment coefficients drop as detailed in the previous section.

A similar impression is gained from the second quarter of figure 5.2. The cointegration statistic $\hat{\tau}$ is calculated according to Engle/Granger (1987) as the t-statistic testing for a zero coefficient in a regression of Δu_t on u_{t-1} (without constant). The statistic thus tests the null of integrated residuals, or absence of cointegration. As shown in section 4.1 the statistic equivalently tests the null of a zero adjustment coefficient, so that the similarities between the first and second quarter do not surprise. The dotted straight lines represent the 5% and 1% critical values according to MacKinnon (1991). Absence of cointegration is correctly rejected for both micro equations, and for the macro equation around the consistent parameter constellation. The stability measures $\hat{\sigma}^2$, $\hat{\alpha}$ and $\hat{\tau}$ therefore all convey the same message, namely an increasing aggregation loss. The estimates for the long run parameters, shown in the third quarter of figure 5.2, converge to simple averages of the micro parameters, albeit with a small bias in the case of quasilinear aggregation. The fourth quarter finally summarizes the residual variances obtained under quasilinear aggregation. The macro variance always exceeds both micro variances. Thus, under the present simulation setup, the aggregation loss clearly prevails over the portfolio gain in large samples.

At this stage is is necessary to pause for a short theoretical reflection on the meaning of "large samples" in the present setup. The textbook meaning is that large samples more closely resemble a true population picture than small samples. This is not the meaning applicable here. Rather, in the present non-stationary simulation setup it is the population picture itself which changes under different time horizons. A pertinent example is the population variance of integrated variables, which diverges at rate T with time. This feature can here be detected in the fourth quarter of figure 5.2: the surrogate variance is disproportionately large in comparison to the principal and the micro variance. The culprit is the aggregation loss, which is part of the surrogate but not of the other variances (see (5.3) and (5.6)). The aggregation loss is defined as the variance of the aggregation error. The aggregation error in turn is an integrated variable in the present simulation setup, due to non-cointegration between the explanatory micro variables z_1 and z_2 (case 2 in section 5.1.3)

The time-dependency of the aggregation loss has a serious consequence: aggregation effects can be different (on a population level) under different time horizons. The following small sample simulation in fact reveals one such instance, namely in the comparison of the (time-dependent) aggregation loss and the (time-invariant) portfolio gain.

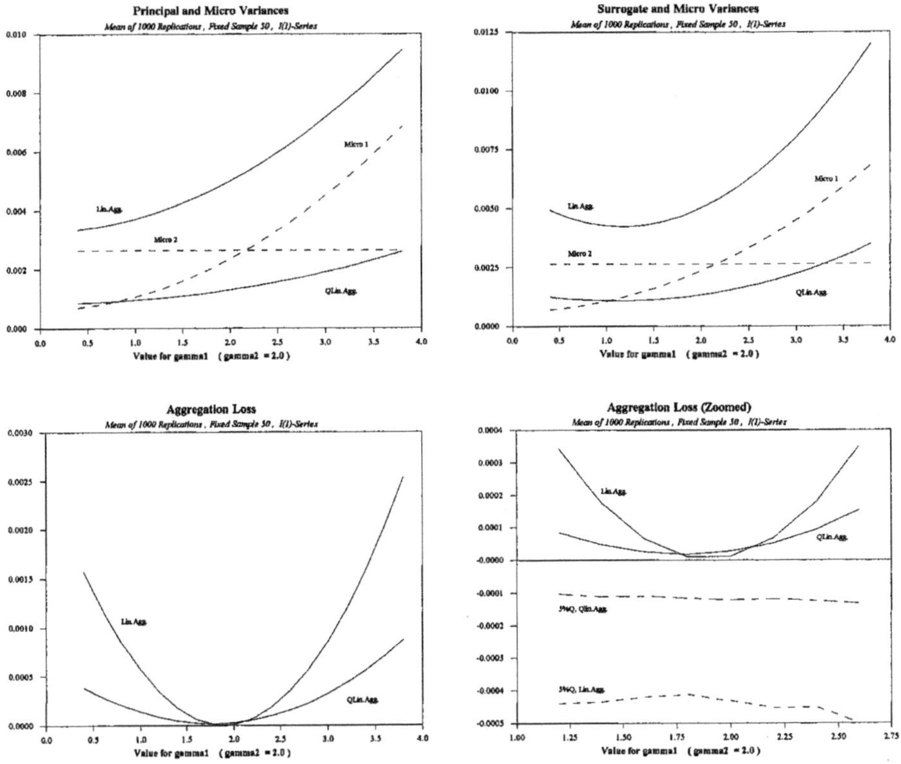

Fig. 5.3. Small Sample Simulation

The results of small sample simulation ($T = 50$) are shown in figures 5.3 and 5.4. In contrast to the large sample case, the principal and surrogate variances are here relatively close and the aggregation losses consequently relatively small in magnitude. In case of quasilinear aggregation the portfolio gain therefore clearly dominates in the macro variance. Moreover, the 5%-quantiles in the fourth quarter of figure 5.3 indicate a non-negligible probability of actually observing an improved prediction performance ($\hat{\sigma}^2 < \hat{\sigma}_p^2$). This corresponds to empirical results (Läufer 1992b, 1995 for quasilinear and Fagan/Henry 1998 for linear aggregation) which compare principal and surrogate residual variances of European money demand functions.

In figure 5.4, the adjustment parameters and the cointegration statistics again show a parallel behaviour. In contrast to the large sample case, however, the macro estimates stay closely together and remain largely within the bounds provided by the respective micro estimates, although a small downward bias is still perceptible. The bias in the long-run parameters is the familiar finite-sample cointegration bias and does not result from aggregation.

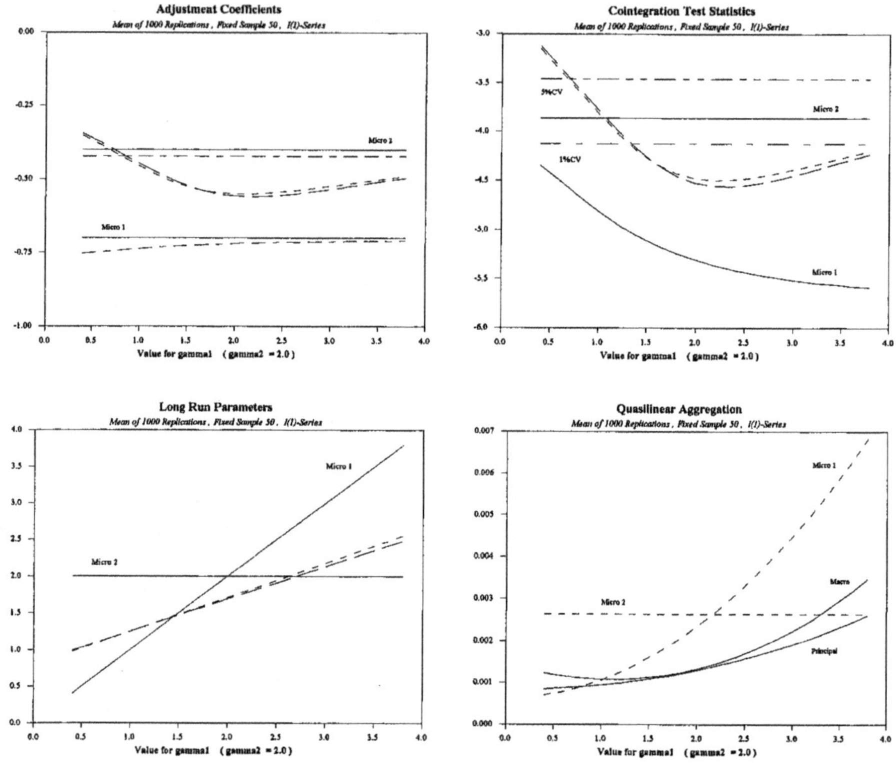

Fig. 5.4. Small Sample Simulation

The fourth quarter of figure 5.4 finally shows that under quasilinear aggregation the surrogate and principal variance stay well below both micro variances over a considerable range of parameters. Thus in small samples the portfolio gain perceptibly prevails over the aggregation loss. This stands in contrast to the large-sample case, where a converse dominance obtained. The reason behind this reversal of dominance is the present non-stationary simulation setup: the micro variances $var(u_{nt})$, being derived from stationary cointegration relations, are time-invariant. As a result, the principal variance and hence the portfolio gain are likewise time-invariant (see equation (5.8)). The aggregation loss, in contrast, is linearly time-dependent in the present setup (see discussion above). This discrepancy, which is unknown in the stationary world of conventional aggregation theory, explains the observed reversal in the ranking between aggregation loss and portfolio gain.

In summary, the above simulation portrayed the effects of linear and quasilinear aggregation against departures from the micro homogeneity restriction, or the degree of global consistency, which provided the x-axis in each graph.

An alternative x-axis could have been the degree of local consistency, that is, departures from the compositional stability restriction. Both cases provide an instance of cointegration carrying through from the micro to the macro level (cf section 5.1.3). Therefore the above simulation results, in particular the shown behaviour of cointegration statistics and adjustment coefficients, would similarly pertain to this alternative x-axis.

There are, however, two subtle exceptions to this rule. First, while global consistency cannot be achieved under quasilinear aggregation, local consistency is possible (cf section 5.1.2). Therefore it would be possible to observe a zero aggregation error even under quasilinear aggregation in this alternative scenario. Second, and more important, the aggregation error otherwise constitutes a stationary rather than an integrated variable in this alternative scenario (cf section 5.1.3). Consequently its variance, the aggregation loss, would be time-invariant rather than time-dependent. A time related reversal in the relative importance of two effects - namely the above reversal between aggregation loss and portfolio gain - would therefore not be possible in this alternative scenario. This topic will resurface in the aggregation-theoretic interpretation of certain empirical results in chapter 7 below.

Summary: From the preceding discussion four interrelated features of aggregation can be distinguished which center around the notions of aggregation structure, aggregation loss, portfolio gain, and cointegration. These features are now briefly summarized.

The notion of an aggregation loss arises from comparing principal and surrogate prediction. Since active aggregation wastes information on individual behaviour, the principal invariably outperforms the surrogate prediction to the extent that micro units indeed behave differently (absence of micro homogeneity and/or compositional stability). Consequently the surrogate variance is generally larger than the principal variance, which defines an aggregation loss. In contrast to this theoretical result, however, some empirical studies actually report a gain rather than a loss from a comparison of the two variances. One explanation for this phenomenon pertains to the estimation procedure: Zellner (1962) and Sasaki (1978) demonstrate the inefficiency of OLS relative to GLS in case of contemporaneous error correlations. Pesaran/Pierse/Kumar (1989) however show that both OLS- and GLS-based estimators of the principal variance suffer from finite sample bias, and propose a suitably adjusted unbiased estimator.

Another explanation concerns the aggregation structure itself: in the present framework the aggregation loss rests on the assumption of correctly specified microfunctions, rendering the principal an unbeatable benchmark. Consequently, as soon as misspecification at the micro level is allowed for, a *specification gain* favouring the surrogate may arise. To motivate such a gain,

Grunfeld/Griliches (1960) suggest omitted variables on the micro level which cancel out in the aggregate (e.g., foreign opportunity costs not included in national money demand specifications[80]). Similarly, Aigner/Goldfeld (1974) suggest measurement errors in micro variables which cancel out in the aggregate (e.g., cross-border deposits not included in national money definitions). Pesaran/Pierse/Kumar (1989) provide a formal treatment and show that a specification gain may but need not outweigh an aggregation loss.

The second feature arises from comparing linear and quasilinear aggregation structures. Globally consistent aggregation, which is possible in a linear structure, is unfortunately not possible in a quasilinear structure, that is, if either the aggregation rules or the behavioural equations are nonlinear. The resulting aggregation error, however, does not appear to inflict serious distortions: at least in the present simulation setup, the differences between the two types of aggregation structures are not dramatic with regard to long run parameters, adjustment parameters, and cointegration test statistics. This may justify the application of statistical tools originally developed for linear structures (such as parameter-equality tests or the GG-criterion) also to quasilinear structures, as for example in Artis/Bladen-Hovell/Zhang (1993), Angeloni/Cottarelli/Levy (1994), or Wesche (1997). There is, however, one exception to this result: under quasilinear aggregation the principal variance is subject to the type of portfolio gain pointed out by Läufer (1992a, 1992b), which is not present under linear aggregation.

The notion of a portfolio gain arises from comparing the principal and the micro prediction. Since the principal error constitutes a linear combination of micro errors, the familiar portfolio effect may reduce the principal variance below even the smallest micro variance. This reduction is called a portfolio gain. The linear combination itself involves deterministic factors (h_n) under linear aggregation, and stochastic weights (w_{nt}) under quasilinear aggregation. The necessary conditions for a portfolio gain therefore depend on the respective aggregation structure. Under linear aggregation it is required that the aggregation factors h_n be proper weights, which is the setup used by Kremers/Lane (1992c), Monticelli/Papi (1996, p.78), and Fagan/Henry (1998, 'index method'). In contrast, under quasilinear aggregation it is required that the approximation $\exp u_{nt} \approx 1 + u_{nt}$ be valid, which is the setup used by Läufer (1992a, 1992b, 1995). Given that almost all empirical studies

[80] The argument led VanRiet (1992, p.38) to conclude that " *... as integration progresses, it will be ever-less possible to explain the demand for money in the individual EC countries from national variables.*" This confuses economic and statistical explanation. Omitted variables (and also omitted error correlations) become statistically less problematical if the explanatory variables become more correlated. For example, if national interest rates were perfectly collinear as a result of European integration, then the statistical gain from including foreign opportunity costs would be zero.

employ simple-sum aggregation rules and a quasilinear aggregation structure, the second type of portfolio gain is clearly the more relevant type, and offers a robust explanation for a superior performance of European money demand specifications.

The portfolio gain also influences the comparison of surrogate and micro prediction, for the simple reason that the surrogate variance contains the principal variance (compare equation (5.6)). The portfolio gain therefore directly competes with the aggregation loss in its influence on the surrogate macro variance. In a cointegration setup, the portfolio gain is time-invariant while the aggregation loss is either time-invariant or linearly time-dependent. Therefore the portfolio gain may well prevail either generally or in small samples over the aggregation loss, so that the macro variance is lower than any of the micro variances. Consequently a macro prediction can appear 'bad' if compared with the principal prediction, but 'good' if compared to the constituent micro predictions. For a choice between, say, national and European monetary targeting the latter type of comparison is certainly of more interest than the former.

The feature of cointegration arises from replacing the conventional assumption of stationary variables with the empirically more plausible assumption of integrated variables. In a linear aggregation structure, the property of cointegration can be shown to carry through from the micro to the macro level only under local or global consistency (cf section 5.1.3). This theoretical result is corroborated by the simulation experiment, and apparently applies also under quasilinear aggregation. Consequently, a cointegration test on the macro level indirectly constitutes a test for consistent aggregation. This point is completely ignored in the empirical literature on European money demand functions, where in the tradition of conventional aggregation theory cointegration and consistency are treated as independent problems (see for example Artis/Bladen-Hovell/Zhang 1993, Wesche 1997, Fagan/Henry 1998). Moreover, since the variance of a static cointegration relation is linked to the adjustment coefficient of an embedding dynamic ECM via Grangers representation theorem, an aggregation loss in the surrogate variance induces a downward bias in the adjustment coefficient of a macro ECM, imparting the impression of sluggish adjustment.

A tacit justification underlying the formulation of some analog macro model, in either a linear or a quasilinear aggregation structure, is of course the assumption that its constituent aggregate variables make economic sense. It is by no means guaranteed that the summations employed by the above aggregation rules preserve whatever economic sense could be attached to the original micro variables. This aspect of aggregation is discussed in the following section.

5.2 Aggregation of Variables

Theoretical variables, like money or price level, are defined in the context of an economic or statistical model. Empirical variables, like M3 or CPI, are defined by some measurement system superimposed on reality and but hypothetically linked within an econometric model. The distinction of economic or statistical models versus econometric models is a problem of econometric methodology and discussed in section 2. The measurement of macroeconomic reality is a problem of index number theory and discussed now.

5.2.1 Index Number Theory

The index number problem is essentially an aggregation problem: In an economy, millions of agents engage in millions of transactions involving millions of prices and quantities. Index numbers are used to reduce and summarize this abundance of information by aggregating over time (into quarterly data) and over agents (into national or European data). To introduce some notation, let all quantities transacted in some current and some base period be recorded in vectors $\mathbf{q}_c$ and $\mathbf{q}_b$. Let the corresponding transaction prices be recorded in vectors $\mathbf{p}_c$ and $\mathbf{p}_b$. The inner product $\mathbf{p}_c\mathbf{q}_c$ then gives the transaction value for period c. A function aggregating vectors of a single period c into a representative absolute price $P(\mathbf{p}_c, \mathbf{q}_c)$ is called a *price level* if it is monotone and linear homogeneous in prices, and invariant to the measurement of quantities.[81] A function aggregating vectors of different periods into a representative relative price $P(\mathbf{p}_c, \mathbf{p}_b, \mathbf{q}_c, \mathbf{q}_b)$ is called a *price index* if, in addition, it is unity for equal price vectors and invariant to the measurement of prices.[82] A quantity level and a quantity index are defined analogously. Many economic variables are measured by indices or levels. For example, consumer prices are measured by a Laspeyres price index $\mathbf{p}_c\mathbf{q}_b/\mathbf{p}_b\mathbf{q}_b$, while the GDP-deflator is given by a Paasche price index $\mathbf{p}_c\mathbf{q}_c/\mathbf{p}_b\mathbf{q}_c$. Nominal output constitutes a quantity level $\mathbf{p}_c\mathbf{q}_c$, while real output constitutes a quantity level scaled by a Laspeyres quantity index, namely $\mathbf{p}_b\mathbf{q}_b \cdot (\mathbf{p}_b\mathbf{q}_c/\mathbf{p}_b\mathbf{q}_b)$.

In order to be truly representative, indices can be required to satisfy certain criteria in addition to their defining properties. According to the origin of these criteria there exists an axiomatic approach and an economic approach to index number theory. Surveys are given by Hill (1988) or Diewert (1995). Under the economic approach, an index incorporates quantities indirectly via some aggregator function and relates them to prices via some cost function.

---

[81] The definition is due to Eichhorn (1978, p.144). The defining properties are known as Monotonicity Axiom, Linear Homogeneity Axiom, and Commensurability Axiom.

[82] The definition is due to Eichhorn (1978, p.160). The additional defining properties are known as Identity Axiom and Price Dimensionality Axiom.

For example, quantities entering via an utility function allow to define a cost-of-living price index as a ratio of minimum costs required to attain a certain utility level under two different price vectors. Under the axiomatic approach, an index incorporates quantities and prices directly and independently. The index is, however, required to pass certain 'tests'.

An important test for any money demand specification is the *product test* for levels, requiring $P(\mathbf{p}_c, \mathbf{q}_c)\, Q(\mathbf{p}_c, \mathbf{q}_c) = \mathbf{p}_c \mathbf{q}_c$. A price level and a quantity level satisfying this functional equation could reasonably claim to represent the arguments of a quantity-style money demand function. However, Eichhorn (1978, Theorem 7.3.13) shows that price- and quantity levels passing the product test simply do not exist.[83] Another test is the *proportionality test* for indices, requiring $P(\mathbf{p}_c, \mathbf{p}_b, \mathbf{q}_c, \mathbf{q}_b) = \lambda$ whenever $\mathbf{p}_c = \lambda \mathbf{p}_b$. Proportionality holds for all price indices, but not necessarily for ratios of price indices: A ratio of consecutive Laspeyres indices (e.g., first difference of logged CPI) passes this test, whereas a ratio of consecutive Paasche indices (e.g., first difference of logged deflator) fails it. Possibly relevant for an European money demand specification is the *transitivity test* for indices[84], requiring $P(\mathbf{p}_c, \mathbf{p}_a, \mathbf{q}_c, \mathbf{q}_a)\, P(\mathbf{p}_a, \mathbf{p}_b, \mathbf{q}_a, \mathbf{q}_b) = P(\mathbf{p}_c, \mathbf{p}_b, \mathbf{q}_c, \mathbf{q}_b)$. Price indices satisfying this functional equation could be used as purchasing power parities converting national variables into an arbitrary common denomination. However, Eichhorn (1978, Theorem 8.5.20) shows that no price index can pass the product test and the transitivity test together. Moreover, Balk (1995, Theorem 11) shows that the only price index passing the transitivity test is a geometric mean of prices independent of quantities.

The decisive tests, however, for the construction of European aggregates are the *consistency test* and the *equality test*. The first test requires that the respective index can equivalently be obtained as an index of analog subindices calculated from disjoint subsets of the underlying transactions. The second test requires that this index indicates an increase of λ whenever all its subindices do so. Balk (1995, Corollary 16) shows that the only indices passing both tests together are Laspeyres and Paasche indices. This important result implies that (i) genuine European price- and quantity indices can be obtained indirectly by summing available national indices, and (ii) rival aggregation-consistent indices do not exist. The result is employed in the following construction of European aggregate variables.

[83] Consider for example the textbook exposition in Jarchow (1998, p.175): Nominal output is defined by $YN \equiv \Sigma p_i q_i$, the general price level by $P \equiv \Sigma p_i \pi_i$ with fixed weights π_i, and real output is determined by $Y = YN\,/\,P$ using the product test. The aggregate quantity Y does not satisfy the Commensurability Axiom: Redimensioning all quantities by a factor λ and readjusting their prices would change real output.

[84] This test is also known as circularity test. If the price indices are taken to be exchange rates the test is known as triangular arbitrage condition.

5.2.2 Construction of European Aggregates

To aggregate nominal variables, let the vectors $\mathbf{p}_t, \mathbf{q}_t$ (the subvectors $\mathbf{p}_{nt}, \mathbf{q}_{nt}$) contain all prices and quantities from transactions in Europe (in the n-th country), the former denominated in some common currency. Let e_{nt} denote the rate converting national prices of period t into common denomination prices $\mathbf{p}_{nt}$. The same rate converts national 'stores of value' into the common denomination. Aggregate money (M) and aggregate nominal output (YN) then constitute simple sums of national contributions:

$$M_t = \sum_{n=1}^{N} e_{nt} M_{nt} \tag{5.14}$$

$$YN_t \equiv \mathbf{p}_t \mathbf{q}_t = \sum_{n=1}^{N} \mathbf{p}_{nt} \mathbf{q}_{nt} = \sum_{n=1}^{N} e_{nt} YN_{nt} \quad . \tag{5.15}$$

The consistency-in-aggregation property now allows a convenient breakdown of nominal output (5.15). The Paasche price index PPI describing the aggregate price level can be expressed as a weighted harmonic mean of corresponding converted national indices. Similarly, the Laspeyres quantity index LQI underlying aggregate real output can be expressed as a weighted arithmetic mean of corresponding national indices. Precisely (see appendix A.4):

$$PPI_t \equiv \frac{\mathbf{p}_t \mathbf{q}_t}{\mathbf{p}_0 \mathbf{q}_t} = \left(\sum_{n=1}^{N} w_{nt} \left(\frac{e_{nt}}{e_{n0}} \right)^{-1} PPI_{nt}^{-1} \right)^{-1} \tag{5.16}$$

$$LQI_t \equiv \frac{\mathbf{p}_0 \mathbf{q}_t}{\mathbf{p}_0 \mathbf{q}_0} = \sum_{n=1}^{N} w_{n0} \, LQI_{nt} \quad , \tag{5.17}$$

where $w_{nt} \equiv \mathbf{p}_{nt}\mathbf{q}_{nt} \,/\, \mathbf{p}_t\mathbf{q}_t$ (current value share) and $w_{n0} \equiv \mathbf{p}_{n0}\mathbf{q}_{n0} \,/\, \mathbf{p}_0\mathbf{q}_0$ (base-period value share). From (5.17) it follows that European real output constitutes a sum of national contributions converted by e_{n0}. It is again noted that rival indices allowing a similar breakdown do not exist. However, as a precondition for (5.14) and (5.15) to constitute sensible aggregation rules the national variables M_{nt} and YN_{nt} must both be disjoint across countries. Given the prevailing measurement systems this is however not necessarily the case in open and integrating economies.

First, traditional definitions of national money may either double-count or exclude *cross-border deposits (CBD's)*. These deposits denote monetary bank liabilities for which the residency of the nonbank holder, the currency of denomination, and the location of the issuing bank do not coincide in the same country. Such deposits are created to protect money holdings against devaluation risk (currency substitution) or country risk (deposit relocation). As a simple example, suppose residents hold money partly with domestic (D_1) and partly with foreign (D_1^*) banks. Similarly, foreigners may hold money partly with foreign (D_2^*) and partly with domestic (D_2) banks. According to traditional definitions[85] the respective national quantities of money are measured by D_1 and D_2^*. These measures understate the true national money stock since also the cross-border deposits (D_1^* or D_2) can be used to finance transactions in the respective country. Moreover, an aggregate constructed indirectly according to (5.14) also understates the true total money stock.[86] Given the prevailing measurement system, CBD's therefore induce measurement errors on both the national and the European level.

Second, since money is used to finance transactions, there is some mirror-image of CBD's on the real side of the economy. Thus one may define *cross-border transactions (CBT's)*, i.e. transactions in goods or assets for which the residency of the buyer, the currency of denomination, or the location of the seller do not coincide in the same country. Traditional measures of national transaction volume may now either double-count or exclude such CBT's. As a simple example, suppose domestic nominal output is sold partly at home (T_1) and partly abroad (T_1^*). Similarly, foreign nominal output is sold partly abroad (T_2^*) and partly at home (T_2). Suppose that all CBT's are financed using domestic currency. The foreign transaction volume is then T_2^* (foreign output minus foreign exports), while the domestic transaction volume is $T_1 + T_1^* + T_2$ (domestic output plus domestic imports). The traditional measure 'nominal output' then overstates the true volume for the foreign country and understates it for the home country. The true total transaction volume is however correctly measured by an aggregate constructed indirectly according to (5.15). Given the prevailing measurement system, CBT's therefore may induce measurement errors on the national but not on the European level.

In the literature on money demand in Europe, the problem of CBT's is completely neglected. The problem of CBD's and their impact on the stability of empirical money demand functions has though received some attention: Giucca/Levy (1992) construct CBD series for six European countries over 1977 to 1990. Some of them even reach double-digit percentages of the respective national stock of broad money. From Granger-causality tests within VAR's of logarithmic first differences for France and Germany the authors conclude that a CBD-correction of national definitions does not help to improve the statistical relationship between broad money, nominal output, and interest rates in both countries. Angeloni/Cottarelli/Levy (1994) put the total of intra-European CBD's to roughly 8% of European broad money in 1990.

[85] The definitions used by all EMS countries comprise but deposits held by residents with domestic banks irrespective of their denomination (see Monticelli/Papi 1996, p.108).

[86] A direct definition of the total money stock as the sum of monetary liabilities from a consolidated balance sheet of all European banks would of course avoid this problem. This is the motivation behind the list of 'Monetary Financial Institutions' drawn up by the European Central Bank (see ECB 1999b).

From an information-content measure obtained within a multicountry SURE system for five European countries they find that the CBD-correction of national definitions only in the case of Germany decisively improves the information in money for nominal output. Monticelli (1996) and Monticelli/Papi (1996) discuss in detail the measurement of money in an open economy. Their series show intra-European CBD's rising from 2% to 8% of European broad money over 1978 to 1992. The aggregates constructed from CBD-corrected national definitions are then confronted with those constructed from traditional definitions within single-equation money demand specifications. Comparing the cointegration test statistics and ECM adjustment coefficients the authors conclude that a CBD correction does not improve the statistical qualities of the aggregate specification.

To aggregate interest rates, let v_{nt} denote some possibly time-varying weights. The European interest rate constitutes a weighted arithmetic average of national interest rates

$$i_t = \sum_{n=1}^{N} v_{nt}\, i_{nt} \quad . \tag{5.18}$$

If the national interest rates are perceived as the own rate or as the opportunity cost of money, then a logical choice for the weight v_{nt} is the share of national money in its aggregate, namely $v_{nt} = e_{nt}M_{nt} \,/\, M_t$. In this case the aggregate i_t constitutes a proper own rate or opportunity cost of the aggregate money stock. The weighting schemes found in the literature usually comprise the share of national currency in the ECU basket (Kremers/Lane 1990, Artis/Bladen-Hovell/Zhang 1993, Monticelli/Strauss-Kahn 1993), or alternatively the share of national real output in the aggregate (Tullio/DeSouza/Giucca 1996, Monticelli/Papi 1996, Wesche 1997).

The final problem in the construction of European aggregates is the choice of an appropriate conversion rate. The first choice concerns the common denomination. This is a minor issue for quasilinear aggregation structures: Multiplying the original variables by some conversion rate e amounts to adding $\ln(e)$ to the logged variables. This operation affects only the intercept in the micro equations. Any currency or currency basket can thus be used for denomination, the literature frequently employs Dollar or DM. Second, some rate converting national currencies into the common denomination must be chosen. The relative magnitude of this rate affects the size of national contributions in aggregate nominal output, and hence the weights w_n. Possible candidates are market rates and purchasing power parity (PPP) rates. While market rates are usually observable variables, PPP-rates are price indices and rival methods of defining and calculating such indices exist (cf Balk 1989 and Gulde/Schulze-Ghattas 1992). If the system of conversion rates lacks transitivity, converting aggregate output into a new denomination is not equivalent to converting each national component directly into the new denomination.

Third, possible variations over time in the conversion rate affect the ratio e_{nt}/e_{n0} and hence also the aggregate price index. The alternatives found in the literature comprise variable current rates and fixed base-period rates.

To evaluate the effect of current rates, let country N be the numeraire country whose currency serves as common denomination so that $e_{Nt} = 1\,\forall t$. Against this benchmark, the aggregate deflator (5.16) can be rewritten as

$$PPI_t \;=\; PPI_{Nt}\left(\sum_{n=1}^{N} w_{nt}\left(\frac{e_{nt}}{e_{n0}}\,\frac{PPI_{nt}}{PPI_{Nt}}\right)^{-1}\right)^{-1} . \tag{5.19}$$

In period $t = 0$ by construction holds $e_{nt}/e_{n0} = PPI_{nt}/\,PPI_{Nt} = 1$. Subsequent devaluation of country n currency against the numeraire currency is expressed as $e_{nt}/e_{n0} < 1$, and subsequent inflation in country n relative to the numeraire country as $PPI_{nt}/\,PPI_{Nt} > 1$. Suppose now the conversion rate e_{nt} is taken to be the current PPP rate. In this case the bracketed terms in equation (5.19) equal unity, so that every converted national price index and hence also the aggregate price index identically equals the numeraire price index. If the conversion rate e_{nt} is taken to be the current market rate, then the aggregate price index equals the numeraire price index to the extent that observable exchange rates correspond to their PPP values.

To illustrate this point, several deflators aggregated according to (5.19) are calculated for the present data set.[87] The underlying countries comprise Germany, Netherlands, Austria (DM-Block), Belgium/Luxemburg, Denmark, France, Ireland (BE,DK,FR,IR), and Italy, Spain, Portugal (IT,SP,PO), which together aggregate into an 'Euro10' area. The various deflators obtained for these groups are collected in figure 5.5, starting at 79:1 to trace the development over the ERM era. The common denomination is Deutsche Mark, so that all 'current PPP' deflators by construction equal the German deflator. The respective 'current market' deflators are now repeatedly driven back towards this benchmark by a devaluation of inflating national currencies. This is particularly obvious for the ERM-realignments in the early 1980's and for the ERM-crises in the early 1990's. In summary, converting national price indices via current rates imposes a cross-country common trend on these indices to the extent that PPP holds. Testing for cointegration in aggregate money demand insofar constitutes an indirect test of PPP holding between component countries, cf section 5.1.3.

Fixed conversion rates ($e_{nt} = e_{n0}\,\forall t$) keep an aggregate free of exchange rate movements, and thus preserve the 'pure' movements of the underlying national variables. To illustrate this point, figure 5.5 contains deflators aggre-

[87] The data set is described in detail in section 6.2 and in appendix A.7.

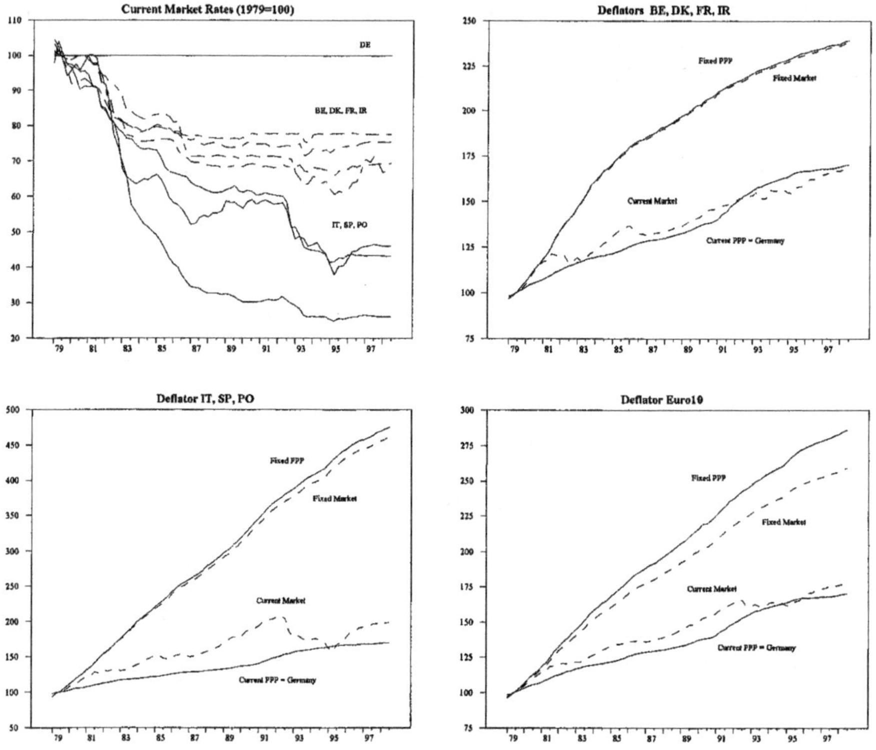

Fig. 5.5. Aggregated Deflators (1979=100)

gated by fixed PPP rates and fixed market rates.[88] These fixed rate deflators nicely trace, for example, the poor inflation performance within the 'Club Med' relative to the DM-Block (third quarter), and keep the aggregate price index free of the exchange rate gyrations of the 1990's. Fixed rates therefore put a much tougher condition on the appearance of cross-country common trends in national variables: if devaluations can not be (ab-)used to keep national price indices (and hence also the aggregate price index) in line with the numeraire price index, then a common trend in prices can be brought about only by a genuinely similar inflation performance. This rather attractive aspect of fixed conversion rates of course involves a drawback: Historically the available time series simply did not evolve under a regime of fixed conversion rates, and their behaviour would have been (most likely) significantly different had such a system actually been in operation.

88 Precisely, these rates are base period rates for 1979. The base period PPP rates are from OECD (1998), the base period market rates are averages of current rates over 79:1 to 79:4.

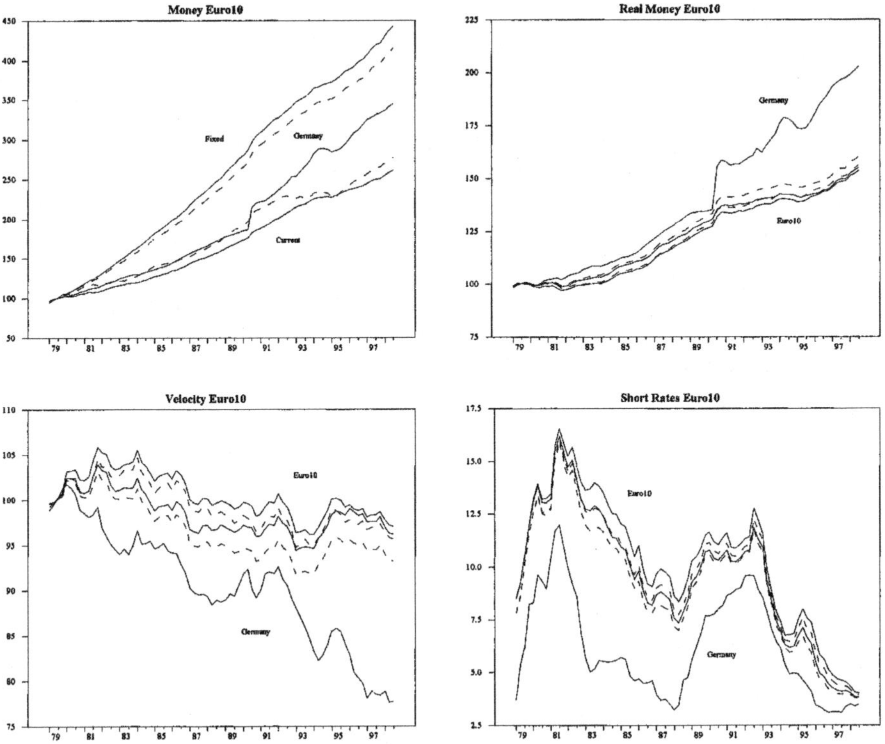

Fig. 5.6. Aggregated Variables (1979=100)

The whole conversion-rate problem is, however, somewhat moderated in that exchange rate movements may cancel out in certain variables or combinations of variables. Figure 5.6 contains the Euro10 series for money, real money, velocity, and the short interest rate. Solid lines indicate aggregates from PPP rates, and dotted lines those from market rates. The series on money clearly exhibit characteristics similar to those shown by the Euro10 deflator-series in figure 5.5. But in real money, and even more so in velocity, the difference between current-rate aggregation and fixed-rate aggregation largely vanishes. The same applies for the share of national money in aggregate money, so that interest rates aggregated according to (5.18) also appear invariant to the choice of a conversion rate. Real output, finally, is aggregated according to (5.17) using only fixed rates anyway. An empirical study involving real money, real output, and interest rates can therefore be expected to find but little difference between rival conversion methods. And in fact, even with money and deflator left unrestricted, the empirical results in chapter 6 show no substantial difference between fixed-rate and current-rate aggregation.

Summary: Aggregation rules for the construction of European variables are given by 5.14 for money, 5.16 for prices, 5.17 for real output, and 5.18 for interest rates. A consistency result from index number theory justifies the construction of the European price- and quantity indices from available national Paasche- and Laspeyres indices. Both the national and the aggregate variables may, however, suffer from measurement errors induced by cross-border activities. Moreover, several conversion rates are available to convert national variables into a common denomination. A compelling a-priori choice between market-rates and PPP-rates, or fixed-rates and current-rates, could not be derived. Therefore different sets of European variables can be constructed from the present aggregation rules. The empirical analysis of the resulting variables is the topic of the following chapter.

6 Empirical Money Demand

An econometric assessment of the 'stability of money demand' faces a number of problems which, essentially, provided the content for the previous chapters. Specifically, the notion of money demand being first of all a theoretical idea and not necessarily a hidden empirical truth is expressed in the concept of an unknown DGP introduced in chapter 2. As a methodological consequence, the proper task of a probability model is not to cast some economic theory into estimable form, but to summarize statistical properties of the analyzed data series. A probability model particularly suited to capture the dynamic interdependencies between macroeconomic data series is the VAR model introduced in chapter 3. However, even if the empirical truth of this model could somehow be established, the isolation of money demand therein remained to some extent arbitrary since other equilibrium relations could likewise be effective in the data. The reformulation of a (conditional) VAR in the light of some (arbitrary) a-priori information leads to the just-identified structural ECM introduced in chapter 4.

In the present chapter these methods are applied to actual data series to obtain an empirical model for money demand. In section 6.1, the autoregressive probability model is fitted to data series for Germany. The model's subtleties and possible pitfalls motivate a systematic approach: First the present data are related to the literature by estimating typical single-equation ECM's over the former to replicate stylized facts from the latter. Then the data series are individually screened by scalar unit-root tests, and an empirical model for velocity is derived. Finally the data series are jointly modelled as a VAR, and in this framework subjected to extensive sequential and recursive vector unit-root tests. Section 6.2 then proceeds similarly with data series for Europe. In section 6.3, finally, the resulting VAR-submodels are converted into structural ECM's by implementing hypotheses about the existence and stability of money demand. This allows to (destructively) identify the shortcomings of single-equation models, and to (constructively) propose a multi-equation alternative.

6.1 Probability Model for Germany

6.1.1 Data and Recent Literature

The data for Germany comprise seasonally adjusted quarterly series covering a sample period from 81:1 to 98:3 (T=71), with suitable presample periods allowing for initial conditions. All data refer to West-Germany until 90:2, and to united Germany from 90:3 onwards. Money (m) is measured by its broad definition M3, which is the Bundesbank's official target variable. Output (y) is measured by the real gross national product (GNP) in 1979 prices. The ratio of nominal to real GNP gives a Paasche price index measuring the general price level (p), normalized at 1979=100. Money's own rate (is) is measured by a short term interest rate, namely the rate on 3-month time deposits which are a major component in M3. Money's opportunity costs (il) are measured by a long term interest rate, namely the yield on government bonds. The data on money, income, and prices are expressed in natural logarithms of the respective original series, while the interest rate series are left untransformed. Consequently real money is here defined as $mr \equiv m - p$ and velocity as $v \equiv y + p - m$. Graphs of the respective series are given in figure 6.1, and the data sources are detailed in appendix A.7.[89]

Of course there are numerous empirical studies investigating similar data. The majority employs single-equation error-correction models. Within this ECM class, most studies choose real money as a dependent variable and purport to estimate money demand. Hansen/Kim (1995) analyze seasonally adjusted data on real broad money, real GNP, and two interest rates over 74:1 to 92:4 (T=76). They find cointegration before and after reunification, and explicitly test weak exogeneity of real GNP and interest rates for the cointegration parameters. Formal tests on parameter constancy suggest time-invariance of the cointegration relation. Wolters/Lütkepohl (1997), Wolters/Teräsvirta/Lütkepohl (1998), and Lütkepohl/Wolters (1998) analyze seasonally unadjusted data on real broad money, real GNP, an interest rate spread, and inflation over 76:1 to 96:1 (T=81), 94:1 (T=73), 96:4 (T=84), respectively. They find cointegration with an unit income elasticity, and confirm, by recursive estimation, parameter constancy over reunification. The Bundesbank (1997) analyses seasonally unadjusted data on real broad money, real GDP, inflation, and a long interest rate over 75:1 to 96:4 (T=88). Excluding further variables from the long-run a-priori, cointegration is found between real money and real GDP with an income elasticity significantly greater than one. In all studies, the cointegration residuals are interpreted as 'excess money' and subsequently embedded into a dynamic ECM for real money. The adjustment coefficients obtained from these ECM's are $\hat{\alpha} = -0.22$ (Hansen/Kim) and $\hat{\alpha} = -0.10$ (other studies).

[89] In the graphs, the unification break in the series for money and output is partially cut off for better resolution.

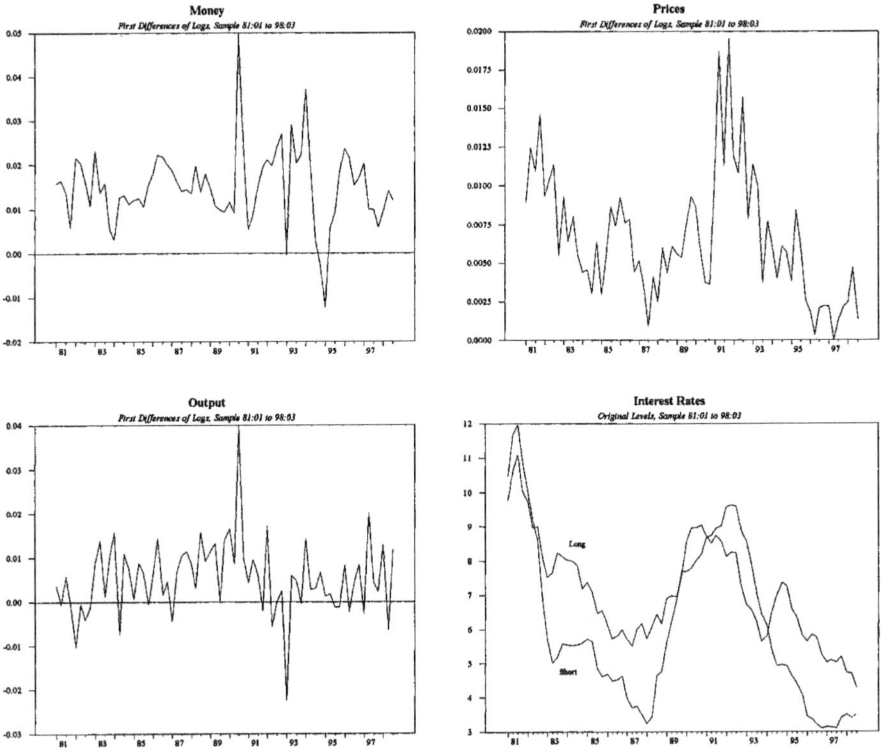

Fig. 6.1. Data Series for Germany

Other studies within the ECM class choose the price level as a dependent variable and purport to estimate an equilibrium price level (P-star) by turning a money demand equation on its head. Tödter/Reimers (1994) analyze seasonally unadjusted data on real broad money and real potential GDP over 71:1 to 92:4 (T=88), while Issing/Tödter (1995) analyze seasonally unadjusted data on real broad money, real GDP, and an interest rate spread over 75:1 to 93:2 (T=74). Both studies find cointegration, with an income elasticity above one reflecting the observed downward trend in velocity. The cointegration residuals are subsequently interpreted as a 'price gap' and inserted into an error-correction model for inflation, yielding an adjustment coefficient $\hat{\alpha} = -0.08$ in both studies. A similar approach is presented in Bundesbank (1992) for West-Germany.

The preceding single-equation models suffer from two drawbacks. First, by construction at most one cointegration relation is permitted, although up to $p-1$ such relations can possibly hold between p variables. Second, the exogeneity status of the conditioning right-hand-side variables is always presumed rather than tested. Both problems can be addressed within a multi-equation VAR-framework. Several studies indeed manage to develop a single-equation ECM out of an initial general VAR, with a cointegration rank $r = 1$ inferred by the Johansen-procedure.

Gerdesmeier (1996) analyses seasonally adjusted data on broad money, GDP, an interest rate spread, and a wealth variable over 75:1 to 94:4 (T=80). Both in real and in nominal terms these data indicate a single cointegration relation, with adjustment coefficients $\hat{\alpha} = -0.14$ for real and $\hat{\alpha} = -0.16$ for nominal money. Funke (1996) analyses seasonally adjusted data on real narrow money, real GDP, and a short term interest rate over 74:1 to 94:2 (T=82) within a VAR(2) model. He finds weak evidence for one cointegration relation, and strong evidence for structural change after reunification from a parameter-constancy test. Given that no dummies are included in his model this result is not particularly surprising. In a careful and thorough study, Beyer (1998) analyses seasonally adjusted data on real broad money, real GDP, a short and a long interest rate, and inflation over 76:3 to 94:4 (T=74). Under the restriction of a single cointegration relation inferred from the Johansen procedure, he finds weak exogeneity of output, interest rates, and inflation within a VAR(2) model, and tests for Granger-Causality within a VAR(4) model. With this justification he proceeds to sequentially reduce a general four lag ADL model to a simpler ECM for real money, yielding an adjustment coefficient $\hat{\alpha} = -0.08$. Four different stability tests on the conditional and the marginal model confirm parameter constancy and super exogeneity. The ECM is then shown to encompass similar models derived in other studies. Scharnagl (1998) finally analyses seasonally unadjusted data on real broad money, real GDP, and an interest rate over 75:1 to 96:4 (T=88) within a VAR(4) model. He finds weak exogeneity of output and interest rate for the cointegration vector, the adjustment for real money is then $\hat{\alpha} = -0.13$.

Albeit apparently data inferred, the detection of but a single cointegration relation in the preceding studies seems somewhat surprising given the number of equilibrium relations proposed by economic theory for these variables. Juselius (1996) analyses seasonally unadjusted data on real broad money, real GDP, a short and a long interest rate, and inflation over 75:2 to 94:4 (T=79) within a VAR(2) model. She finds 3 cointegration relations, on which over-identifying structural restrictions are extensively tested. The final long-run identification scheme includes a money demand relation, a central bank reaction function, and some sort of Phillips curve. The resulting structural coefficients reveal significantly different monetary regimes before and after 1983. Similar data are analyzed by Hubrich (1999) over 79:1 to 94:2 (T=62), also within a VAR(2) model. She likewise finds 3 cointegration relations, and her final long-run identification scheme includes a money demand relation, a Fisher-equation, and an interest-rate spread.

Given the recent literature and the present data set, a natural next step is to relate the two by replicating from the latter salient results of the former. To this end, two typical money demand specifications (one using m, p and one using $mr, \Delta p$) are tried on two versions of the present data set (seasonally adjusted, SA, and unadjusted, NSA) within the usual single-equation ECM framework. Table 6.1 contains the results from one-step estimation over the full sample 81:1-98:3. All four models include a constant and impulse dummies ID90:3, ID93:1, ID95:1 in their deterministic regressor, for the NSA-data moreover centered seasonal dummies. All models pass the usual battery of diagnostic tests (white noise, autocorrelation, conditional and unconditional homoscedasticity) for possible misspecification.

Data	$\hat{\alpha}$	$\hat{\beta}'$					t_α
	Δm	m	p	y	is	il	
SA	−0.09	1.00	−1.61	−0.69	−0.03	0.06	−2.7
NSA	−0.13	1.00	−1.16	−1.07	−0.02	0.05	−2.4
	Δmr	mr	Δp	y	is	il	
SA	−0.08	1.00	8.75	−1.17	−0.03	0.06	−2.3
NSA	−0.12	1.00	6.03	−1.20	−0.02	0.05	−2.1

First Block: cointegration relation between $[m, p, y, is, il]$ inserted into dynamic ECM for nominal broad money (Δm). Second Block: cointegration relation between $[mr, \Delta p, y, is, il]$ inserted into dynamic ECM for real broad money (Δmr). Labels SA and NSA denote seasonally adjusted and unadjusted data. The 5% critical value for t_α-statistics on $\hat{\alpha}$ is -4.4 (one-step estimation).

Table 6.1. Single Equation Specifications for Germany

The long-run coefficients, assembled in a vector $\hat{\beta}'$, show usual and theoretically plausible properties, namely a unit elasticity for income, a positive semi-elasticity for the own rate, and a negative semi-elasticity for the opportunity cost. The corresponding adjustment coefficients $\hat{\alpha}$ do not seem invariant to seasonal adjustment, but in magnitude completely in line with the values reported in the cited literature. Disappointing though are the test statistics t_a : applying the critical value -4.4 from Banerjee/Dolado/Mestre (1998, Table I.B) gives but scarce evidence for cointegration. Applying, as a cross-check, also the critical value from MacKinnon (1991, Table 1) within the Engle/Granger procedure yields similarly disappointing results. One explanation could be the presence of dummies in the model, which usually necessitates lower critical values. Another explanation could be a failure of weak exogeneity of the chosen regressors for the long-run parameters. Both explanations are explicitly considered in sections 6.1.3 and 6.3.1 below.

6.1.2 Scalar Autoregressive Modelling

As a first characterization of the stochastic properties of the chosen data, the time series on money, output, prices, velocity and interest rates are individually modelled as scalar autoregressive sequences. The scalar model's lag length is selected using the Schwarz (SC) and the Hannan-Quinn (HQ) information criteria, and its statistical adequacy is evaluated using the modified Q-statistic (Ljung/Box 1978) and the LM-statistic (Breusch/Pagan (1980) for autocorrelation. These statistics recommend, quite unanimously, an AR(2) model for m, y, v and an AR(3) model for p, is, il. Table 6.2 summarizes a menu of unit-root statistics obtained from these models. The graphs in figure 6.1 suggest the presence of a linear trend in the deterministic component of m, y, p, v, and the presence of a constant for is and il. The indicated null hypotheses are thus tested against their most plausible alternatives. The employed tests have been detailed in section 3.1 (tables 3.1 and 3.2). One extension, the τ-statistic under a break, is briefly discussed here.

The time series on money and output jump by 14% and 11% in 90:3 because of reunification. Breaks in an underlying DGP affect the behaviour of unit root statistics: Hendry/Neale (1991) show the $\hat{\tau}_\mu$ statistic to be biased towards zero under a stationary DGP with intercept shift, and Perron (1989) shows the $\hat{\tau}_\tau$ statistic to biased to zero under a trend-stationary DGP with intercept shift. To adequately model the above breaking series, the deterministic component of their AR models should contain some permanent level shift. This is achieved by including into the regressor d_t an impulse dummy in the I(1) case and a stepdummy in the I(0) case. For this setup Perron (1989, model A) derives a unit root statistic similar to $\hat{\tau}_\tau$ in two steps. First, by means of an auxiliary regression on constant, time trend, and step dummy the deterministics postulated by the alternative hypothesis are removed from the raw series. Second, over the resulting residuals an ADF regression (without constant) is run, and the t-statistic on the lagged level regressor computed.[90] The distribution of this statistic depends on the relative time of the break. Perron (1989, Table IV.B) tabulates the asymptotic critical values, Silvestre/Rossello/Ortuno (1999) provide finite-sample values via response surface regressions.

In finite samples, the appropriate critical values for unit-root statistics depend on the actual sample size (T) and on the lag order (k) of the fitted autoregressive model. Refining the limiting distributions listed in table 3.1, MacKinnon (1991,1996) provides critical values for any finite sample size, using response surface regressions to interpolate and summarize simulation

[90] Using a similar auxiliary regression Park/Sung (1994) extend Phillips' (1987) Z-test to accomodate breaks. In contrast to Perron (1989) they incorporate the a-priori information about the break time into the test statistic rather than into the limiting distribution.

results. Cheung/Lai (1995a,1995b) provide critical values for any finite sample and any known lag order, also via response surface regressions. Hall (1994) and Ng/Perron (1995) derive the asymptotic distribution of the ADF-statistic for a data-based lag order selection. This distribution coincides with the usual Dickey-Fuller distribution if the chosen lag order is not smaller than the true order. Since the HQ- and SC-criteria select the true order with probability one in the limit, a selection guided by these information criteria asymptotically preserves the appropriateness of the distributions in table 3.1. In finite samples, however, the criteria may either underestimate or overestimate the true lag order. For the ADF test-this results in either size distortions or power losses, respectively. Simulation evidence in Hall (1994) and Ng/Perron (1995) suggests that an order selection based on the HQ- and SC-criteria is more powerful than a general-to-specific lag testing procedure.

Null:	I(2)			I(1)+Trend		
Statistic:	$\hat{\tau}_\mu$	GLS_μ	$\Phi_3(4)$	$\hat{\tau}_\tau$	GLS_τ	Φ_3
5% CV	**−2.9**	**−2.2**	**5.8**	**−3.5**	**−3.1**	**6.7**
Money	−7.6*	−7.4*	15.9*	-3.3^{b}	−2.0	2.3
Prices	−2.2	−2.2	3.0	−2.3	−2.4	3.3
Output	−8.0*	−7.3*	17.1*	-1.6^{b}	−1.6	1.5
Velocity	−6.2*	−4.7*	11.7*	−2.3	−2.4	2.8

Null:	I(2)		I(1)		
Statistic:	$\hat{\tau}$	$\Phi_2(2)$	$\hat{\tau}_\mu$	GLS_μ	Φ_1
5% CV	**−2.0**	**6.6**	**−2.9**	**−2.2**	**4.9**
Short Rate	−4.2*	14.3*	−2.8	−1.7	4.7
Long Rate	−5.4*	17.1*	−1.7	−1.5	2.3

Statistics from AR(3)-model (Prices,Rates) or AR(2)-model (Money,Output, Velocity). Description of tests and critical values (CV) in tables 3.1 and 3.2. Superscript 'b' denotes statistic from Perron (1989, model A) with critical value -3.8 for λ=0.6 as relative time of break. Superscript '' denotes rejection of null with at most 5% error probability.*

Table 6.2. Scalar Unit Root Tests for Germany

For the present data, the tests reported in table 6.2 indicate the presence of possibly two unit roots in the AR-model for prices, and the presence of one unit root in the respective AR-models for money, output, velocity, and interest rates. The hypothesis of three unit roots (not reported) is rejected for all variables, in particular also for prices. Estimation over a reduced sample 81:1 - 89:4 (also not reported) did not significantly alter the respective test statistics. Some qualifying comments seem appropriate. First, although the

I(1)-null for interest rates is empirically not rejected, integratedness or lack of mean reversion is a theoretically implausible property for such variables. To resolve this contradiction, it is noted that in finite samples an integrated and a stationary process can have similar observational implications in that their likelihood functions are arbitrarily close (see Cochrane 1991 and Blough 1992). Thus here one may proceed *as if* interest rates were integrated without implying this property in an asymptotic or even ontological sense. Second, although the I(2)-null for prices is narrowly accepted in the recommended AR(3) model, it is rejected in an equally possible AR(2) model. This ambiguity in testing for a second unit root is well known in the empirical literature on long memory in inflation rates. One explanation, offered by Hassler/Wolters (1995), could be that inflation is better represented by a fractionally integrated I($d < 1$) process. As shown by Granger (1980), such a process may arise from aggregating a large number of prices into a single price index. A further hint is the behaviour of velocity: if prices were actually I(2), then this property should likewise surface in the derived series for velocity. The null of two unit roots is, however, clearly rejected in the velocity series.

As a side product of the unit root tests, an AR(2) model with one unit root emerges for velocity. Since the level shifts in money and output are of nearly the same magnitude and thus cancel out in velocity (compare figure 5.6), the initial deterministic regressor is specified without dummies as $d_t = m_0 + m_1 t$. The restriction $m_1 = 0$ is subsequently accepted by Φ_3 and $\hat{\tau}_{\beta\tau}$, so that a quadratic trend can be ruled out. Although the further restriction $m_0 = 0$ is also accepted by Φ_2, the absence of a linear trend is not yet imposed in accordance with the visual appearance of the series. Estimation over 81:1 to 98:3 then gives the empirical model[91]

$$\Delta v_t = \underset{(0.01)}{0.29}\, \Delta v_{t-1} - \underset{(0.07)}{0.0023} + \hat{e}_t \quad , \quad \hat{\sigma}_e = 1.0\,\% \quad . \tag{6.1}$$

This specification passes a battery of diagnostic tests evaluating the model against the relative past and the relative future of its own data. The quarterly drift $m_0 = -0.0023$ translates into a yearly velocity decline of 0.92%.[92] If the coefficient on the lagged difference is (invalidly) restricted to zero, the quarterly drift becomes $m_0 = -0.0033$. This simply depicts the average change in velocity and translates into a yearly decline of 1.32%. For all crudeness of model (6.1), these two long-run forecasts are quite 'realistic': in the derivation of its annual monetary targets, the Bundesbank (since 1993) regularly allowed for a yearly velocity decline of 1%.

---

[91] The values in brackets report the marginal probability (p-value) of the t-statistic testing a zero restriction on the respective coefficient.

[92] A quarterly growth rate g_q translates into a yearly growth rate g_y through $g_y = (1 + g_q)^4 - 1$. Recall that m, y, p are all in natural logarithms, so that Δv approximates a growth rate.

6.1.3 Vector Autoregressive Modelling

Following their individual characterization as scalar autoregressions, the German data series are modelled jointly as a vector autoregression in the present section. In a first paragraph the statistical adequacy of the general VAR model is ascertained via misspecification tests. Within this (adequate) general model a second paragraph then tests for integration and cointegration to achieve a more informative submodel. Since this submodel forms the basis of the structural ECM in section 6.3, some care is taken in the determination of the cointegration rank and the deterministic degree. In particular, vector I(1) tests are conducted sequentially over all submodels and recursively over time. Moreover, the possible influence of dummies is evaluated, and the constancy of the cointegration space over break dates is tested. Finally vector I(2) tests are conducted to rule out higher order integration. In a final paragraph two rival VAR specifications are briefly considered.

The General Model: The initial VAR is formulated according to (3.15) for a vector $x_t = [m,\, p,\, y,\, is,\, il]$ and two lags (k=2). To account for breaks, three impulse dummies are included in the deterministic regressor, which is formulated as $d_t = [1, t,\text{ID90:3,ID93:1,ID95:1}]$.[93] This specification constitutes the maintained hypothesis, or the general unrestricted model (GUM) in the sense of section 2.3. Its statistical adequacy is therefore checked by misspecification tests. These tests evaluate the initial VAR against the relative past and the relative future of its own data, both equationwise and for the whole system. Table 6.3 reports several diagnostic tests on the VAR-residuals. A detailed description of these tests is available in Doornik/Hendry (1997). Figure 6.2 shows a recursive test on the VAR-forecast errors. Similar to a CUSUMSQ-test, the VAR is here recursively fitted over an estimation period 81:1 to 88:4+H-1 (for H=1,...,39) and then Chow-tested over the remaining forecast period 88:4+H to 98:3. The resulting sequence of F-statistics is then scaled by the respective 5% critical values, so that statistics below unity indicate non-rejection of the hypothesis of parameter constancy.

The misspecification tests indicate two minor problems: serial correlation appears in the price equation over the full sample, and parameter nonconstancy appears in the money equation over 1993. The first problem can be attributed to the difficulties of measuring prices in East-Germany after reunification[94], in particular by the statistical difficulties of seasonally adjusting

[93] Impulse dummies assume the value 1 in the quarter indicated, and the value 0 otherwise. Dummy ID90:3 captures reunification, ID93:1 the introduction of a withholding tax, and ID95:1 a redefinition of M3 combined with a wealth-tax exemption of money market mutual-funds. All effects are visible in figure 6.1.

[94] Prices in East-Germany were initially driven by a gradual adjustment of artificially low levels towards higher West-German market levels. This base effect induces a relatively high non-monetary inflation.

these data. Fitting a VAR(4) model removes all serial correlation, but depletes the available degrees of freedom. Therefore two lags are maintained, following the recommendation of the SC- and HQ- information criteria. Otherwise, the forecasts do not exceed their 5% critical values, and the diagnostics indicate well behaved residuals.

Null:	White Noise[1]		Normality[2]		Cond.Homosc.[3]		Uncond.Homosc.[4]	
Statistic:	$F(4,20)$	$F(4,52)$	$\chi^2(2)$	$\chi^2(2)$	$F(4,16)$	$F(4,48)$	$F(20,3)$	$F(20,35)$
Sample:	89:4	98:3	89:4	98:3	89:4	98:4	89:4	98:3
Money	1.36	0.31	3.05	1.35	0.32	0.97	0.43	0.76
Prices	2.44	3.94*	0.10	0.72	0.17	1.30	0.10	1.40
Output	1.51	1.62	0.80	0.23	0.22	0.27	0.19	0.81
Short Rate	0.41	1.03	2.60	4.35	0.17	0.64	0.22	0.75
Long Rate	2.14	1.11	0.62	0.56	1.22	1.78	0.15	0.62
System		1.31	9.08	3.76				0.66

1) LM-Test against up to fourth order serial correlation. 2) Parametric LM-Test against skewness and excess kurtosis. 3) LM-Test against up to fourth order ARCH. 4) LM-Test against general non-linear forms of heteroscedasticity. The superscript '' denotes rejection of null with at most 5% error probability.*

Table 6.3. Misspecification Tests for Germany

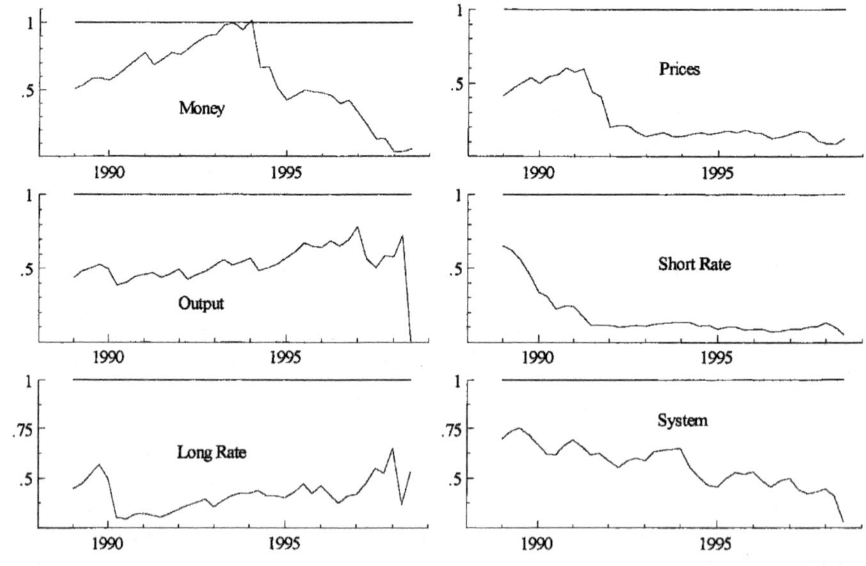

Fig. 6.2. Recursive Chow Test for Germany

The Submodel: Given the data congruency of the maintained hypothesis, restrictions concerning the cointegration rank and the deterministic component can now be tested. The asymptotic properties of cointegration tests remain unchanged under a data-based lag order selection using the HQ and SC information criteria (cf Lütkepohl/Saikkonen 1999). In finite samples, however, the vector unit root tests suffer from a bias which is a function of sample size (T), lag order (k), and number of variables (p). The bias can be accounted for by scaling either the asymptotic quantiles up or the test statistics down by a correction factor $T/(T-pk)$; see Reimers (1992), Cheung/Lai (1993) or Lee/Siklos (1995).

Case	Null:	$\hat{r}=0$	$\hat{r}\leq 1$	$\hat{r}\leq 2$	$\hat{r}\leq 3$	$\hat{r}\leq 4$
$\mathcal{H}(\hat{r},0)$	ME	62.8* (30.0)	47.7* (23.8)	34.4* (17.9)	13.8* (11.4)	0.3 (3.8)
	TR	158.8* (59.5)	96.0* (39.9)	48.4* (24.3)	14.0* (12.5)	0.3 (3.8)
$\mathcal{H}(\hat{r},1^*)$	ME	69.9* (34.4)	54.5* (28.1)	34.4* (22.0)	13.9 (15.7)	6.6 (9.2)
	TR	178.5* (76.1)	108.5* (53.1)	54.0* (34.9)	19.6 (20.0)	6.6 (9.2)
$\mathcal{H}(\hat{r},1)$	ME	56.2* (33.5)	39.8* (27.1)	25.2* (21.0)	**6.8** (14.1)	0.1 (3.8)
	TR	128.1* (68.5)	71.9* (47.2)	32.1* (29.7)	**6.9** (15.4)	0.1 (3.8)
$\mathcal{H}(\hat{r},2^*)$	ME	56.3* (37.5)	41.9* (31.5)	25.3 (25.5)	9.0 (18.9)	0.5 (12.3)
	TR	132.9* (87.3)	76.6* (63.0)	34.7 (42.4)	9.4 (25.3)	0.5 (12.3)
$\mathcal{H}(\hat{r},2)$	ME	54.3* (36.4)	41.8* (30.3)	25.2* (23.7)	8.3 (16.9)	0.3 (3.7)
	TR	129.9* (77.7)	75.5* (54.6)	33.8 (34.5)	8.6 (18.1)	0.3 (3.7)

ME tests for $p-\hat{r}>0$ common I(1)-trends within restricted model $rk\,\Pi_1 \leq \hat{r}+1$.
TR tests for $p-\hat{r}>0$ common I(1)-trends within unrestricted model $rk\,\Pi_1 \leq p$.
Critical values (5%) from Osterwald-Lenum (1992) are shown in brackets.

Table 6.4. Vector I(1) Test for Germany

Table 6.4 reports the maximal eigenvalue statistics (ME) and the trace statistics (TR) obtained from the Johansen procedure over the full sample 81:1 - 98:3 and scaled by the finite-sample correction factor. The sequential cointegration testing procedure detailed in section 3.2.3 now stipulates that any hypothesis be tested only after all other hypotheses nested therein have been rejected before. Therefore table 6.4 is read columnwise from top to bottom. That is, beginning with column $\hat{r}=0$, the hypotheses $\mathcal{H}(\hat{r},i)$ are successively rejected in the order $i=0,1^*,1,2^*,2$. This then repeats downwards column $\hat{r}\leq 1$, and so on, until the first non-rejected hypothesis occurs. In this way the statistics indicate, albeit narrowly, a cointegration rank $r=2$ with case 2^* deterministics. Unfortunately, this borderline result is not confirmed by the likelihood ratios from page 58 testing the deterministics against each other for a given cointegration rank. Here these statistics, reported in table 6.5, accept a restriction from case 2^* to case 1 deterministics at every possible rank r. Therefore the sequential testing procedure is continued until a more decisive stop, which occurs at rank $r = 3$ with case 1 deterministics (typed in bold-face). This outcome agrees with the statistics in table 6.5, where any further restriction of case 1 deterministics is firmly rejected.

Null:	0 vs 1*	1 vs 2*		1* vs 1	2* vs 2	
Restriction:	$m_0 = 0$	$m_1 = 0$	$\chi^2(r)$	$m_0 = \hat{\alpha}\, n_0$	$m_1 = \hat{\alpha}\, n_1$	$\chi^2(p-r)$
Statistic:	$q(r, 0)$	$q(r, 1)$	5%CV	$q(r, 1^*)$	$q(r, 2^*)$	5%CV
$r = 0$				58.6*	3.5	11.1
$r = 1$	8.3*	0.2	3.8	42.7*	1.2	9.5
$r = 2$	16.3*	2.6	6.0	25.6*	1.1	7.8
$r = 3$	16.3*	2.7	7.8	14.8*	1.0	6.0
$r = 4$	16.5*	5.3	9.5	6.5*	0.1	3.8
$r = 5$	22.9*	5.6	11.1			

Statistics test indicated restrictions on deterministic regressor $d_t = m_0 + m_1 t$.

Table 6.5. Test of Deterministics for Germany

To resolve the apparent contradiction between the outcomes of table 6.4 and table 6.5, a plausible guess is that the critical values in the former are not entirely appropriate: like scalar unit root tests, cointegration tests are also influenced, even asymptotically, by breaks in the underlying DGP. Campos/Ericsson/Hendry (1996) for example trace the influence of breaks on the t_α statistic in the popular single-equation ECM, using simulation methods. For the present multi-equation VAR model the influence of breaks on the trace statistic TR can be studied using the simulation program DisCo of Nielsen (1997). This program allows to simulate the quantiles of the asymptotic TR distribution (see footnote 49) for a wide range of user-specified deterministic regressors d_t, the limitation being that the dimension of d_t be not larger than the dimension $p - r$ of the distribution.

Table 6.6 summarizes the 95% quantiles for various constellations of impulse dummies, each simulated from $N = 10,000$ replications and $T = 400$ as discretization of the Brownian motion. The dummies are ID90:3 and ID93:1 with break-dates expressed relative to the sample-span. Now, the inclusion of such unrestricted impulse dummies obviously lowers the critical values uniformly compared to the standard values from Osterwald-Lenum (1992). This in turn alters the conclusions drawn from table 6.4: the borderline hypothesis $\mathcal{H}(\hat{r}, 2^*)$ with $\hat{r} \leq 2$ is but narrowly accepted under ID1 (critical value 36.1 instead of 42.4) and decidedly rejected under ID1 plus ID2 (critical value 29.1 instead of 42.4). In this way the contradictory results from table 6.4 and table 6.5 can be reconciled, and hypothesis $\mathcal{H}(r, 1)$ with $r = 3$ is tentatively entertained as an data-admissible restriction of the initial VAR.

	Dimension p-r :	1	2	3	4	5
Case 1	ID1, ID2			16.6	34.5	55.1
	ID1		9.4	23.3	41.2	62.1
	Standard	3.8	15.4	29.7	47.2	68.5
Case 2*	ID1, ID2			29.1	49.4	72.3
	ID1		19.6	36.1	56.3	79.8
	Standard	12.3	25.3	42.4	63.0	87.3
Case 2	ID1			26.6	46.6	69.3
	Standard	3.7	18.1	34.5	54.6	77.7

ID1 and ID2 are impulse dummies at relative dates 0.60 and 0.75.
Standard values are taken from Osterwald-Lenum (1992).

Table 6.6. Asymptotic Critical Values (5%) for Trace Statistic

To further corroborate this choice, the robustness of the respective cointegration tests is explored by recursive estimation over time, in particular over reunification. Figure 6.3 contains graphs of the trace statistic and the maximal eigenvalue statistics obtained from the recursive model (4.21) detailed in in section 4.2.1, again scaled by the respective finite-sample correction factor.[95] Following a recommendation in Hansen/Johansen (1993), the recursive model (4.21) is here concentrated by the full-sample matrix $P_{(F)}$. This modification, denoted by *short-run (SR) fixed*, eliminates the influence of short-run fluctuations which possibly contaminate the test in finite samples. The modification also reduces distortions caused by recursively varying degrees of freedom.

The recursion shown in figure 6.3 starts with an estimation over an initial sample 81:1 - 89:1, and successively adds further observations until the full sample 81:1 - 98:3 is reached. For increasing t, the trace- and maximal eigenvalue statistics should diverge if $\hat{r} \leq r$, that is, if the tested rank is lower than the unknown true rank (cf section 3.2.3). In figure 6.3 this is clearly the case for $\hat{r} \leq 0, 1$. In the borderline case $\hat{r} \leq 2$ the statistics seem insignificant until reunification but divergent thereafter. For $\hat{r} \leq 3, 4$ the statistics are insignificant over the whole sample period. The recursive tests therefore support hypothesis $\mathcal{H}(r, 1)$ with $r = 3$ as a sensible choice, albeit with some doubt around reunification. An alternative type of recursion would start with a full sample 81:1 - 98:3 and successively drop initial observations until a reduced sample 89:1 - 98:3 is reached. This experiment (not shown here) confirms the choice of $r = 3$ as surprisingly invariant to the model's initial conditions.

[95] Note that the critical values in table 6.6 can not be applied for reinterpretation of the recursive tests in figure 6.3, since the former depend on relative time of the break (which changes in the course of the recursion).

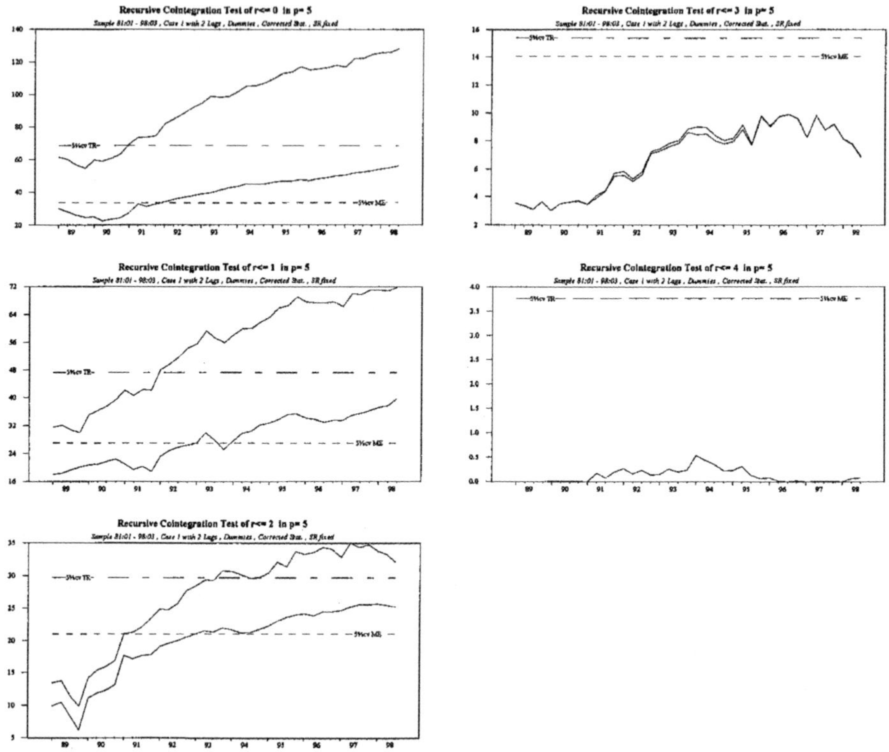

Fig. 6.3. Recursive Vector I(1) Test for Germany

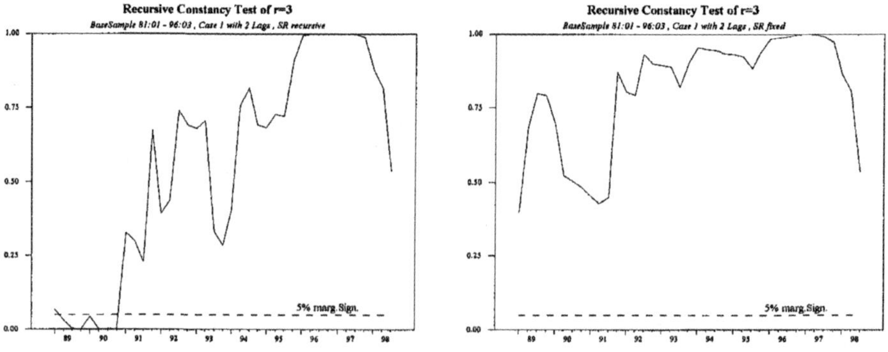

Fig. 6.4. Recursive Constancy Test for Germany

Another application of recursive testing concerns the time-invariance, or constancy, of the cointegration space. As detailed in section 4.2.1, this hypothesis can be formulated as a special case of the over-identifying restriction (4.17). The resulting $\chi^2(pr-r^2)$ distributed likelihood-ratio checks the cointegration space spanned by a recursive estimate $\hat{\beta}_t$ for equality with the space spanned by a given, constant reference matrix.

Figure 6.4 contains marginal significance levels of such a likelihood-ratio testing the present three-dimensional cointegration space. The recursion for $\hat{\beta}_t$ starts again with an initial sample 81:1 - 89:1 and continues until the full sample 81:1 - 98:3. The reference matrix chosen as the β-estimate over a fixed period 81:1 - 96:3. The null of constancy is rejected for marginal significance values below the dotted 5% line. The first graph in the figure contains the recursive-short-run version of the constancy test (matrix $P_{(R)}$ in (4.21)), which accepts constancy only after 91:1. The second graph contains the fixed-short-run version (matrix $P_{(F)}$ in (4.21)), which accepts constancy over the whole recursion. This difference suggests the presence of otherwise constant long-run relations overshadowed by sudden turbulences in the short-run dynamics. Indeed, the 'break' date in figure 6.4 (namely 91:1) exactly coincides with the perceptible, though transitory change in the behaviour of the price series observable in figure 6.1 and explained in footnote 94.

To sum up, the preceding battery of sequential and recursive cointegration tests seems to support, in the language of table 3.3, a choice of submodel $\mathcal{M}(r,1)$ with $r = 3$ as a statistically valid reduction of the initial VAR. This conclusion, however, is slightly premature: the statistical evidence presented so far supports, in fact, merely the weaker assertion that the VAR is integrated of *some* order $d \geq 1$. To justify a choice of the particular I(1)-submodel $\mathcal{M}(r,1)$ it is therefore necessary to rule out higher order integration. Since the scalar unit root tests presented in table 6.2 caused suspicions about two unit roots in the price level series, the problem of higher order integration is also addressed in the present VAR framework. Specifically, ruling out $d \geq 3$ on a-priori grounds, the null hypothesis of $p-r-s$ I(2) trends is tested. The respective tests, detailed in section 3.2.3, are constructed from imposing the reduced rank restrictions (3.32) on the concentrated model (3.47).

Table 6.7 reports the test results for $\mathcal{H}(\hat{r},1;\hat{s},1^*)$, the particular subhypothesis of $\mathcal{H}(\hat{r},1)$ allowing for a linear trend in the deterministic component (cf table 3.3). Note that in the borderline case $\hat{s} = p-\hat{r}$ the former collapses into the latter, so that the corresponding test statistics (typed in italics) actually constitute I(1)-tests. As detailed in section 3.2.3, there are two sequential test procedures in the I(2) model. The first procedure is based on the trace statistic $TR(\hat{r},i;\hat{s},j)$, or TRp for short. This statistic tests the two rank restrictions (3.32) simultaneously. In the procedure one therefore proceeds along the respective TRp-row of table 6.7 in the order $\hat{s} = 0, 1, ..., p-\hat{r}$ for each rank $\hat{r}$. This repeats over $\hat{r} = 1, 2, 3, 4$ until the first non-rejected hypothesis occurs. The second procedure is based on the trace statistic $TR(\hat{s}, j|\hat{r}, i)$, or TRr for short, which tests but the critical I(2)-restriction. The procedure therefore tests the two rank restrictions (3.32) successively: beginning with the rank $r = 3$ recommended by the I(1)-tests in table 6.4 one then proceeds along the respective TRr-row of table 6.7 in the order $\hat{s} = 0, 1, ..., p-\hat{r}-1$ until the first non-rejected hypothesis occurs. In this way both procedures decisively reject the I(2)-hypothesis $s < p - r$ for all ranks r, indicating an absence of I(2)-trends. The I(1)-hypothesis $s = p - r$ is accepted by the first procedure for $r = 3$, which restates the conclusion drawn from table 6.4.

$p-\hat{r}$	$\hat{r}$	Null:	$\hat{s}=0$	$\hat{s}\leq 1$	$\hat{s}\leq 2$	$\hat{s}\leq 3$	$\hat{s}\leq 4$
4	1	TRp	295.3* (116.3)	158.9* (91.4)	120.4* (73.0)	97.1* (57.9)	*83.7* (47.2)*
		TRr	211.6* (53.1)	75.3* (34.9)	36.7* (20.0)	13.4* (9.2)	
3	2	TRp	196.8* (70.9)	85.3* (51.4)	54.0* (38.8)	*37.3* (29.7)*	
		TRr	159.5* (34.9)	47.9* (20.0)	16.7* (9.2)		
2	3	TRp	110.5* (36.1)	25.4* (22.6)	*8.0 (15.4)*		
		TRr	102.5* (20.0)	17.3* (9.2)			
1	4	TRp	72.0* (12.9)	*0.1 (3.8)*			
		TRr	71.9* (9.2)				

TRp tests for $p-\hat{r}-\hat{s} \geq 0$ common I(2)-Trends in unrestricted model $rk\,\Pi_1 \leq p$.
TRr tests for $p-\hat{r}-\hat{s} > 0$ common I(2)-Trends in restricted model $rk\,\Pi_1 = \hat{r}$.
Critical values from Paruolo (1996, Table 6), Osterwald-Lenum (1992, Table 1).*

Table 6.7. Vector I(2) Test for Germany

Rival Specifications: In this paragraph two alternative specifications for the initial unrestricted VAR are briefly considered. The first specification employs real money ($mr \equiv m-p$) and inflation (Δp) instead of nominal money and the price level as input variables for the VAR. The second specification employs seasonally unadjusted data. Both alternatives are routinely used in empirical studies on macroeconomic data series, in particular also in the VAR models specified for German data by Juselius (1996) and Hubrich (1999). The rival specifications are therefore also tried on the present data set.

The specification in real money and inflation is often motivated by economic theory. It is argued that a money demand function of agents free of money-illusion contains but real balances mr as endogenous variable, and that inflation represents additional opportunity cost for holding money instead of real assets (cf Ericsson 1998). The specification in real money and inflation is also statistically convenient, namely if both m and p are individually I(2). As shown by Johansen (1992b), the corresponding I(2)-trends can be expected to cancel out in real money mr, leaving only I(1) variables in the VAR specification. This rival specification is not adopted here, for two reasons. First, the formulation in real money imposes an untested homogeneity restriction not only on the long-run cointegration relations, but also on the entire short-run dynamics of the VAR. Second, the empirical results from this specification on the present data set are decidedly less satisfactory, in particular with respect to the misspecification tests and to the recursive cointegration tests.

The specification in seasonally unadjusted data can be motivated by the single-equation estimation results in table 6.1, where the adjustment coefficient perceptibly changed under seasonal adjustment. Indeed, Ericsson/Hendry/Tran (1994) show that the adjustment matrix α in a VAR model is dependent on seasonal adjustment, whereas the cointegration rank r and the cointegration vectors β are actually independent of it. Seasonality is usually accounted for by including centered seasonal dummies into the deterministic regressor. As shown by Lee/Siklos (1995) this type of dummy does not alter the stochastic matrix underlying the asymptotic distribution of the TR- and ME-statistics testing for cointegration at zero frequency. In accordance with this theoretical result, the empirical cointegration tests on the seasonally unadjusted data produce here results similar to those obtained in tables 6.4 and 6.7. The misspecification tests, however, reveal autocorrelation, nonnormality, and ARCH-effects in a VAR(2) model, indicating an inability of the seasonal dummies to fully capture the seasonality in the data.

Summary: Scalar and vector autoregressive models were fitted on the German data set, and evaluated by a battery of diagnostic tests. The specification preferred here is 5-dimensional VAR(2)-specification comprising money, prices, output, and two interest rates. Having established their statistical adequacy, the models were systematically tested for unit roots. For the preferred specification, an elaborate menu of sequential and recursive unit-root tests suggests the presence of 2 stochastic I(1)-trends and, correspondingly, 3 cointegration relations. In addition, a linear time trend seems present in the deterministic component of the VAR. The possible presence of stochastic I(2)-trends was explicitly tested and rejected. In the language of table 3.3, the submodel $\mathcal{M}(r,1)$ with $r=3$ is therefore maintained in the sequel as a statistical model for the German data. In the following section, aggregated European data are analyzed in an similar fashion.

6.2 Probability Model for Europe

6.2.1 Data and Recent Literature

The data for Europe likewise comprise seasonally adjusted quarterly series covering a sample period from 81:1 to 98:3 (T=71), with suitable presample periods allowing for initial conditions. The constituent national series correspond to those employed for Germany. Money (m) is generally measured by its broad definition, a narrow definition (n) is used only to reproduce some results from the literature. Output (y) is measured mostly by the real gross domestic product (GDP) in 1979 prices. The ratio of nominal to real GDP gives a Paasche price index measuring the general price level (p), normalized at 1979=100. Money's own rate (is) is measured by a money market rate, its opportunity costs (il) by the yield on government bonds. All data are taken from the International Financial Statistics (IFS) and the Main Economic Indicators (MEI). It is noted that in both databases the data quality is, more often than not, surprisingly poor. For example, quarterly output series are either inexistent (Belgium, Ireland) or incomplete (Austria, Portugal), and quarterly money series incoherent (Denmark). A precise description of all national data series is given in appendix A.7.

The aggregation of variables across countries has been discussed in section 5.2.2. The aggregate data series analyzed in the present section are calculated from the original, un-logged levels of the respective national data series according to the aggregation rules (5.14) - (5.18). Since there is no compelling a-priori choice for a conversion rate, the aggregate series on money, prices, and interest rates appear, throughout the chapter, in two different versions: one using current market rates (denoted by 'c') and one using fixed market rates (denoted by 'f').[96] The aggregate series on output involves only fixed market rates. The common denomination is Deutsche Mark (DM). The aggregate data series on money, output, and prices are subsequently transformed into natural logarithms. Combined with the linear VAR model the whole setup thus amounts to a quasilinear aggregation structure.

The definition of a currency area 'Europe' rests on economic and not on political or legal criteria. One salient criterion is the degree of exchange rate stability, irrespective of whether this stability is brought about by formal participation in the Exchange Rate Mechanism (ERM) or by informal shadow membership. The relative exchange rates against the present numeraire currency, the DM, have been shown in figure 5.5. Their inspection motivates

[96] The fixed market rates are the 1979-averages of the respective current market rates. Conversion by purchasing-power-parity (PPP) rates is not used: Aggregate series from fixed PPP rates are closely related to those from fixed market rates, whereas aggregate series from current PPP rates are, by construction, closely related to those of the numeraire-country.

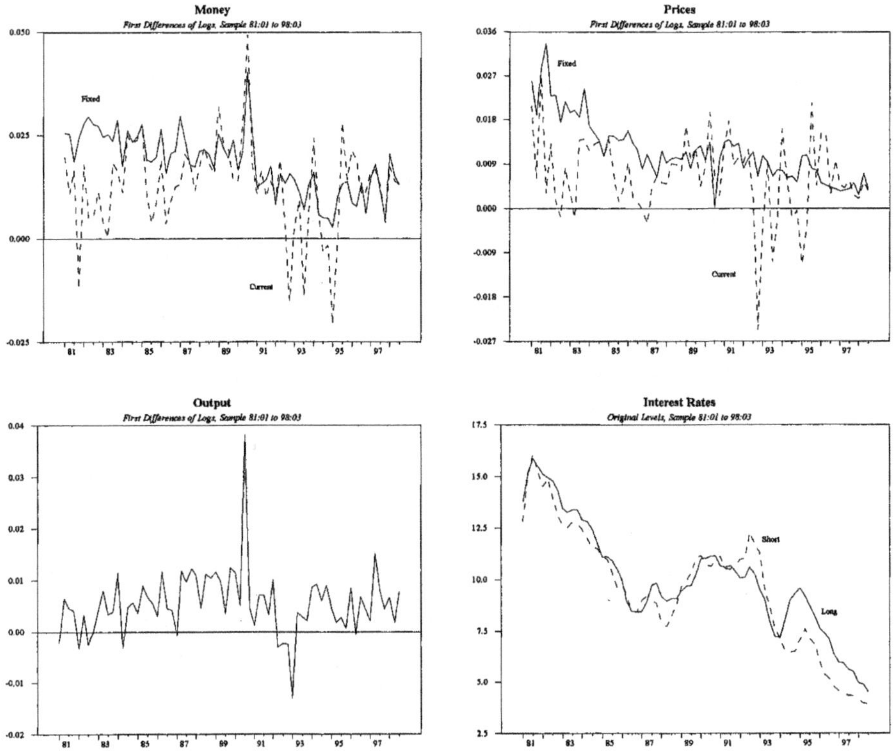

Fig. 6.5. Data Series for Euro10

a currency area with the following internal ordering: Germany, Netherlands, Austria (=DM-Block), Belgium/Luxemburg, Denmark, France, Ireland, Italy (=Euro8), Spain, Portugal (=Euro10). Alternative currency areas include the original ERM-area, which comprises the seven currencies participating in the exchange rate mechanism since 79:1, and the original EMU-area, which comprises the ten currencies participating in the European monetary union since 99:1. These areas fit neatly into above ordering, with Euro8 comprising the original ERM plus its shadow member Austria, and Euro10 comprising the original EMU with Finland replaced by Denmark. Graphs of the aggregate data series for the Euro10 group are shown in figure 6.5.

The frequently cited paper of Kremers/Lane (1990) marks the beginning of a meanwhile considerable body of empirical literature on aggregate European money demand functions. An early survey is given by VanRiet (1993). Again, the bulk of these studies employs single-equation error-correction models with real money as dependent variable.

Kremers/Lane (1990) analyze seasonally adjusted data on consumer-price deflated narrow money, real output, a short and a long interest rate, inflation, and the US$/ECU exchange rate over 78:4 to 87:4 (T=37). The aggregates are constructed for the original ERM, with quantities expressed in DM using current market rates, fixed market rates, and fixed PPP rates. Their preferred final specification relies on fixed PPP-rates and finds, from Engle/Granger's (1987) two-step procedure, cointegration between inverse velocity, the short interest rate, inflation, and the exchange rate. The resulting cointegration residuals are inserted into an ECM for real money which in addition contains a long interest rate. Estimation over 79:1 to 84:4 (T=24) produces a surprisingly large estimate ($\hat{\alpha} = -0.95$) for the adjustment coefficient. From these results the authors conclude that a European money demand function is indeed existent and even superior to its national counterparts. This claim was soon disputed: Barr (1992) replicates Kremers/Lanes's empirical model, finding an adjustment speed of only $\hat{\alpha} = -0.5$, and then reestimates the model over 79:1 to 90:4 using more refined cointegration tests and recursive estimates. His results indicate failure of the model over the extended sample period, which is 'explained' by data revisions in Kremers/Lane's (1992a) reply. Another dispute emerged from Arnold's (1992) misapprehension of Kremers/Lanes's conversion method. In their reply Kremers/Lane (1992b) discuss the effects of converting nominal and real quantities using fixed PPP rates as opposed to current PPP rates, without however clarifying why PPP rates should be used at all.

Artis/Bladen-Hovell/Zhang (1993) and Artis (1996) analyze seasonally adjusted data on consumer-price deflated narrow money, real output, a long term interest rate, and the ECU/US$ exchange rate over 79:2 to 90:2 (T=44) and 79:2 to 92:4 (T=54), respectively. The aggregates are constructed for the original ERM, with quantities expressed in US$ using fixed market rates. Using the Engle/Granger two-step procedure they find a cointegration relation passing several misspecification tests over two sample periods. The subsequent error-correction models produce $\hat{\alpha} = -0.73$ and $\hat{\alpha} = -0.70$. On basis of national cointegration relations the authors then infer the presence of a specification error from significant currency-substitution variables, and the presence of an aggregation error from unequal cointegration vectors across countries.

Cassard/Lane/Masson (1994, 1997) analyze seasonally adjusted data on real broad money, real output, and short and long interest rates, over 82:4 to 90:2 (T=31) and 80:4 to 90:2 (T=39), respectively. The aggregates are constructed for the original ERM minus Italy and Ireland, with quantities expressed in DM using current PPP rates. The Engle/Granger procedure and the Johansen procedure are applied to the aggregate data, and for comparison also to the French and German data. Unfortunately, the reported single equation statistics nowhere exceed their critical values, and the reported Johansen statistics are compared to a wrong set of critical values. Nevertheless the authors classify their results as 'very promising', and proclaim the existence of a stable long-run relation for the ERM whose adjustment coefficients ($\hat{\alpha} = -0.32$ and $\hat{\alpha} = -0.10$) exceed those for Germany ($\hat{\alpha} = -0.06$ and $\hat{\alpha} = -0.07$) in both studies.

Läufer (1995) analyses annual data on narrow and broad real money per capita, real output per capita, and a short interest rate over 1960 to 1990 (T=30). The aggregates are constructed from the original ERM plus Greece, Portugal, Spain, Switzerland and the U.K., and expressed as weighted averages of national growth rates. A single European equation and a system of national equations are formulated on these growth rates, and estimated by static OLS and GLS regressions. The residual (co)variance matrices resulting from the system of national equations are then used to compute a principal variance according to (5.8), while the residual variance of the European equation is taken as surrogate variance. Both for narrow and broad money the two variances roughly equal each other under OLS and GLS, which may indicate the presence of a portfolio gain working against an aggregation loss.

Falk/Funke (1995) analyze seasonally adjusted data on narrow real money, real output, a short interest rate, and the ECU/US$ exchange rate over 77:4 to 92:4 (T=61). The aggregates are constructed once for France, Germany, and the Netherlands, and once for the whole original ERM. Quantities are expressed in DM using current market rates and fixed PPP rates. Using the single-step dynamic-model procedure the authors find a cointegration relation for both currency areas and both conversion methods. The adjustment coefficients under current-rate conversion appear slightly larger than those obtained under fixed-rate conversion, which roughly equal the coefficient found for Germany alone ($\hat{\alpha} = -0.48$). The stability of the respective specifications is further assessed by split-sample Chow tests and recursive coefficient estimation. In both cases the results for current-rate conversion again appeared slightly superior compared to those for Germany or for fixed-rate conversion.

Monticelli (1996) and similarly Monticelli/Papi (1996) analyze seasonally adjusted data on real broad money, real output, and a long term interest rate over 79:1 to 92:1 (T=53). The aggregates are constructed for the original ERM plus United Kingdom and Spain, with quantities expressed in ECU using current market rates. Both studies investigate the possible presence of a specification gain arising from inconsistent national definitions of money due to cross-border deposits (CBD's). The European money aggregate is therefore corrected to account for various measures of CBD's. Evidence of cointegration is then found to be very weak in case of broad CBD-measures, ambiguous in case of narrow CBD-measures, and strong in case of the traditional uncorrected money aggregate. This corresponds to the reported estimates from error-correction models, where the largest adjustment speed ($\hat{\alpha} = -0.52$) is found for the uncorrected aggregate, confirming the irrelevance of CBD's.

Tullio/DeSouza/Giucca (1996) analyze data on consumer-price deflated narrow and broad money, real output, a short interest rate, and the deviation of the US$ exchange rate from its PPP value, over 79:2 to 89:2 (T=40). The aggregates are constructed for the original ERM, with quantities expressed in DM using fixed market rates. The authors find cointegration for both the narrow and broad specification. The error-correction models are estimated by the single-step procedure and produce estimates $\hat{\alpha} = -0.47$ (narrow money) and $\hat{\alpha} = -0.25$ (broad money) for the adjustment coefficients. Virtually the same values are subsequently found in an error-correction model for Germany, and even larger values for Italy. In contrast to their results the authors conclude that money demand on the European level is more stable than on the individual country level.

Some studies finally depart from the convenient single-equation paradigm and venture into VAR modelling: Monticelli/Strauss-Kahn (1993) analyze seasonally adjusted data on real broad money, real output, and a short interest rate over 77:1 to 90:3 (T=55). Aggregates are constructed for the original ERM plus the U.K. and Spain, with quantities expressed in ECU using current and fixed market rates. Wesche (1997) analyses seasonally unadjusted data on consumer-price deflated broad money, real output, and a long interest rate over 73:1 to 93:3 (T=83). Aggregates are constructed for France, Germany, Italy, and the U.K., with quantities expressed in DM using current market rates, fixed market rates, and fixed PPP rates. Fagan/Henry (1998) analyze seasonally adjusted data on narrow and broad real money, real output, and short and long interest rates over 81:1 to 94:4 (T=56). Aggregates are constructed for the 14 EU-countries, with quantities expressed in ECU using current market rates and fixed PPP rates. Gottschalk (1999) analyses seasonally adjusted data on consumer-price deflated broad money, real output, a short and a long interest rate, and inflation over 83:1 to 97:2 (T=58). Aggregates are constructed for the original EMU, with quantities expressed in ECU using fixed rates. All studies fit an initial VAR(2) with unrestricted constant (case 1), and use the Johansen procedure to test for cointegration. Gottschalk finds 2 cointegration vectors, which are subsequently identified into a money-demand relation and a Fisher-equation. The other studies find but a single cointegration vector, which is duly interpreted as money demand.

Some critical comments on this literature are necessary. First, the construction of an aggregate price index proves a tricky operation. Kremers/Lane (1990), Monticelli/Strauss-Kahn (1993), and Wesche (1997) employ the share of current real output in its aggregate ($\mathbf{p}_{n0}\mathbf{q}_{nt}/\mathbf{p}_0\mathbf{q}_t$) to weigh a national price index. This method is correct in that aggregate real output multiplied by this aggregate price index indeed produces aggregate nominal output. All other studies either employ fixed shares ($\mathbf{p}_{n0}\mathbf{q}_{n0}/\mathbf{p}_0\mathbf{q}_0$), or do not bother at all to elaborate in detail on their aggregation methods.[97] Fagan/Henry (1998) even employ, curiously, the share of current nominal money and nominal output in their respective aggregates to weigh a national price index; the resulting two aggregate price indices are then used to separately deflate aggregate money and aggregate nominal output.

Second, the aggregation structures adopted in all studies are in fact quasilinear, that is, log-linear models formulated on aggregate variables constructed as arithmetic averages of un-logged national variables. However, the underlying theoretical framework is always that of conventional aggregation theory. Unsurprisingly, the different implications of cointegration and of quasilinear aggregation are nowhere addressed. The only exception are Fagan/Henry (1998), who in their 'index method' construct aggregates as weighted geometric averages of un-logged national variables, which produces a linear aggregation structure for the log-variables. This choice of an aggregation rule substitutes the economic interpretability of the aggregates for the mathematical tractability of the aggregation structure.[98]

Third, most studies use single-equation error-correction models explaining changes in real money. The reported adjustment coefficients usually exceed (in absolute values) those found for similar specifications on German data. This led to the notion of money demand being more 'stable' in Europe than in Germany. In order to relate the present study to the existing literature, this stylized fact is replicated on the present data set. Precisely, the typical specification of Kremers/Lane (1990) is tried on the present data for their currency area (Euro8) under fixed market rates. Table 6.8 summarizes the results. The first line replicates (with remarkable accuracy) the coefficients obtained by Kremers/Lane from estimating a static long-run regression, normalized on inverse velocity (the liquidity ratio $lr \equiv n-p-y$), over 78:4 - 87:4. The residuals are subsequently inserted into a dynamic short-run regression for real narrow money ($nr \equiv n-p$), which is estimated over 79:1 - 84:4. The large adjustment coefficient of -0.95 could, however, not be reproduced despite considerable experimentation. The second line broadly confirms the preceding results under the alternative one-step dynamic model estimation procedure. The last two lines show the results from re-estimating the Kremers/Lane-specification over a longer sample period 78:4 - 98:3. Whereas neither the long-run coef-

[97] Artis/Bladen-Hovell/Zhang (1993) and Cassard/Lane/Masson (1994) even purport to employ Kremers/Lane's method while actually employing fixed shares.

[98] This is an old debate in aggregation theory: Pu (1946) qualifies such artificial aggregates as "*monsters that are completely void of any economic significance*", whereas Klein (1946) argues that "*there is nothing sacred about a sum*".

ficients nor the statistics t_α are much affected by this sample extension, the adjustment speed decreases perceptibly, which corroborates the objections raised by Barr (1992) against Kremers/Lane's results.

$\hat{\alpha}$	$\hat{\beta}'$				t_α	Sample	Method
Δnr	lr	Δp	is	ecu			
−0.56	1.00	1.52	0.0067	−0.024	−4.0	78:4 - 87:4	Two-Step
−0.50	1.00	3.87	0.0031	−0.033	−3.8	78:4 - 87:4	One-Step
−0.33	1.00	1.35	0.0069	−0.011	−4.8	78:4 - 98:3	Two-Step
−0.31	1.00	3.40	0.0041	−0.004	−3.5	78:4 - 98:3	One-Step
Δm	m	p	y	is	il		
−0.16	1.00	−1.05	−0.97	−0.015	0.018	−2.4	81:1 - 98:3	One-Step

First Block: static relation between liquidity ratio ($lr \equiv n-p-y$), inflation (Δp), short rate (is), and exchange-rate (ecu) inserted into dynamic ECM for narrow real money (Δnr). Second Block: static relation between $[m, p, y, is, il]$ inserted into dynamic ECM for nominal broad money (Δm). The 5% critical values for t_α-statistics on $\hat{\alpha}$ are -4.4 (one-step estimation) and -3.7 (two-step estimation).

Table 6.8. Single Equation Specifications for Europe

Nevertheless, the estimated adjustment coefficients still appear larger for Europe than for Germany. This is somewhat unexpected in view of chapter 5, where a downward bias in the aggregate adjustment coefficient was deduced as a likely result of aggregation. One simple explanation could be that studies for Europe often rely on some narrow definition for money, whereas those for Germany traditionally rely on broad money. To account for this possibility a single-equation ECM for broad money (m) is also included in table 6.8. This specification for Euro10 (fixed rates) is directly comparable to the specification for Germany in table 6.1. Estimation under the one-step procedure produces an apparently perfect money demand equation, whose adjustment coefficient (−0.16) is plausibly smaller than those for narrow money, but larger than those for Germany. The stylized fact of money demand being more 'stable' in Europe than in Germany is therefore replicable also for a broad money specification.

Finally, the cited studies analyzing European data within a multi-equation VAR model are, in several aspects, statistically inadequate. First, the initial VAR in all studies includes but a constant, so that the statistical model is neither able to distinguish difference- and trend-stationarity, nor able to distinguish stochastic and deterministic cointegration (cf section 3.2.2). Second, in all studies the cointegration rank is tested but for the given deterministics, so that, in the terminology of section 3.2.3, only the hypothesis $\mathcal{H}(\hat{r}, 1)$ is tested over all possible cointegration ranks $\hat{r}$. This procedure may lead to statistically invalid conclusions, since a number of further restrictions, in particular the I(2)-restrictions $\mathcal{H}(\hat{r}, 1;\ \hat{s}, j)$, are nested within the tested hypothesis. Therefore a more elaborate testing procedure is required (cf page 57). Third, the topic of weak exogeneity or Granger-noncausality is but rarely discussed, although these properties are crucial for any useful money demand relation. Consequently, the development of an estimated VAR model into a conditional CVAR and its identification into a SECM is nowhere addressed in the empirical literature.

The alleged superior stability of European money demand will be scrutinized in section 6.3, in the framework of a multivariate structural ECM. Before that, the statistical properties of the European data are explored within scalar and vector autoregressive models to provide a valid benchmark for further conclusions.

6.2.2 Scalar Autoregressive Modelling

The European data series in figure 6.5 appear not dramatically different from the German series in figure 6.1, apart of course from the blips in the current-rate series due to discrete exchange rate realignments. For a formal characterization, the aggregated series are likewise individually modelled as scalar autoregressive sequences. The scalar model's lag length is selected using the Schwarz (SC) and Hannan-Quinn (HQ) information criteria, and its statistical adequacy is evaluated using the modified Q-statistic (Ljung/Box 1978) and the LM-statistic (Breusch/Pagan (1980) to test for autocorrelation. These statistics recommend quite unanimously an AR(4) model for the interest rates, and AR(2) models for money, output, and velocity. For the price level the recommendations are inconclusive, an AR(4) model appeared slightly superior. Fitted to the current-rate and the fixed-rate aggregate series, these models yield a number of unit root statistics which are summarized in table 6.9. The employed tests have been detailed in section 3.1.3.

Following the sequential procedure outlined in section 3.1.3 the unit-root tests in table 6.9 are structured in a 'top-down' order. That is, rejection of higher-order integration is required before lower-order integration is tested. Here the empirical rejection of third-order integration (not reported) ensures a valid test of second-order integration. This null is tested directly by formulating an I(2)-null on the sequence of levels (statistics $\Phi_3(4)$ and $\Phi_2(2)$), and also indirectly by formulating an I(1)-null on the sequence of first differences (statistics $\hat{\tau}_\mu$, GLS_μ, and $\hat{\tau}$). The alternatives comprise first-order integration around a linear deterministic trend (for money, prices, velocity, output), and first-order integration around a constant (for the interest-rates). Here the

Null:	I(2)			I(1)+Trend		
Statistic:	$\hat{\tau}_\mu$	GLS_μ	$\Phi_3(4)$	$\hat{\tau}_\tau$	GLS_τ	Φ_3
5% CV	**−2.9**	**−2.2**	**5.8**	**−3.5**	**−3.1**	**6.7**
Money–c	−5.8*	−3.6*	8.9*	-1.2^b	−1.4	1.0
Money–f	−4.0*	−2.7*	9.6*	-0.6^b	−0.2	9.2*
Prices–c	−3.2*	−1.5	4.5	−2.5	−1.9	3.4
Prices–f	−1.6	−0.9	6.5	−3.8*	−1.1	10.7*
Velocity–c	−7.1*	−4.4*	16.7*	−3.2	−3.1	5.2
Velocity–f	−6.9*	−4.3*	13.4*	−2.1	−2.1	2.3
Output–f	−7.2*	−5.8*	14.0*	-1.6^b	−1.3	1.4

Null:	I(2)		I(1)		
Statistic:	$\hat{\tau}$	$\Phi_2(2)$	$\hat{\tau}_\mu$	GLS_μ	Φ_1
5% CV	**−2.0**	**6.6**	**−2.9**	**−2.2**	**4.9**
Short Rate–c	−4.7*	15.5*	−1.8	−0.7	3.9
Short Rate–f	−4.9*	15.6*	−1.4	−0.6	3.2
Long Rate–c	−4.0*	12.0*	−1.6	−0.6	3.8
Long Rate–f	−4.2*	12.1*	−1.3	−0.5	3.1

Series from current-rate (c) and fixed-rate (f) conversion of national series. Statistics from AR(3)-model (Prices,Rates) or AR(2)-model (Money,Output, Velocity). Description of tests and critical values (CV) in tables 3.1 and 3.2. Superscript 'b' denotes statistic from Perron (1989, model A) with critical value -3.8 for λ=0.6 as relative time of break. Superscript '' denotes rejection of null with at most 5% error probability.*

Table 6.9. Scalar Unit Root Tests for Euro10

reported statistics reject the I(2)-null for all series, except for prices. For the remaining series this rejection ensures, subsequently, a valid test of first-order integration. This null is tested directly by converting the above alternatives into null hypotheses, which are then tested against I(0)-alternatives. Here the reported statistics accept the I(1)-null in all cases. As a result, the procedure indicates the presence of two unit roots in the AR model for prices, and the presence of one unit root in the AR models for money, output, velocity, and interest rates. Some qualifying comments of this result are, however, necessary.

First, from their graphs in figure 6.5, the two European inflation series could be I(0) around some downward sloping linear trend. In the indirect I(2)-tests of the respective price series, however, the two inflation series are only tested against an I(0)-around-constant alternative (statistics $\hat{\tau}_\mu$ and GLS_μ). This implausible alternative could favour the I(1)-null in inflation, and hence explain the observed acceptance of the I(2)-null in the prices series. To obviate this bias, an additional ADF-regression (case IIIb in table 3.2) is run over the inflation series, which tests the I(1)-null against a plausible I(0)-around-trend alternative. The resulting Φ_2-statistics, however, again accept the null (value 3.7 for current rates, value 3.2 for fixed rate, critical value 5.1) and hence but confirm the suspicion about two unit roots in the European price series.

Second, the results for money, output, and prices are in fact borderline cases and not invariant to the chosen lag length. In higher order models for money and output the I(2)-null is less decisively rejected or even accepted. Conversely, in lower order models for prices the I(2)-null is less easily accepted or even rejected. This ambiguity cancels out in velocity, where the I(2)-null is always decisively rejected. Finally, the statistics for money and prices seem more prone to reject the I(2)-null if current rates are used to construct the aggregate. This coincides with the visual appearance of the respective time series in figure 6.5.

As a side product of the unit root tests, a scalar AR(2) model with one unit root emerges for velocity. The restriction $m_1 = 0$ is accepted by $\hat{\tau}_{\beta\tau}$ and Φ_3 for both the current- and fixed rate aggregates. Absence of a quadratic trend is hence imposed, in accordance with the visual appearance of these series. The restriction $m_0 = 0$ is accepted by Φ_2. Absence of a linear trend is nevertheless not yet imposed to facilitate comparison with (6.1). Estimation over 81:1 to 97:1 gives for the fixed-rate Euro10 aggregates the empirical model[99]

$$\Delta v_t = \underset{(0.07)}{0.21}\, \Delta v_{t-1} - \underset{(0.34)}{0.0008} + \hat{e}_t \quad , \qquad \hat{\sigma}_e = 0.7\,\% \quad . \tag{6.2}$$

The results for the current rate aggregates are virtually identical, which is not surprising given that conversion rate movements largely cancel out in velocity. Both specifications pass a battery of diagnostic tests evaluating the model against the relative past and the relative future of their own data. The quarterly drift $m_0 = -0.0008$ translates into a yearly velocity decline of 0.32%. If the coefficient on the lagged difference of velocity is (invalidly) restricted to zero, the quarterly drift becomes $m_0 = -0.0011$. This simply depicts the average change in velocity and translates into a yearly decline of 0.44%. However, the drift is statistically far less significant than in (6.1), so that a linear trend seems not really present in the deterministic component of Euro10 velocity. This result coincides with the visual appearance of the series in figure 5.6. It does, however, not coincide with the perceptions of the European Central Bank (1999b), which assumes a trend-stationary behaviour with a yearly decline between 0.5% – 1.0% for Euro-velocity.

---

[99] The values in brackets report the marginal probability (p-value) of the t-statistic testing a zero restriction on the respective coefficient.

6.2.3 Vector Autoregressive Modelling

In this section the European data series are modelled jointly as vector autoregressions. That is, two general VAR models are set up, one for the fixed-rate aggregates and one for the current-rate aggregates. Their statistical adequacy is first ascertained via misspecification tests. Then the full menu of multivariate unit-root tests is applied to determine a cointegration rank and a deterministic degree. The resulting European VAR-submodels are finally handed over to section 6.3 for a direct comparison with the VAR-submodel obtained for Germany before.

The General Model: The initial VAR is again formulated according to (3.15) for a vector $x_t = [m, p, y, is, il]$ and two lags (k=2). The deterministic regressor d_t includes a constant (1), a linear trend (t), and several impulse dummies. For the fixed-rate aggregates these dummies are ID81:2, ID90:3, ID92:3, ID93:1; and for the current-rate aggregates the same except that ID92:3 is replaced by ID92:4. These specifications constitute the maintained hypotheses, or the general unrestricted model (GUM) in the sense of section 2.3. Their statistical adequacy is therefore checked by misspecification tests. These tests evaluate the respective initial VAR against the relative past and the relative future of its own data. Table 6.10 reports several diagnostic tests on the VAR-residuals for both specifications. Figure 6.6 shows a recursive Chow test on the VAR-forecast errors for the current-rate specification. These series appeared more difficult to model (cf figure 6.5), and the recursive Chow test for the fixed-rate specification is not substantially different. Again, values below unity indicate non-rejection of the hypothesis of parameter constancy.

Null:	White Noise[1]		Normality[2]		Cond.Homosc.[3]		Uncond.Homosc.[4]	
Statistic:	$F(4,20)$	$F(4,52)$	$\chi^2(2)$	$\chi^2(2)$	$F(4,16)$	$F(4,48)$	$F(20,3)$	$F(20,35)$
Sample:	Fixed	Current	Fixed	Current	Fixed	Current	Fixed	Current
Money	1.54	0.34	0.36	3.30	0.06	0.53	0.59	0.42
Prices	0.75	1.63	10.2*	0.50	0.54	0.60	0.75	0.70
Output	0.58	1.27	2.96	1.20	0.66	0.69	0.55	0.40
Short Rate	0.66	0.06	3.47	1.96	0.25	0.28	0.49	0.45
Long Rate	2.49	2.37	1.49	0.89	0.15	0.17	0.88	0.64
System	1.13	0.96	15.2	4.01			0.64	0.69

1) LM-Test against up to fourth order serial correlation. 2) Parametric LM-Test against skewness and excess kurtosis. 3) LM-Test against up to fourth order ARCH. 4) LM-Test against general non-linear forms of heteroscedasticity. The superscript '' denotes rejection of null with at most 5% error probability.*

Table 6.10. Misspecification Tests for Euro10

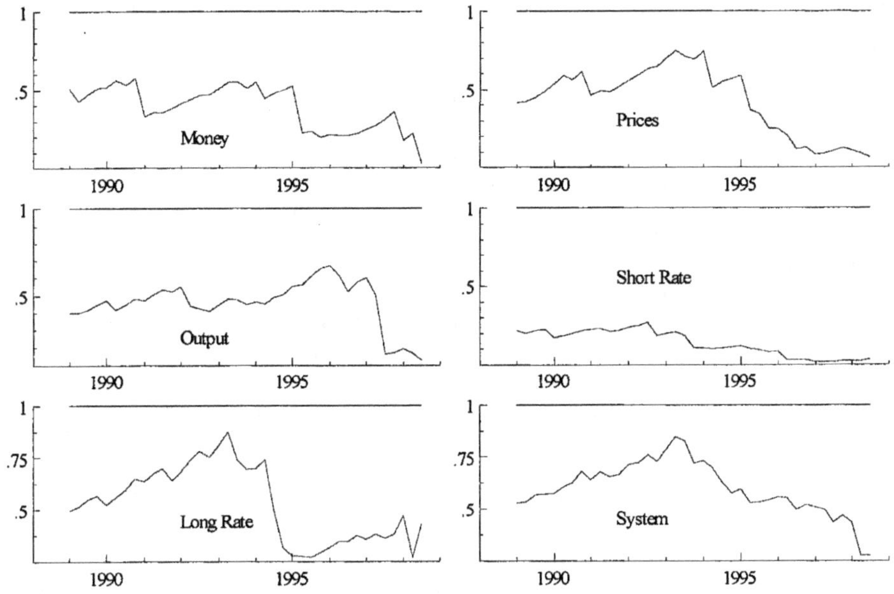

Fig. 6.6. Recursive Chow Test for Euro10

None of these tests indicates misspecification, except for some non-normality in the price equation of the fixed-rate specification. This defect is due to excess kurtosis and vanishes in a VAR(4) model. In order to keep as many degrees of freedom as possible the VAR(2) model is nevertheless maintained.

The Submodel: Having established the data congruency of the respective maintained hypotheses, the next step in the analysis of the European data is to evaluate their cointegration properties. To anticipate the results, these properties are less clear cut than those of the German data, which is hardly surprising given the poor data quality and the consistency requirements deduced in section 5 for cointegration to appear in aggregated data. Nevertheless, some cointegration seems to be present, and this paragraph attempts to detail this assertion.

Table 6.11 contains the finite-sample corrected trace statistics for both European specifications. Again, the table is read columnwise from top to bottom, beginning with column $\hat{r} = 0$. The first decisively non-rejected hypothesis for the fixed-rate version is $\mathcal{H}(\hat{r}, 2)$ with $r = 3$ (typed in bold). This result is corroborated by the likelihood ratios testing for a reduction in the deterministic degree (cf page 58). These statistics, shown in table 6.12, here reject a restriction from case 2 to case 2* deterministics at every possible

Null:	$\hat{r} = 0$	$\hat{r} \leq 1$	$\hat{r} \leq 2$	$\hat{r} \leq 3$	$\hat{r} \leq 4$
Fixed					
$\mathcal{H}(\hat{r},0)$	134.5* (59.5)	66.6* (39.9)	26.6* (24.3)	12.2 (12.5)	4.4* (3.8)
$\mathcal{H}(\hat{r},1^*)$	164.3* (76.1)	91.6* (53.1)	49.0* (34.9)	18.9 (20.0)	7.7 (9.2)
$\mathcal{H}(\hat{r},1)$	138.5* (68.5)	67.9* (47.2)	37.4* (29.7)	13.4 (15.4)	3.3 (3.8)
$\mathcal{H}(\hat{r},2^*)$	160.8* (87.3)	90.3* (63.0)	58.2* (42.4)	29.3* (25.3)	6.3 (12.3)
$\mathcal{H}(\hat{r},2)$	134.5* (77.7)	72.8* (54.6)	40.7* (34.5)	**12.2 (18.1)**	2.3 (3.7)
Current					
$\mathcal{H}(\hat{r},0)$	98.5* (59.5)	49.0* (39.9)	21.3 (24.3)	4.5 (12.5)	2.2 (3.8)
$\mathcal{H}(\hat{r},1^*)$	132.0* (76.1)	71.4* (53.1)	42.6* (34.9)	18.6 (20.0)	2.2 (9.2)
$\mathcal{H}(\hat{r},1)$	90.3* (68.5)	49.4* (47.2)	21.3 (29.7)	5.0 (15.4)	1.4 (3.8)
$\mathcal{H}(\hat{r},2^*)$	115.1* (87.3)	72.0* (63.0)	41.8 (42.4)	**14.9 (25.3)**	3.0 (12.3)
$\mathcal{H}(\hat{r},2)$	112.1* (77.7)	70.2* (54.6)	40.8* (34.5)	13.9 (18.1)	2.2 (3.7)

Trace statistics (TR) testing for $p-\hat{r} > 0$ common I(1)-trends within unrestricted model $rk\,\Pi_1 \leq p$. Critical values (5%, in brackets) from Osterwald-Lenum (1992).

Table 6.11. Vector I(1) Tests for Euro10

cointegration rank. For the current-rate version the situation is less straightforward. Skipping $\mathcal{H}(\hat{r},0)$ as entirely implausible, the first non-rejected trace statistic indicates $\mathcal{H}(\hat{r},1)$ with $r = 2$, and at this rank the deterministics can indeed be reduced down to case 1. However, accounting for the presence of impulse dummies in the deterministic regressor (see table 6.6) turns this acceptance into a rejection (critical value 16.6 instead of 29.7). The next decisively non-rejected plausible hypothesis is $\mathcal{H}(\hat{r},1)$ with $r = 3$, but at this rank the deterministics can only be reduced to case 2* (see table 6.12). Since the trace statistic for $\mathcal{H}(\hat{r},2^*)$ with $r = 3$ (typed in bold) is also safely accepted, this hypothesis is finally chosen for the current rate specification.[100]

These statistical results also coincide with the visual appearance of the respective inflation series in figure 6.5: over the sample period, aggregate fixed-rate inflation appears I(0) around a linear downward trend, reflecting the success of European countries in gradually bringing national inflation down to German levels. The corresponding price level series hence appears I(1) around quadratic trend. Under current rates, in contrast, high national inflation rates are at least partly offset by devaluations, so that aggregate current-rate inflation seems better represented as I(0) around a constant. A

[100] The impact of dummies at $r = 3$ can only be guessed, since the computer program underlying table 6.6 operates under the restriction that the dimension of d_t be not larger than the dimension $p-r$ of the TR-distribution. In case 2* the critical value at dimension 2 drops by 23% from 25.3 to 19.6. In case 2, a similar drop would reduce the critical value from 18.1 to 14.0. Both values still allow to accept the respective hypotheses.

	Null:	0 vs 1*	1 vs 2*		1* vs 1	2* vs 2	
	Restriction:	$m_0 = 0$	$m_1 = 0$	$\chi^2(r)$	$m_0 = \hat{\alpha}\, n_0$	$m_1 = \hat{\alpha}\, n_1$	$\chi^2(p-r)$
	Statistic:	$q(r,0)$	$q(r,1)$	5%CV	$q(r,1^*)$	$q(r,2^*)$	5%CV
Fixed	$r=0$				30.1*	30.7*	11.1
	$r=1$	5.6*	0.0	3.8	27.6*	20.4*	9.5
	$r=2$	8.7*	1.9	6.0	13.5*	20.3*	7.8
	$r=3$	26.9*	7.6	7.8	6.4*	19.9*	6.0
	$r=4$	30.9*	22.6*	9.5	5.1*	4.6*	3.8
	$r=5$	34.7*	26.0*	11.1			
Current	$r=0$				48.5*	3.5	11.1
	$r=1$	12.9*	2.6	3.8	25.6*	2.1	9.5
	$r=2$	14.2*	5.0	6.0	24.8*	1.2	7.8
	$r=3$	22.7*	17.5*	7.8	15.8*	0.9	6.0
	$r=4$	38.9*	27.1*	9.5	0.9	0.9	3.8
	$r=5$	39.0*	28.9*	11.1			

Statistics test indicated restrictions on deterministic regressor $d_t = m_0 + m_1\, t$.

Table 6.12. Test of Deterministics for Euro10

similar behaviour is also shown by the respective money series in their first differences. The choice of case 2 (fixed rates) and case 2* (current rates) deterministics therefore seems fairly uncontentious.

The robustness of the results in table 6.11 is again explored by recursive estimation. This exercise should, in particular, help confirm the cointegration rank chosen in the above borderline cases of the full-sample cointegration tests. Figure 6.7 contains the recursive, finite-sample adjusted trace- and maximal eigenvalue statistics obtained from the current-rate specification. The graphs for the fixed-rate specification (not shown) are not substantially different. The recursion is based on (4.21) with a short-run matrix fixed at its full-sample value (SR fixed), and it re-estimates the long-run beginning with 81:1 - 89:1 until the full sample 81:1 - 98:3 is reached.

The resulting statistics in figure 6.7 clearly diverge for ranks $\hat{r} \leq 0, 1, 2$, although a certain reluctance in crossing the respective critical values is also discernible. This is not entirely surprising given that the critical values are not dummy-adjusted. For ranks $\hat{r} \leq 3, 4$ all statistics remain safely below their critical values. This non-rejection confirms the choice of 3 cointegration relations. Finally, a reversed recursion starting with a full-sample estimation and successively dropping initial observations (not shown here) confirms the choice of $r = 3$ for both specifications as surprisingly invariant to the respective model's initial conditions.

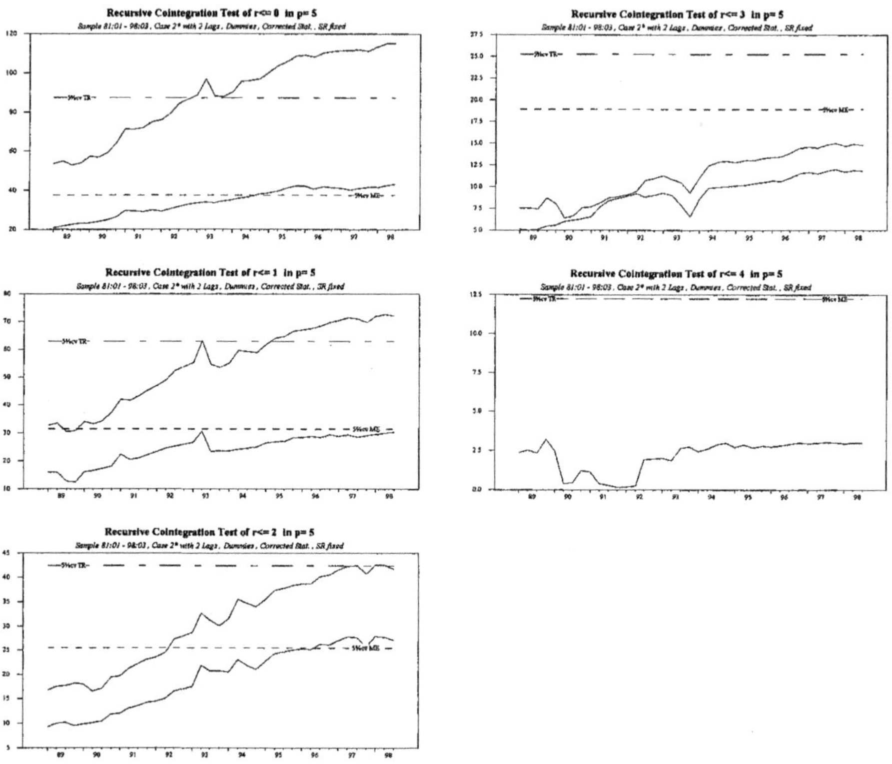

Fig. 6.7. Recursive Vector I(1) Test for Euro10

An interesting similarity between the fixed-rate and current-rate specification is revealed if the respective cointegration spaces are tested for constancy. Figure 6.8 contains the marginal significance levels of likelihood ratios testing the space spanned by each recursive $\hat{\beta}_t$ for equality with that spanned by a fixed reference matrix (cf section 4.2.1). The null of constancy is thus rejected for values below the dotted 5% line. The recursion again starts with 81:1 - 89:1 and continues until 81:1 - 98:3. The reference matrix is set to the β-estimate over a baseperiod 81:1 - 96:3.

The similarity between the specifications becomes apparent if the two alternative ways of treating the short-run in (4.21) are compared. That is, if the short-run is re-estimated recursively (SR recursive), then the constancy-hypothesis experiences a distinctive, sudden transition from the rejection region into the acceptance region in both specifications, at exactly the same date 94:2. If, in contrast, the short-run is kept fixed at its estimate over the baseperiod (SR fixed), then the constancy-hypothesis of the underlying long-run relations is throughout accepted, although the turbulent period between

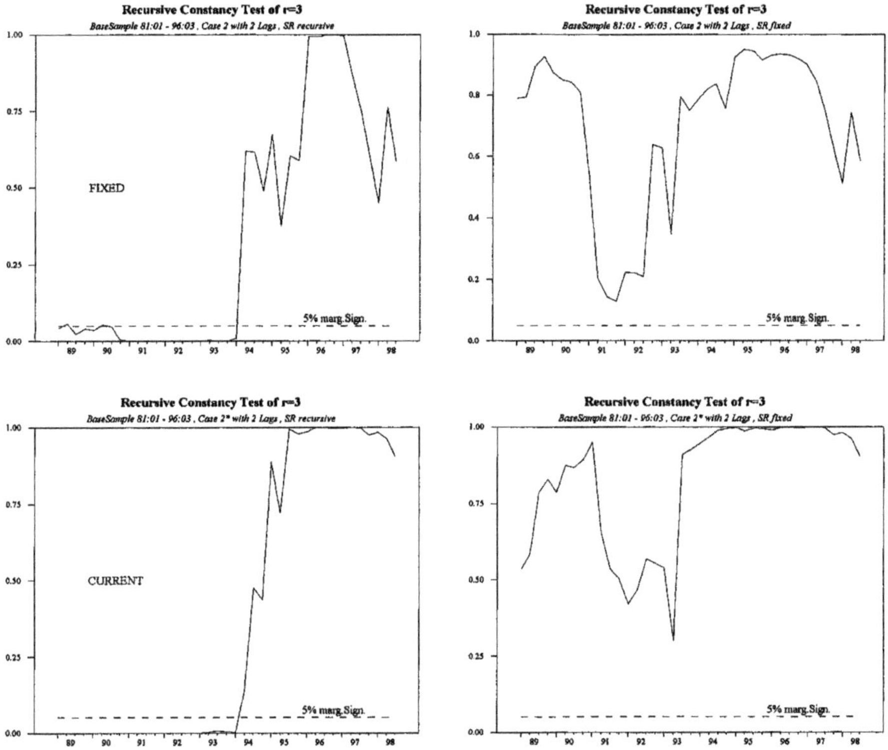

Fig. 6.8. Recursive Constancy Test for Euro10

German reunification (90:3) and the second EMS crisis (93:3) is still visible in the recursive statistics. It is worth noting that these features equally pertain to both specifications and not to the current-rate version alone. This suggests that the turbulences between 90-93 extended well beyond the currency markets and perceptibly disturbed also the intricate balances between national money markets.

The final step in the statistical analysis of the European data is a test for the possible presence of higher order integration, i.e. stochastic I(2) trends. Judging from the univariate unit root tests in table 6.9 such trends can be expected in the series for money and prices. As discussed before, the multivariate unit-root tests in this case impose the rank restrictions (3.32), and check the joint null of r I(0)-relations and s I(1)-relations, implying integration of order two for the remaining $p - r - s$ linear combinations. The specific hypotheses of interest here are $\mathcal{H}(\hat{r}, 1; \hat{s}, 1)$ for the fixed-rate specification, which allows for a quadratic trend in the data, and $\mathcal{H}(\hat{r}, 1; \hat{s}, 1^*)$ for the current-rate specification (compare table 3.3). The trace statistics TRr

Case	$p-\hat{r}$	$\hat{r}$	Null:	$\hat{s}=0$	$\hat{s}\leq 1$	$\hat{s}\leq 2$	$\hat{s}\leq 3$
Fixed $\mathcal{H}(\hat{r},1;\hat{s},1)$	3	2	TRp	166.4* (63.8)	93.3* (47.8)	62.5* (36.3)	*43.6* (29.7)*
			TRr	122.9* (29.7)	49.7* (15.4)	18.9* (3.8)	
	2	3	TRp	94.3* (30.2)	29.1* (19.8)	*15.6* (15.4)*	
			TRr	78.7* (15.4)	13.5* (3.8)		
	1	4	TRp	46.7* (6.0)	*3.8 (3.8)*		
			TRr	42.8* (3.8)			
Current $\mathcal{H}(\hat{r},1;\hat{s},1^*)$	3	2	TRp	135.0* (70.9)	73.3* (51.3)	48.1* (38.8)	*24.8 (29.7)*
			TRr	110.2* (34.9)	48.5* (20.0)	23.3* (9.2)	
	2	3	TRp	82.0* (36.1)	28.6* (22.6)	*5.8 (15.4)*	
			TRr	76.2* (20.0)	22.8* (9.2)		
	1	4	TRp	29.2* (12.9)	*1.7 (3.8)*		
			TRr	27.5* (9.2)			

TRp tests for $p-\hat{r}-\hat{s}\geq 0$ common I(2)-Trends in unrestricted model $rk\,\Pi_1\leq p$. TRr tests for $p-\hat{r}-\hat{s}>0$ common I(2)-Trends in restricted model $rk\,\Pi_1=\hat{r}$. Critical values (5%, in brackets) are from Paruolo (1996, Tables 13 & 6) and from Osterwald-Lenum (1992, Tables 1 & 1).*

Table 6.13. Vector I(2) Tests for Euro10

and TRp obtained under these hypotheses are summarized in table 6.13. Note that for $\hat{s}=p-\hat{r}$ both hypotheses again collapse into $\mathcal{H}(\hat{r},1)$, so that the respective TRp statistics (typed in italics) correspond to the TR statistics of that row in table 6.11. In the proper I(2)-cases, represented by $\hat{s}<p-\hat{r}$, the statistics consistently reject their null at all ranks $\hat{r}$ for both specifications. For the European data, a cointegration rank $r=3$ and absence of stochastic I(2) trends is therefore maintained in the sequel.

Summary: Two versions of data series for Europe were obtained through consistent aggregation of available national data series. These versions use fixed base-period market rates and current market rates, respectively, to convert national values into a common denomination (Deutsche Mark). On both versions, scalar and vector autoregressive models were fitted, evaluated, and then systematically tested for unit roots. For a 5-dimensional VAR model comprising money, prices, output, and two interest rates these tests suggest the presence of 2 stochastic I(1)-trends and hence 3 cointegration relations in both versions of the data.

The appearance of cointegration in the European data has encouraging implications. In terms of statistical theory (chapter 3), cointegration establishes the existence of economically interesting long-run relations by means of a 'neutral' statistical criterion. In terms of aggregation theory (chapter 5), cointegration in the European data implies either the existence of common stochastic trends across national data series ('compositional stability restriction'), or the existence of similar cointegration vectors within the national data series ('parameter-equality restriction'). Succinctly, cointegration on an European level implies consistent aggregation over the constituent countries (cf section 5.1.3).

To complete the summary of statistical results, the deterministic component of the European VAR's contains a quadratic time trend in the fixed-rate version, and a linear time trend in the current-rate version. In contrast to the results obtained for Germany, the European cointegration relations also contain a linear time trend, which raises the problem of stochastic versus deterministic cointegration. In the terminology of table 3.3, the submodels $\mathcal{M}(r,2)$ and $\mathcal{M}(r,2^*)$ with $r = 3$ are eventually maintained as statistical models for the fixed-rate and the current-rate version of the European data, respectively. These statistical models can now be subjected to an economic analysis aiming at money demand. This is done in the following section.

6.3 Money Demand in Germany and Europe

In the previous two sections, the concepts of integration and cointegration were established as empirically important statistical properties of the German and European data series. In particular, submodels showing these properties were deduced from a general VAR model through valid, data acceptable parameter restrictions. Each submodel - $\mathcal{M}(r,1)$ for Germany, $\mathcal{M}(r,2^*)$ for current-rate Euro10, $\mathcal{M}(r,2)$ for fixed-rate Euro10 - isolates $r = 3$ statistically identified cointegration relations. In the present section these statistical submodels are used as a benchmark against which further structural properties of the analyzed data series are analyzed.

The structural properties of interest are, of course, those relating to the existence and stability of money demand. As detailed in chapter 4, their implementation into the present probability model involves two steps. First the respective VAR submodel is split into a conditional and a marginal VAR submodel as in equations (4.2) and (4.3). This allows to test for properties separating an interesting conditional model from some uninteresting marginal model, i.e., exogeneity and noncausality properties. Second, the resulting conditional VAR submodel (CVAR) is identified into a structural error-correction model (SECM) as in equation (4.16). This allows to reformulate the statistical cointegration relations as structural equilibrium relations (long-run identification), and to implant these static relations into separate dynamic adjustment equations (short-run identification). Such a dynamic equation, describing the empirical reaction of some conditioned variable to the deviations ('errors') from a single structural equilibrium relation, can then be used to assess the stability of money demand.

6.3.1 Conditional VAR Model

In order to obtain a conditional VAR submodel possibly containing money demand, this section applies two different sets of (over-identifying) restrictions. The first set is destructive: the restrictions leading to a CVAR are derived from economic theory and then imposed onto the data. This procedure is shown to be tempting, but invalid. The second set is constructive: the restrictions leading to a CVAR are derived from the empirical data via a systematic testing procedure.

The destructive set of restrictions aims at the shortcomings of the popular single-equation ECM dominating the literature. According to economic theory, a log-linear long-run money demand function determines desired money holdings m^* in terms of explanatory variables $z = [p, y, is, il]$. Allowing for non-instantaneous adjustment of actual money holdings m towards desired holdings m^* then leads to a dynamic adjustment equation, whose estimable form is a single-equation ECM for Δm. A typical example for this economic 'straightjacket approach' are Wolters/Lütkepohl (1997). The approach can be incorporated into the present framework by noting that the conditional VAR model (4.2) collapses into a single-equation ECM under certain restrictions. These restrictions comprise the choice of but one conditioned variable ($g = 1$) and the imposition of but a single cointegration vector ($r = 1$) plus weak exogeneity of all remaining variables ($\alpha_z = 0$). The validity of these restrictions is a-priori assumed by the ECM, but explicitly testable within the VAR. This suggests to replicate some of the previous single-equation models as special cases of the present VAR's, and to check the validity of the underlying assumptions or, rather, the consequences of their violation.

Table 6.14 summarizes the empirical single-equation CVAR's obtained from the present VAR submodels for Germany and Europe by choosing money as the sole conditioned variable. The table's upper block imposes a single cointegration vector, the invalidity of this restriction was demonstrated in the previous sections. The table's lower block imposes, in addition, weak exogeneity of $[p, y, is, il]$ for the long-run parameters. This restriction simplifies the adjustment coefficients from α_y-$\omega\alpha_z$ in the upper block to but α_y in the lower block, and transforms the single-equation CVAR into a proper short-run adjustment equation for money. The resulting equations for Germany and Fixed-Euro consequently collapse into the ECM's already shown in tables 6.1 and 6.8, respectively. A comparison of the two blocks in table 6.14 reveals its seductive effects: the adjustment coefficients change from instable to 'plausibly large' negative values, and the long-run coefficients change from meaningless to 'theory consistent' money demand values. As could be expected, however, the weak exogeneity restriction underlying this outcome is

$\hat{\alpha}_y - \hat{\omega}\,\hat{\alpha}_z$ Δm	$\hat{\beta}'$ m	p	y	is	il	Data Set
0.02	1	1.52	−3.37	0.003	0.005	Germany
−0.01	1	0.27	−2.47	−0.019	−0.006	Fixed Euro
0.04	1	−0.63	−2.04	−0.003	0.006	Current Euro
	Single Cointegrationvector ($r = 1$)					
−0.09	1	−1.61	−0.69	−0.028	0.057	Germany
−0.16	1	−1.04	−0.97	−0.015	0.018	Fixed Euro
−0.21	1	−0.85	−1.06	−0.010	0.020	Current Euro
	Single Equation ($r = 1$ *and* $\hat{\alpha}_z = 0$)					

Conditional model (4.2) for money (g=1) with restrictions as indicated.

Table 6.14. Invalid Restrictions on Conditional VAR's

actually grossly invalid.[101] The alleged superior stability of European money demand functions, or indeed the very existence of money demand functions at a German or European level, should not be inferred from such statistically invalid results.

As an auxiliary exercise, the VAR submodels for Germany and Europe are also tested for the restriction that money and prices enter the entire cointegration space but as real money ($m - p$), or that the interest rates enter but as a spread ($il - is$). This type of restriction is easily implemented via the generic hypothesis $\mathcal{H}_1(r, i)$ detailed in section 4.2. On the present data, a formulation of the cointegration relations in terms of real money or in terms of an interest rate spread is decidedly rejected, for Germany as well as for Europe. Thus, the widespread practice of specifying probability models in terms of real money could also not be replicated as a statistically valid special case.

[101] The cointegration restriction here suggests two approaches to test weak exogeneity. The first is to (invalidly) assume $r = 1$, and to test $\alpha_z = 0$ for r=g=1 according to (4.23). This gives $\chi^2(4)$-statistics 36.2, 58.7, 20.8 for Germany, fixed Euro, current Euro, respectively. The second approach is to (validly) assume $r = 3$, and to test $\alpha_{z1} = 0$ and $\beta_{y2} = 0$ for r_1=g=1 according to (4.27). This gives $\chi^2(4)$-statistics 17.8, 23.5, 26.4 in the same order. In both approaches the parameters of interest (α_{y1} and β_1) occur but in the conditional model under the null hypothesis. This null of weak exogeneity is always rejected (5% critical value for $\chi^2(4)$-statistic is 9.5).

The inadequacy of the single-equation model now leads to the second, the constructive set of restrictions. Accepting a cointegration rank $r = 3$ these constructive restrictions attempt to establish a conditional VAR model (4.2) which allows to isolate money demand within a system of other long-run relations. To determine such a CVAR from the data, the noncausality hypothesis $\mathcal{H}_4(r, i)$ detailed in section 4.2.3 is systematically tested over all possible combinations of variables $g + q = p$ and cointegration relations $r_1 + r_2 = r$. Note that these combinations include (for $r_2 = 0$) also the weak exogeneity hypothesis $\mathcal{H}_3(r, i)$. The testing procedure gives a total of 70 likelihood ratio statistics for each data set.[102]

$p = 5,\ r = 3$	y	z	Cointegration	Restriction	Statistic
Germany	m, il ($g = 2$)	p, y, is ($q = 3$)	$r_1 = 1$ $r_2 = 2$	$\alpha_{z1} = 0$ $\beta_{y2} = 0$	$\chi^2(5) = 11.9$ [4 %]
Fixed Euro	p, y, is ($g = 3$)	m, il ($q = 2$)	$r_1 = 3$ $r_2 = 0$	$\alpha_z = 0$	$\chi^2(6) = 9.9$ [13 %]
Current Euro	p, y, is ($g = 3$)	m, il ($q = 2$)	$r_1 = 3$ $r_2 = 0$	$\alpha_z = 0$	$\chi^2(6) = 9.3$ [15 %]

Combinations of conditioned (y) and marginalized (z) variables and of systemwide (r_1) and marginal (r_2) cointegration relations accepted by the noncausality test (4.27). Marginal significance levels (p-values) in brackets below statistics.

Table 6.15. Conditional VAR's Accepted by Noncausality Tests

Table 6.15 summarizes the instances of an acceptance, which suggest the following situation. For Germany, the variables $z = [p, y, is]$ are jointly self-causal in the long run with $r_2 = 2$ cointegration relations holding only among these marginal variables. This implies a CVAR for $y = [m, il]$ containing but a single systemwide cointegration relation. Thus, under the accepted restriction the VAR-model $\mathcal{M}(r, 1)$ for Germany can be split into a conditional and a marginal submodel similar to (4.26). For Europe, in contrast, the variables $z = [m, il]$ are jointly self-causal in the long run with no cointegration relation holding exclusively among them. This implies a CVAR for $y = [p, y, is]$ containing three systemwide cointegration relations. Thus, under the accepted restriction the two VAR-models $\mathcal{M}(r, 2)$ and $\mathcal{M}(r, 2^*)$ for Europe can both

[102] The possible combinations are delimited by the requirement $r_2 < q$ (integrated z-variables) and $r_1 \leq g$ (reduced rank regression). Thus the switching algorithm maximizing the concentrated likelihood (3.36) under restriction (4.27) was programmed to run at each combination (q, r_2) satisfying $r_2 < q \leq p - r_1$ for $r_1 = 1, ..., r$.

be split into a conditional and a marginal submodel similar to (4.22). The statistical validity of these splitting-restrictions, as judged by the marginal significance levels associated with the test statistics in table 6.15, appears nevertheless somewhat disappointing. This is particularly true for Germany, where long-run noncausality is accepted at only a 4% significance level.[103] It is, however, emphasized that these restrictions are the *only ones* that are accepted at all.[104]

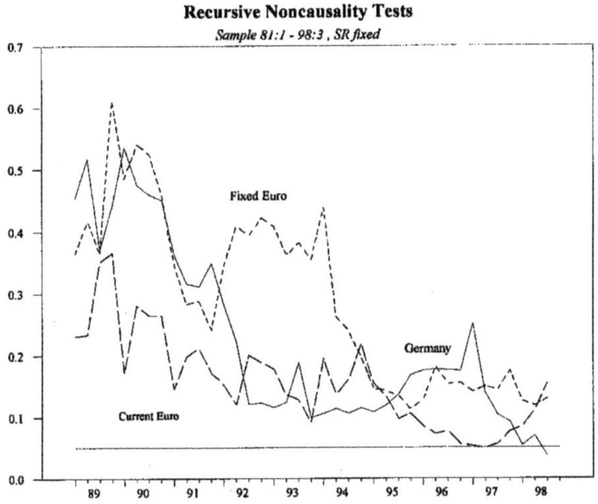

Fig. 6.9. Recursive Noncausality Tests

The weak statistical validity of the results in table 6.15 suggests to test the respective noncausality restrictions also recursively, again over 89:1 - 98:3. The marginal significance levels of the resulting sequences of likelihood ratio statistics are shown in figure 6.9. It emerges from this analysis that the validity of the test statistics does not really deteriorate until the end of the sample period, in fact, the validity of the European tests even starts to improve again in the run-up to full monetary union. Since, moreover, the present set of restrictions also constitutes the only accepted instance of noncausality over several shorter sample periods, the results from table 6.15 are maintained in the sequel.

103 This corresponds to a result in Hubrich (1999), where the simple weak-exogeneity hypothesis $\mathcal{H}_3(r, i)$ is throughout rejected for similar German data series.

104 The only exception is one instance of noncausality in the current-rate Euro10 data involving $z = [m, p, il]$. An identification of the corresponding CVAR for $[y, is]$ into an IS-curve and a central-bank reaction function however produced meaningless results, and was therefore not adopted.

In summary, the indicated z-variables in the above hypotheses are (i) self-causal in the long-run within the marginal model, and (ii) weakly exogenous for the parameters α_{y1} and β_1 in the conditional model. The statistics in table 6.15 now suggest an interesting reversal of this structural property during the transition from the national to an aggregate level: in the recommended CVAR for Germany the causation runs from $[p, y, is]$ to $[m, il]$, whereas this direction is just the opposite in both recommended CVAR's for Europe.[105]

Whether this outcome actually reflects a structural property of economic reality or but some whimsical trait of the data is certainly disputable. Taken at face value, however, this empirical result immediately pertains to the economic debate motivating this study: in section 1.1 it was argued, essentially, that for policy purposes money demand is not necessarily equal to money demand. That is, several rival approaches to price-level determination are known from monetary economics. In a version dubbed as *domestic monetarism* national money determines the national price level. The same causation underlies another version dubbed as *hegemonic EMS*, where German money determines German and eventually also European prices. In a third version, the *symmetric EMS*, European money conversely determines European and German prices, leaving the national money stock endogenous.

The present empirical evidence clearly supports the third version: European money is causal for European prices regardless of the chosen conversion rate. Under the assumption of purchasing-power-parity, the observed flip-side of this aggregate relation on the national level is noncausality of German money for German prices. The present result therefore indicates an inability of German money demand to anchor nominal prices, and recommends a shift of this task to an European level.[106] On this level, the result contradicts the banking-theoretic perceptions prevailing in the concept of inflation targeting, and instead recommends a policy of monetary targeting for the European Central Bank. It is finally noted that the tested hypothesis of long-run noncausality does not preclude an economically plausible endogeneity of money in the short-run.

A further economic interpretation of the isolated CVAR's is now undertaken in the following section.

[105] This corresponds to a result in Monticelli/Papi (1996, appendix 1), who find causality from money to nominal output in a bivariate VAR for European data.

[106] This corresponds to a result in MacKinnon (1984), who finds US-prices statistically better explained by world-money than by US-money. The argument is reformulated by Läufer (1992b) in terms of German prices being dependent on European money, and empirically confirmed by Bayoumi/Kenen (1993), who in a trivariate VAR framework find national prices better predicted by European money than by the respective national money stock for a number of countries including Germany.

6.3.2 Structural ECM Model

Defying convention, the estimates of the long-run parameters $\alpha\beta' = \Pi_1$ obtained from the likelihood procedure in sections 6.1.3 and 6.2.3 have not been reported so far. The reason was detailed in chapter 4: the factorization of the matrix Π_1 is not unique, so that the parameters α and β are statistically not identified. To solve this problem the likelihood procedure employs the nonlinear a-priori restriction that the covariance matrix of the concentrated disequilibria, $\beta' S_{ll} \beta$, be diagonal. This condition can be replaced by an alternative set of just-identifying linear restrictions (4.9) satisfying (4.11). Although both identification schemes are equally arbitrary, the latter allows a reinterpretation of statistical cointegration relations (β) as structural equilibrium relations (b). This reinterpretation is implemented in the present section. Moreover, to obtain a precise correspondence between disequilibrium and adjustment, the dynamics of the CVAR are just-identified such that its adjustment matrix (α_c) becomes diagonal (a). Combining the long-run and short-run identification scheme turns the CVAR (4.2) into a SECM (4.16).

For Europe, the restrictions accepted in table 6.15 recommend a CVAR in conditioned variables $y = [p, y, is]$ isolating three systemwide cointegration relations. This suggests a long-run identification scheme containing a money demand relation for p, an IS-curve for y, and a central bank reaction function for is. Under the present analogy-approach to aggregation (cf section 5.1), such aggregate structural relations represent the collective behaviour of national agents and national central banks which, if sufficiently aligned or coordinated, should induce a theoretically meaningful structure also on the European level. Specifically, within the present ordering $x = [m, p, y, is, il]$ of variables, the 3 European cointegration vectors are required to satisfy (4.9) for the design matrices

$$H_1 = \begin{bmatrix} -1\,0\,0 \\ \mathbf{1}\,0\,0 \\ 1\,0\,0 \\ 0\,1\,0 \\ 0\,0\,1 \end{bmatrix}, \quad H_2 = \begin{bmatrix} 0\,0\,0 \\ 0\,0\,0 \\ \mathbf{1}\,0\,0 \\ 0\,1\,0 \\ 0\,0\,1 \end{bmatrix}, \quad H_3 = \begin{bmatrix} 0\,0\,0 \\ 1\,0\,0 \\ 0\,0\,0 \\ 0\,\mathbf{1}\,0 \\ 0\,0\,1 \end{bmatrix}. \qquad (6.3)$$

Each matrix H_i imposes $r - 1 = 2$ restrictions on the respective cointegration vector. The matrix H_1 for example restricts the first vector such that the coefficients on $-m$ and y equal the coefficient on p. The matrix H_2 restricts the second vector such that the coefficients on m and p become zero, and H_3 similarly excludes the variables m and y from the third vector. To obtain a set of structural relations $b_{p\times r}$ from the statistical relations $\beta_{p\times r}$ these design matrices are inserted, one by one, into the eigenvalue problem (4.12). This gives a nonsingular transformation matrix N_1. The relations are then normalized on the respective conditioned variables (typed bold in (6.3)) by means of a diagonal normalization matrix N_2. Combining both steps in (4.13) gives the desired structural relations as $b = \beta N_1 N_2$. The first column of b contains a money demand relation with unit price- and income-elasticity. The second column contains an IS-curve linking real output to the interest rates. The third column links a central-bank instrument, namely the short rate, to possible central-bank targets, namely prices and the long rate. The short-run identification scheme finally comprises a diagonalization of the corresponding adjustment matrix. For the European CVAR's this diagonalization is easily achieved by application of (4.14), with α_z set to zero.

Since the restrictions implied by (6.3) are not necessarily identifying, the generic rank condition (4.11) is checked. In the present case ($r = 3$) this condition requires that $\mathrm{rk}\,(R_i' H_{j_1}) \geq 1$ and $\mathrm{rk}\,(R_i'[H_{j_1}; H_{j_2}]) \geq 2$ for all indices $i \neq j_1 \neq j_2$. For the first restriction-matrix $R_1 \equiv H_{1\perp}$ this gives $\mathrm{rk}_{\,1.2} = 1$, $\mathrm{rk}_{\,1.3} = 1$, and $\mathrm{rk}_{\,1.23} = 2$ (compare appendix A.5). Thus the first cointegration vector is just-identified. Similar results obtain for $R_2 \equiv H_{2\perp}$ and $R_3 \equiv H_{3\perp}$. It follows that the chosen scheme is generically identifying for 'almost all' vectors from a 3-dimensional cointegration space. Of course the design matrices H_i can be 'narrowed' to accommodate additional, over-identifying restrictions. For example, canceling the third column and changing the second column's last element from 0 to -1 in H_1 imposes the restriction that the two interest rates enter the money demand relation only as a spread.

For Germany, the restrictions accepted in table 6.15 recommend a CVAR in $y = [m, il]$ isolating but a single systemwide cointegration relation (β_1) and two cointegration relations holding among only the marginalized variables (β_2). This slightly complicates the long-run identification. The systemwide β_1-relation is, as usual, just-identified by $r - 1 = 2$ freely imposable restrictions. In each β_2-relation, however, the noncausality hypothesis consumes $r_1 = 1$ just-identifying and $g - r_1 = 1$ over-identifying exclusion restrictions in order to produce $\beta_{y2} = 0$ (see footnote 66). This leaves but $r_2 - 1 = 1$ freely imposable just-identifying restrictions per relation. Therefore, within the present ordering $x = [m, p, y, is, il]$ of variables, the German cointegration vectors are here required to satisfy (4.9) for the design matrices

$$H_1 = \begin{bmatrix} 1 & 0 & 0 \\ -1 & 0 & 0 \\ 0 & 1 & 0 \\ 0 & 0 & 1 \\ 0 & 0 & -1 \end{bmatrix}, \qquad H_2 = \begin{bmatrix} 0 & 0 \\ 0 & 0 \\ 1 & 0 \\ 0 & 1 \\ 0 & 0 \end{bmatrix}, \qquad H_3 = \begin{bmatrix} 0 & 0 \\ 1 & 0 \\ 0 & 0 \\ 0 & 1 \\ 0 & 0 \end{bmatrix}. \tag{6.4}$$

The identification scheme in H_1 is designed to generate a money demand relation similar to the European relations, but normalized on money rather than prices. Since the switching algorithm failed to converge under the restriction of a unit income elasticity, the interest rates were instead restricted to enter as a spread. The design matrices H_2 and H_3 impose exclusion restrictions on the relations holding among the marginalized variables $z = [p, y, is]$. The interpretation of the resulting CVAR is, however, not straightforward: since there are more conditioned variables than systemwide cointegration relations ($g > r_1$), the conditional model is dynamically instable due to insufficient targets (one target for two variables). An identification of its short-run through a diagonalization (4.14) is therefore not possible. Consequently the German CVAR can not be developed into a proper SECM, although in the sequel it is sometimes also subsumed under that label for convenience.

Conditioned Variables	$\hat{a}$			$\hat{b}'$ m	p	y	is	il	$W(\hat{\delta}_i)$
Germany									
Δm		-0.05		1	-1	-1.1	-0.100	0.100	
Δil		-0.24[1]							
Fixed Euro									
Δp	-0.21	$*$	$*$	-1	1	1	0.020	-0.020	19.9
Δy	$*$	-1.75	$*$	$*$	$*$	1	-0.023	0.015	31.0
$\Delta$is	$*$	$*$	-0.46	$*$	-38.4	$*$	1	$*$	33.4
Current Euro									
Δp	-0.13	$*$	$*$	-1	1	1	0.010	-0.020	22.6
Δy	$*$	-0.65	$*$	$*$	$*$	1	-0.015	0.015	34.6
$\Delta$is	$*$	$*$	-0.41	$*$	-39.2	$*$	1	$*$	27.6

1) Coefficient under renormalization of structural cointegration relation on il.

Table 6.16. Structural ECM's for Germany and Euro10

Table 6.16 now summarizes the structural ECM's obtained from the above identification schemes. The table's first column indicates the respective conditioned variables, whose dynamic changes respond to the disequilibria implied by the SECM. The second column contains the structural adjustment coefficients ($\hat{a}$) which isolate and quantify these responses. All coefficients are within the stable range $-2 < \hat{a}_{ii} < 0$ (cf page 66), although that on Fixed-Euro-Δy implies an overshooting behaviour. The third column contains the identified systemwide cointegration vectors ($\hat{b}$) which can be interpreted as economic equilibrium relations. For these relations, some additional over-identifying restrictions were accepted and hence also imposed. For the Fixed-Euro data, the interest rates enter as a spread in the first relation and the long rate is excluded from the third relation. Implemented jointly with weak exogeneity these additional restrictions produce a test statistic

$\chi^2(8) = 13.9$ [8%]. For the Current-Euro data, the linear time trend is excluded from the first relation, the interest rates enter as a spread in the second relation, and the long rate is excluded from the third relation. Implemented jointly with weak exogeneity these additional restrictions produce a test statistic $\chi^2(9) = 10.1$ [34%]. Note that, for Germany as well as for Europe, all coefficients in $\hat{a}$ and $\hat{b}$ share the important property of likelihood-independence from the respective marginal model. That is, all information regarding these structural coefficients is captured in the respective (identified) conditional models. The table's final column contains the Wald statistic testing the European SECM's for instability as detailed in section 4.2.4.

The coefficients shown in the respective blocks of table 6.16 now admit an economic interpretation in terms of dynamic equilibrium-adjustment equations. In each block, the first long-run relation resembles a conventional money demand relation, with money related positively to its own rate and negatively to its opportunity cost.[107] Despite their formal similarity these relations are, however, qualitatively very different. For Germany, an excess money supply induces downward changes in actual money holdings and in the long interest rate, without any long-run effect on the price level.[108] For Europe, in contrast, an excess money supply induces upward changes in the price level, without any long-run effect on money holdings or the long interest rate. This illustrates a point already stressed in chapter 1, namely that an empirical money demand relation as such is of little practical interest unless the direction of causality has been established.

The second equation in each European block resembles an IS-curve relating output inversely to an interest rate differential approximating perhaps the real interest rate. An excess output supply correctly induces downward changes in output. The respective third equation may be interpreted as a (collective) central bank reaction function, relating the policy instrument is inversely to detrended movements in the ultimate target p. Again, an above-target value of the instrument correctly induces downward changes in is. Although these structural equilibrium relations and associated adjustment coefficients appear quite sensible, it is again emphasized that, due to the inevitable arbitrariness of any identification scheme, table 6.16 contains an only hypothetical isolation of money demand.

---

[107] Precisely, the statistical relation $b'x_t \sim I(0)$ is interpreted as reflecting an underlying equilibrium relation $b'x_t = 0$. The entries, e.g. for Germany, thus read in conventional form as $m = p + 1.1y + 0.10\,(il - is)$.

[108] This corresponds to a result in Juselius (1996), where over a similar sample period the German money stock is found to respond to an interest-rate elastic money demand relation. This endogeneity of money is attributed to increasing difficulties in protecting the national money stock by sterilizing EMS-related capital movements.

6.3.3 Stability of Money Demand

The SECM's derived in the previous section can now be used to assess the stability of the money demand relations isolated therein. Owing to the diffuse usage of the term 'stability', its assessment involves a number of semantic traps. In economics, stability is usually formalized by the variance of structural shocks. For example, casting the theoretical money demand relation (1.1) into a log-linear format produces something like

$$y_t \;=\; \mu + \gamma' z_t + u_t \quad , \qquad u_t \sim i.d.(0, \sigma^2) \quad , \tag{6.5}$$

which is the type of relation used in chapter 5 to compare the properties of national versus European money demand. In such theoretical relations, stability can be measured by the variance of structural shocks, both absolutely ($\sigma^2 < \infty$) and relatively ($\sigma^2 \lessgtr \sigma_n^2$), and conditions were derived for the European relation to be more stable than any national relation ($\sigma^2 < \sigma_n^2$). This concept of stability is, however, not quite applicable to empirical relations in econometric models: as shown in chapter 2, an interpretation of (6.5) as a probability model immediately changes the status of u_t from an autonomous structural shock to a residual innovation depending on the probability model's design criteria (see also Hendry 1987, p.32).

In econometrics it is therefore preferable to employ a purely statistical criterion for stability. A powerful statistical criterion is cointegration, i.e., the requirement that some linear combination of integrated variables be of finite variance and hence absolutely stable. This criterion immediately provides a first assessment: the structural money demand relations in table 6.16 are cointegration relations, and from this very fact follows their absolute stability. Moreover, in terms of aggregation theory the cointegration criterion also provides an indirect test of the compositional-stability/parameter-equality restrictions that imply a zero (or at least low) aggregation loss.

This leaves the problem of relative stability. A natural statistical criterion for relative stability is the 'strength' of the respective cointegration relation. In the present framework, a simple measure for this strength are the nonzero eigenvalues returned by the Johansen procedure, or indeed, any cointegration test statistic constructed from them. Precisely, each eigenvalue in the diagonal matrix $\Lambda_{r\times r}$ defined by (3.41) measures the strength of a cointegration relation with respect to the first differences of the entire system in terms of canonical correlations (cf page 52). This measure, however, lacks a straightforward economic interpretation. Therefore the cointegrated VAR (3.24) is reparameterized into a reduced-form ECM (3.30) and thence into a structural ECM (4.16). The resulting diagonal matrix $a_{r\times r}$ of structural adjustment coefficients is linked to the reduced-form coefficients α by (4.14), and thence to the eigenvalues by the relation $\alpha' S_{dd}^{-1}\, \alpha = \Lambda$. Thus it inherits the information about the strength of the cointegration relations, but presents this information in a more accessible form: each structural coefficient in a measures the strength of an economically identified cointegration relation with respect to the first differences of a single variable in terms of adjustments towards equilibrium. Moreover, due to the dynamic stability of the embedding SECM (cf section 4.1) the coefficients inform not only about the speed but also about the causal direction of this adjustment.

The latter point highlights a problem in the comparison of German and European money demand relations: the relations are, at least over the present data, quantitatively similar but qualitatively different. Specifically, while the German relation induces adjustments in money and the long rate within a dynamically instable CVAR, the European relations both govern inflation within a dynamically stable SECM. In view of such fundamental differences the question of relative stability appears of but secondary importance. Under this caveat of limited comparability several statistics assessing the relative stability of German and European money demand are compiled in table 6.17.

	$\hat{a}_{11}$	$\hat{\sigma}_{11}$	$W(\hat{\delta}_1)$	$\det B(1)$
Germany	−0.05	0.088	20.7	0.000
Fixed Euro	−0.21	0.013	19.9	0.012
Current Euro	−0.13	0.016	22.6	0.016

Adjustment coefficient ($\hat{a}_{11}$), disequilibrium variance ($\hat{\sigma}_{11}$), and Wald-statistic of structural money demand equations; stability matrix of corresponding CVAR.

Table 6.17. Relative Stability of Structural Money Demand

The second column in table 6.17 contains the adjustment coefficients ($\hat{a}_{11}$) on the money demand relations identified in table 6.16. It is noted that thanks to the diagonal adjustment matrix these coefficients are actually invariant to the identification of the other equations within the SECM, as long as the number of (over-) identifying restrictions is not changed. The numerical magnitude of the adjustment coefficients implies for (say) the Fixed-Euro data a time span of roughly 3 quarters for the log-prices to close an initial disequilibrium by one half.[109] The third column contains the square root of the disequilibrium variances implied by the respective money demand relations ($\hat{\sigma}_{11}$). Because of the unit price elasticity in each relation these variances are

[109] The adjustment equation is $\Delta x_t = \alpha\,(x_{t-1} - x^*_{t-1})$. For a fixed target $x^*_{t-1} = x^*$ it relates a present to an initial disequilibrium via $(x_t - x^*) = (1+\alpha)^t\,(x_0 - x^*)$. To close an initial disequilibrium to some extent $ext \equiv (x_t - x^*)/(x_0 - x^*)$ then requires $t = \ln(ext) \,/\, \ln(1+\alpha)$ time periods for a given α.

directly comparable, and restate the ordering in the adjustment coefficients. The last column contains, as a reminder of the system-context, the determinants of the CVAR stability matrix $B(1)$. Here the CVAR for Current Euro seems dynamically slightly more stable than that for Fixed Euro, whereas that for Germany is dynamically instable.

The remaining fourth column in table 6.17 contains the Wald statistic (4.30) obtained for the two European money demand relations, restated from table 6.16. As detailed in section 4.2.4, these statistics incorporate the structural model's identifying information and perform a double task. First, the set of statistics obtained from all equations of a SECM jointly tests for instability in the underlying CVAR. Here the Wald statistics in table 6.16 together reject the hypothesis of instability if compared to the 5% critical values 17.2 (Fixed Euro) and 18.0 (Current-Euro) tabulated by Boswijk (1994, Tables B.4 and B.5). Given the complementary nature of weak exogeneity and dynamic stability, this result corroborates the outcome of the tests in table 6.15. Second, the individual statistic obtained from the i-th equation of a SECM tests the particular significance of the i-th structural cointegration relation and measures how safely the random variable $\hat{a}_{ii}$ is away from zero. The Wald statistics in table 6.17 indicate that European prices react indeed significantly to the identified structural money demand relations.

For the German money demand relation identified in table 6.16 a proper Wald statistic in the sense of section 4.2.4 does not exist. To nevertheless obtain a comparable measure for Germany, recall that the construction of a Wald statistic resembles the square of an ordinary t-statistic. Therefore the adjustment coefficient measuring the reaction of German money to the identified money demand relation is here divided by its standard error, and the square of the resulting t-ratio inserted into table 6.17. This allows a rough comparison of the German relation with the two European relations. Here the isolated reactions to the respective money-market disequilibria show but little difference in significance, despite considerable difference in magnitude.

An equally rough but in a way illustrative comparison is obtained by estimating a SECM analog to the European versions shown in table 6.16 also over the German data. The results of this exercise are summarized in appendix A.6, and they are disastrous: the same apparently plausible economic theory employed to structuralize the European data utterly fails, in terms of statistical validity, if applied to the German data.

A final piece of empirical evidence concerns an aspect of stability which is irrelevant in economics, but quite a challenge in econometrics. This aspect is the time-invariance of a relation, denoted here as constancy. The constancy of the cointegration space was already tested for in figures 6.4 and 6.8. This analysis is now augmented by a recursive estimation of the European SECM's. Figure 6.10 graphs the recursive estimates of the structural adjustments $\hat{a}_{11}$ for the two European money demand relations. In 98:3 these graphs consequently arrive at the values shown in table 6.17. As before, the recursions are run in two different versions: the solid lines depict estimates obtained from (4.28) with the short-run matrix X fixed at its full sample value (SR fixed), whereas the dotted lines show the estimates obtained from (4.28) with the matrix X included into the recursion (SR recursive).

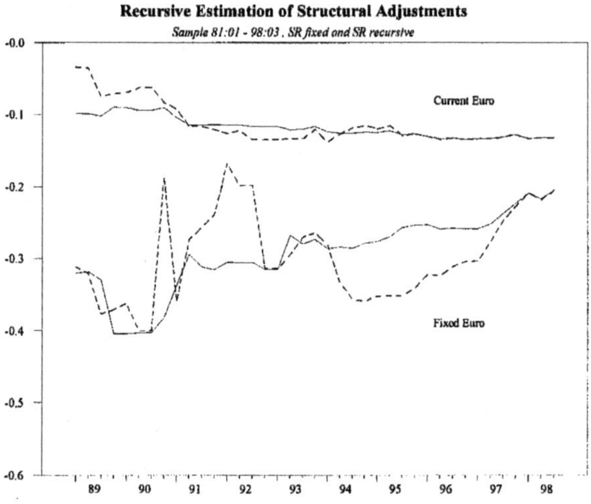

Fig. 6.10. Recursive Estimation of Structural Money Demand

The graphs in figure 6.10 strongly support the structural money demand relations isolated in table 6.16. The fixed-rate specification shows variation between German reunification (90:3) and the second EMS crisis (93:3), but if the contamination by short-run turbulences is filtered out the corresponding structural adjustment coefficient remains fairly time-invariant within a range -0.3 to -0.2. Nearly spectacular, however, is the behaviour of the current-rate specification, where the structural adjustment coefficient remains virtually time-invariant in both versions of the recursion. In fact, it might be tempting to conclude that the corresponding SECM managed to isolate some (usually elusive) 'deep' behavioural parameter of European money demand. However, as argued in chapter 2, such a conclusion precariously mixed the notions of theoretical and empirical models. Therefore the result is interpreted as an implication of the unknown DGP for the theoretical framework of the present SECM. Apparently this SECM managed to capture one of the regular DGP features in an economically interpretable way. This is the best an econometrician can hope for.

Summary: Proceeding from the VAR-submodels derived in section 6.1 for Germany and section 6.2 for Europe, the present section confronted these statistical models with economic theory. Statistically valid noncausality restrictions led to the isolation of a CVAR for $[m, il]$ in the German data set, and of a CVAR for $[p, y, is]$ in both European data sets. These CVAR's were subsequently identified into meaningful SECM's containing 'economic' money demand relations. The significance of these relations and their adjustment coefficients was corroborated by Wald statistics derived from the SECM.

The multivariate framework also allowed to establish several qualitative results about these money demand relations, both destructive and constructive. As to the destructive side, the popular single-equation ECM for money could not be justified as a statistically valid special case of a general VAR. Similarly, the popular formulation of long-run relations in terms of real money proved not statistically valid here.

As to the more important constructive side, distinct directions of causality could be established for the money demand relations in Germany and Europe. This was achieved by testing an extensive set of Granger-noncausality restrictions over all possible combinations of conditioned and marginalized variables. As a result, causation from prices to money could be established for the German relation, and exactly the opposite causation, from money to prices, for both European relations. This result indicates an inability of German money demand to anchor the price level, and recommends a shift of this task to an European level. Concomitantly, the implied policy strategy for the European level would be one of monetary targeting as opposed to inflation targeting.

If the various structural money demand relations - although qualitatively different - are nevertheless compared by their adjustment speed, both European relations appear more stable than the German relation. Among the two European data sets, the current-rate specification appears preferable: its money demand relation is also deterministically cointegrated, and its structural adjustment coefficient is surprisingly time-invariant.

7 Conclusions

The purpose of this study, as stated in its title, has been to provide an econometric assessment of money demand in Europe. This assessment concerned two alternative concepts of monetary policy cooperation, namely a hegemonic EMS based on German money demand and a symmetric EMU based on European money demand (chapter 1). The alleged empirical existence of these two money demand relations therefore defined the main problems to be dealt with in this study. These involved, as likewise stated in the title, the problem of econometric modelling and the problem of cross-sectional aggregation.

As a potential lever of monetary policy, European money demand is primarily an econometric problem. Since any empirical evidence decisively depends on the chosen methodological spectacles, this study was throughout concerned with a particularly interesting pair of spectacles, namely the vector-autoregressive model (VAR) and the structural error-correction model (SECM). These models conveniently combine several existing approaches to econometric modelling (chapter 2). They also involve, as a chance as well as a cost, a considerable sophistication of modelling alternatives and inference procedures (chapter 3 and chapter 4).

As a convenient alternative to a set of national money demand relations, European money demand is also an aggregation problem. The theoretical analysis of the transition from a national to an European level required here some extensions to the conventional framework of cross-sectional aggregation theory (chapter 5). In particular, the concept of a quasilinear aggregation structure and the link between aggregation and cointegration had to be considered. Moreover, an excursion into index theory was required for consistent aggregation of European data series from available national indices.

In this section the lessons and conclusions of the preceding theoretical arguments are structured around their performance in an empirical analysis of money demand (chapter 6). This analysis was conducted for Germany and for Europe using quarterly time series over 81:1 - 98:3, namely money (m), prices (p), output (y), and two interest rates (il and is). Two European data sets were constructed, using fixed and current exchange rates to convert national nominal magnitudes into a common denomination (cf section 5.2.2).

The conclusion from chapter 2 is that econometric modelling constitutes a tentative and inevitably theory-guided reconstruction of some unknown data generation process (DGP). The relevant theory enters at two different stages: statistical theory at the transition from sample to population, and economic theory at the transition from population to structure (cf table 2.1). The primary tool in the first stage is the probability model. Its task is not to cast some economic theory into estimable form, but to summarize salient statistical properties of the analyzed data series. For this summary, lack of precise a-priori information about the DGP recommends a general-to-specific modelling strategy: an initial probability model, sufficiently general as to let 'the data speak for themselves', establishes a data-consistent baseline against which subsequent simplifications can be validly tested in order to derive a more specific and (hence) more informative submodel. The second piece of theory in the DGP reconstruction is economic theory. Its indispensability derives from the fact that any statistical submodel constitutes, at best, but the reduced form of some unknown structural economic model. This identification problem likewise plagues the present VAR model, whose decisive cointegration parameters are neither statistically (cf section 2.1.1) nor structurally (cf section 2.2.1) identified without a-priori theory.

As a methodological consequence, money demand is here interpreted as a first of all theoretical idea rather than an empirical truth waiting for estimation. This distinction of theoretical and empirical models (cf section 2.2.2) has serious implications for the intended econometric assessment of money demand. In particular, the empirical existence of money demand is not taken for granted, but instead established through a neutral statistical criterion, namely cointegration. Moreover, it is acknowledged that an empirical model's residuals generally constitute a compound of information losses resulting from model simplification, and hence cannot sustain an interpretation as genuine structural shocks (cf section 2.1.2). The severity of information losses can, however, be mitigated through a careful, statistically valid model reduction procedure.

In the empirical analysis this conclusion motivated the choice of a general 'statistical' VAR model as the basic framework of analysis, instead of the 'economic' single-equation ECM model dominating the literature. With hindsight for good reason: the statistical assumptions underlying the single-equation ECM - in particular that of but one cointegration relation and that of exogenous regressors - are explicitly testable within a VAR. As it turned out, both assumptions were violated for the present data, so that the single-equation ECM could not be reproduced as a statistically valid reduction of the general VAR model (cf table 6.14). This result raises doubts about the common practice of resting empirical evidence on single-equation ECM's. Moreover, and on the constructive side, the economically crucial question of causality between money to prices could be explicitly formulated, among others, as a reduction strategy within present VAR framework (cf table 6.15), which had not been possible in a single-equation ECM.

The conclusion from chapter 3 is that salient dynamic features of macroeconomic data series, namely an intrinsic unforecastability combined with a discernible tendency of synchronized long-run movements, can be adequately captured by autoregressive probability models. Specifically, the general VAR model allows to combine the interesting properties of integration and cointegration with various constellations of deterministic trends. It also allows to separate the long-run behaviour of a multivariate data series from its short-run behaviour within a single closed model, that is, without imposing untested exogeneity restrictions. The truly appealing feature from a methodological point of view, however, is that the VAR model allows to detect interesting long-run 'equilibrium' relations by means of a purely statistical criterion, namely that linear combinations of I(d)-variables be I(d-1). This in turn relieves economic theory from proving the existence of these relations to the more adequate task of their structural interpretation. The empirical distinction of the respective VAR-submodels is, however, a decidedly non-trivial affair. In particular, the multilaterally nested structure of these submodels, and the interaction of stochastic and deterministic trends, require a carefully tailored testing procedure utilizing a wide menu of test statistics and limiting distributions. These statistical difficulties may explain the conspicuous rarity of VAR models in the empirical literature on money demand (cf section 6.1.1 and section 6.2.1).

In the present empirical analysis these inferential difficulties were tackled within a sequential cointegration testing procedure. This procedure allows to simultaneously determine the cointegration rank and the deterministic degree (cf tables 6.4 and 6.11), and to also simultaneously determine the number of I(1)- and I(2)-trends (cf tables 6.7 and 6.13) present in the data. Here the procedure indicated narrow absence of I(2)-trends and distinct presence of two I(1)-trends both for Germany and Europe. This implied a same number of 3 cointegration relations for all data sets, although the resulting VAR submodels differed by their respective deterministic degree. The results were further corroborated by recursive tests on the divergence of the cointegration statistics and on the constancy of the cointegration space. Moreover, to account for the dummies included in the respective initial VAR-models, appropriate critical values were simulated for all cointegration tests.

The conclusion from chapter 4 is that the occurrence of cointegration in a VAR raises some new questions which are also rarely addressed in applied research. These questions concern the statistical model's economic interpretation, which is impeded by the fact that, even under a reparameterization of the VAR into a reduced-form ECM, the estimated cointegration relations lack statistical identification and the embedding ECM equations lack structural identification (section 4.1.2). To introduce economic theory into the statistical model, the cointegrated VAR was here factorized into a conditional and a marginal submodel, and systemwide cointegration relations were distinguished from relations holding only among marginalized variables. These two distinctions then allowed the formulation of additional restrictions carving out an open, and in a well defined sense stable, SECM from the closed VAR. The necessary additional hypotheses comprise testable over-identifying exogeneity and noncausality restrictions which isolate a stable conditional model (section 4.2). The additional hypotheses also comprise suitable just-identifying restrictions which isolate economic adjustment equations for individual variables within the conditional model (section 4.1).

In the empirical analysis, this conclusion motivated a systematic testing scheme searching for data-acceptable noncausality restrictions. It emerged that noncausality, often but casually postulated by economic theory, is an extremely tough restriction for actual data series. The statistical tests (cf table 6.15) here indicated an interesting reversal of causality in the transition from the national to an aggregate level: in the recommended CVAR for Germany, causation runs from the variables $[p, y, is]$ to the variables $[m, il]$, whereas in the recommended CVAR's for Europe this direction is just the opposite. This result nicely fits into the economic motivation given in section 1.1. It suggests an inability of German money demand to anchor nominal prices, and recommends a shift of this task onto an European level. On this level, the result recommends a policy of monetary targeting as opposed to inflation targeting for the European Central Bank.

To add to these qualitative differences, the CVAR obtained for Germany contained but a single systemwide cointegration relation, whereas the CVAR's obtained for Europe accommodated all three original relations. From these systemwide cointegration relations, a meaningful money demand relation was subsequently isolated, along with an IS-curve and a Central-Bank reaction function, for each data set via suitable long-run identification schemes. In a second step, the empirical response of the conditioned variables (money m for Germany, prices p for Europe) to the implied structural disequilibrium between its actual and its target value was isolated through a short-run identification scheme. Both schemes together turned the empirical CVAR's into proper SECM's (cf table 6.16).

The conclusion from chapter 5 is that the alleged effects of aggregating several national money demand relations into a single European relation are difficult enough to disentangle even in an idealized theoretical setting. The reason is that the nature and the occurrence of aggregation effects crucially depend on the chosen aggregation structure. The observable reluctance in much of the literature to exactly specify the aggregation structure in which alleged aggregation effects are supposed to occur may help explain a certain fuzziness about the existence and properties of 'the' European money demand relation. Here two precisely defined aggregation structures involving linear and quasilinear aggregation rules were considered (section 5.1.1 and section 5.1.2). The concept of an aggregation structure immediately showed that, in contrast to widespread presupposition, no such thing as 'the' European money demand relation exists. Rather, two such relations actually exist, namely a principal relation and a surrogate relation. The properties of these aggregate relations depend on the chosen aggregation rules. An aggregation loss is not necessary under linear aggregation, but inevitable under quasilinear aggregation. Conversely, a portfolio gain is not reasonable under linear aggregation, but very likely under quasilinear aggregation. The portfolio gain directly competes with the aggregation loss in its effect on the innovation-variance of the derived surrogate relation.

However, an attempt to disentangle these properties also in the empirical analysis faced the methodological problem that empirical relations defined on some data set do not necessarily correspond to autonomous theoretical relations defined in an aggregation structure (cf section 2.1.1). Nevertheless, much of the outlined aggregation theory turned out to deliver implications also for the statistical property of cointegration: given its existence on the respective national levels, this property could be shown to carry through to the European level under conditions resembling those for consistent aggregation (section 5.1.3). Therefore tests for cointegration in aggregated data can actually be interpreted as tests for what in the idealized setting of aggregation theory is called a zero aggregation loss. This point seems completely overlooked in the empirical literature on European money demand, where (in the tradition of conventional aggregation theory) cointegration and consistent aggregation are always treated as independent problems.

In this respect the empirical occurrence of cointegration in the European data set (section 6.2) constitutes a surprising but encouraging result. In the light of aggregation theory, this result evidences an internationalization either in the behaviour of national macroeconomic variables (compositional stability) or in the parameters of national cointegration relations (micro homogeneity). Given that micro homogeneity across 10 countries seems a fairly tough restriction on a 3-dimensional cointegration space, one might well conclude that national macroeconomic variables indeed synchronized as a result of European integration. In terms of economic theory, this implies an existence of cross-country parities including purchasing power parity, interest rate parity, and some productivity parity. In terms of aggregation theory, compositional stability implies a stationary aggregation error and hence a time-invariant rather than a time-dependent aggregation loss (cf section 5.1.3). This implication is supported by the recursive estimates of the structural ECM adjustment coefficients shown in figure 6.10: a time-invariant aggregation loss implies a time-invariant macro variance and hence, via (5.12), also a time-invariant adjustment coefficient. And exactly this time-invariance is revealed by the recursive estimates in figure 6.10.

As to the European data themselves, a consistency result from index number theory justifies the construction of European price- and quantity indices from available national Paasche- and Laspeyres indices (section 5.2.2).

In summary, this study addressed a number of shortcomings in the present empirical literature on money demand in Europe. These shortcomings concern, first, the choice of an initial probability model. Few empirical studies employ the multivariate VAR model and no study employs a statistically consistent testing procedure covering deterministic trends or stochastic I(2) trends. Given that the VAR model is a demanding but otherwise well developed generalization of the popular single-equation ECM, its conspicuous rarity in the empirical literature appears somewhat surprising. The second shortcoming concerns the economic interpretation of estimated cointegration relations and conditional models, whose lack of statistical and structural identification goes mainly unnoticed. Therefore in this study the innovative model class of structural error-correction models (SECM's) was detailed as an extension of the cointegrated VAR model, and tried on actual data series for Germany and Europe. The third shortcoming in the empirical literature involves its observable reluctance to clarify the relevant aggregation theory. Therefore this study employed a consistent framework to compare the consequences of linear and quasilinear aggregation, to explore the link between aggregation and cointegration, and to consistently aggregate European variables from available national indices.

The properties of the derived empirical money demand relations, identified in structural conditional models for the German and European data sets, were finally compared by several statistical stability criteria (section 6.3.3). The corresponding structural adjustment coefficients were significant in all three cases. Judging from the numerical values of the adjustment coefficients and the corresponding disequilibrium-variances, the European relations appeared more stable than the German relation. Among the European relations, the version using fixed conversion rates appeared slightly more stable, whereas the version using current conversion rates appeared statistically better behaved. Indeed, recursive estimation of the structural adjustment coefficients revealed an almost perfect time-invariance of the parameter obtained from current-rate conversion (figure 6.10).

Irrespective of the specific reason for these results, the truly important conclusion however is that for both versions of the European data a dynamic money demand relation could be isolated which is (i) data-consistent via cointegration, (ii) time-invariant in recursive constancy tests, (ii) reasonably stable in a SECM, (iv) theory-consistent after statistically valid restrictions, and (v) causal for European prices. Although, in terms of the introducing quotation on page 1, these properties might still not reveal all the secrets of some golden rule for the European Central Bank's monetary policy, they seem impressive enough to encourage further torture.

A Technical Appendix

A.1 Expansion of Polynomials

The autoregressive models in chapter 3 rely on roots of their characteristic polynomials to generate certain statistical properties. Precisely, the scalar model (3.1) relies on the roots of the k-th order polynomial $a(z)$, while the vector model (3.15) relies on the roots of the pk-th order polynomial $\det A(z)$. These characteristic polynomials can be expanded around particular roots of interest. The expansions produce reparameterizations of the original model which isolate roots of interest as explicit parameters restrictions. Expansions around unit roots are used here to obtain the reparameterization (3.11) for a scalar model, and the reparameterizations (3.24) and (3.31) for a vector model. These so-called *interim multiplier representations* form the basis for all subsequent unit-root tests. The present appendix details the underlying expansions of the characteristic polynomials. The expansions apply, mutatis mutandis, also to infinite power series, namely to the scalar $c(z)$ defined by (3.5) and the matrix $C(z)$ defined by (3.19).

Scalar Model: Recall the scalar polynomial $a(z)$ and its factorization introduced in (3.2). From the parameters of $a(z)$, two auxiliary polynomials $a^*(z)$ and $a^{**}(z)$ are defined. In total:

$$a(z) = 1 - \sum_{i=1}^{k} a_i\, z^i = \Pi_{i=1}^{k} (1 - l_i^{-1} z)\,, \tag{A.1}$$

$$a^*(z) = \sum_{j=0}^{k-1} a_j^*\, z^j \quad \text{with} \quad a_j^* \equiv -\sum_{i=j+1}^{k} a_i\,, \tag{A.2}$$

$$a^{**}(z) = \sum_{m=0}^{k-2} a_m^{**}\, z^m \quad \text{with} \quad a_m^{**} \equiv \sum_{j=m+1}^{k-1} a_j^*\,. \tag{A.3}$$

Evaluation of the polynomial $a(z)$ at point $z=0$ returns its normalization $a(0) = 1$, and evaluation at $z=1$ the total impact $a(1) = 1 - \Sigma_{i=1}^{k} a_i$. The newly defined polynomials $a^*(z)$ and $a^{**}(z)$ are in fact also linked to their original: the first derivative of $a(z)$ at $z=1$ is given by $a^*(1) = -\Sigma_{i=1}^{k} i\, a_i$ (the mean lag), while the second derivative at this point is similarly given by $a^{**}(1) = \Sigma_{j=1}^{k-1} j\, a_j^* = -\frac{1}{2} \Sigma_{i=2}^{k} (i-1)\, i\, a_i$.

With these definitions in mind the polynomial $a(z)$ can now be partially expanded around $z = 1$ as[1]

$$a(z) = a(1) - (1-z)\,a^*(z) \tag{A.4}$$
$$= a(1) - (1-z)\,a^*(1) + (1-z)^2\,a^{**}(z)\ . \tag{A.5}$$

The scalar numbers $a(1)$ and $a^*(1)$ in this expansion can be related to the roots l_i of the polynomial $a(z)$. This relation provides a useful basis for testing hypotheses about these roots via parameter restrictions.

To derive this relation, note that $a(1) = \Pi_{i=1}^{k}(1-l_i^{-1})$ by virtue of (A.1). In this expression, complex roots occur but in conjugate pairs, as $l_1 = m\,e^{i\varphi}$ and $l_2 = m\,e^{-i\varphi}$ with common modulus $m = |l_i|$. Complex roots therefore enter $a(1)$ only as a product $ccp \equiv (1-l_1^{-1})(1-l_2^{-1}) = (1-\frac{1}{m}e^{-i\varphi})(1-\frac{1}{m}e^{i\varphi}) = 1-\frac{2}{m}\cos\varphi+\frac{1}{m^2}$. For complex roots l_i it thus holds that $0 < ccp < 4$ provided that $|l_i| > 1$. Similarly, for real roots l_i it holds that $0 < (1-l_i^{-1}) < 2$ provided that $|l_i| > 1$. The factorization of $a(1)$ therefore involves only positive factors if all roots of $a(z)$ are outside the unit circle. It follows that $a(1) > 0$ is a necessary condition for stable roots.[2] Conversely, the factorization of $a(1)$ immediately yields $a(1) = 0$ if at least one unit root occurs in $a(z)$. A similar argument applies to the polynomial $a^*(z)$, which inherits the remaining roots from $a(z)$. This gives the following conditions:[3]

$a(1) \neq 0$	*only stable and explosive roots*
$a(1) > 0$	*only stable roots*
$a(1) = 0$	*at least one unit root*
$a(1) = 0,\ a^* < 0$	*one unit root, other roots stable*
$a(1) = 0,\ a^* = 0$	*at least two unit roots*

Using the above expansion of $a(z)$, the general autoregressive model can now be reparameterized so as to transform these expressions into proper parameter restrictions.

[1] From the general geometric series follows $(1-z^i) = (1-z)\,\Sigma_{j=0}^{i-1} z^j$. Therefore $a(z) - a(1) = \Sigma_{i=1}^{k} a_i\,(1-z^i) = (1-z)\ \Sigma_{i=1}^{k} a_i\,\Sigma_{j=0}^{i-1} z^j$. Multiplying out and collecting terms of equal power in z then produces $a(z)-a(1) = (1-z)\,(-1)\,a^*(z)$. The polynomial $a^*(z)$ can be expanded in a similar fashion. The expansions do not depend on the normalization $a(0) = 1$.

[2] Necessary and sufficient conditions for the stability of higher order difference equations exist in two rather complicated forms (Schur's form and Samuelson's form); see for example Gandolfo (1996, Section 7).

[3] Under $a(1) = 0$ the difference equation in levels, $a(L)x_t$, becomes a difference equation in first differences, namely $-a^*(L)\Delta x_t$. The condition $-a^*(1) > 0$ is then necessary for the stability of this equation.

To begin with, exploiting that $a_0^* = a(1) - 1$ the expansion (A.4) gives

$$a(z) \;=\; (1-z) \;+\; a(1)\,z \;-\; (1-z)\sum_{j=1}^{k-1} a_j^*\, z^j \;. \qquad \text{(A.6)}$$

Defining the polynomial $g(L) \equiv 1 - \Sigma_{j=1}^{k-1} a_j^* L^j \;=\; a(1) - a^*(L)$ and the parameter $\pi_1 \equiv -a(1)$ then allows to identically rewrite the general autoregressive model (3.1) as

$$g(L)\,\Delta x_t \;=\; \pi_1\, x_{t-1} \;+\; e_t \;+\; d_t \;. \qquad \text{(A.7)}$$

This alternative representation of the general model allows to formulate the restriction $\pi_1 = 0$ (at least one unit root) against $\pi_1 < 0$ (only stable roots). This is the basis for the unit-root tests in table 3.1. Turning to the I(2)-case, exploiting that $a_0^{**} \;=\; a^*(1) - a_0^*$ the expansion (A.5) gives

$$\begin{aligned} a(z) \;&=\; (1-z)^2 \;+\; a(1)\,z \;+\; [a(1) - a^*(1)]\,z\,(1-z) \qquad \text{(A.8)} \\ &\qquad - (1-z)^2 \sum_{m=1}^{k-2} a_j^{**}\, z^m \;. \end{aligned}$$

Defining the polynomial $g(L) \;\equiv\; 1 - \Sigma_{m=1}^{k-2} a_m^{**} L^m$ and the two parameters $\pi_1 \;\equiv\; -a(1)$ and $\pi_2 \;\equiv\; a^*(1) - a(1)$ then allows to identically rewrite the general autoregressive model (3.1) as

$$g(L)\,\Delta^2 x_t \;=\; \pi_1\, x_{t-1} \;+\; \pi_2\,\Delta x_{t-1} \;+\; e_t \;+\; d_t \;. \qquad \text{(A.9)}$$

This alternative representation of the general model allows to formulate the restriction $\pi_2 = \pi_1 = 0$ (at least two unit roots) against $\pi_2 < \pi_1 = 0$ (exactly one unit root) or against $\pi_2 \in \mathbb{R}$, $\pi_1 < 0$ (only stable roots). This is the basis for the unit root tests in table 3.2.

It is noted that the above expansions neglect other roots of $a(z)$, like seasonal roots on the unit circle. For example, setting and $\pi_1 = 0$ and $\pi_2 = -2$ in an AR(2) model produces $(1-L)(1+L)x_t \;=\; e_t + d_t$, which is an I(1)-sequence with a stochastic two-period cycle. Expansions isolating such other roots of interest are discussed in Burke (1996).

Vector Model: The definitions and expansions in the vector case proceed analogous to those in the scalar case. Recall the $p \times p$ polynomial matrix $A(z)$ defined in (3.16). A general formula for the full expansion of a polynomial matrix around $z = 1$ is given in Davidson (1991, Lemma 2.1). Applied to $A(z)$ this formula produces (A.10) below. In addition, from the parameters of $A(z)$ two auxiliary polynomial matrices $A^*(z)$ and $A^{**}(z)$ are defined in analogy to (A.2) and (A.2). In summary:

$$A(z) \;=\; I - \sum_{i=1}^{k} A_i\, z^i \qquad = \qquad \sum_{i=0}^{k} A^{\{i\}}\,(1-z)^i \;, \qquad \text{(A.10)}$$

$$A^*(z) \;=\; \sum_{j=0}^{k-1} A_j^*\, z^j \qquad \text{with} \qquad A_j^* \;\equiv\; -\sum_{i=j+1}^{k} A_i \;, \qquad \text{(A.11)}$$

$$A^{**}(z) \;=\; \sum_{m=0}^{k-2} A_m^{**}\, z^m \qquad \text{with} \qquad A_m^{**} \;\equiv\; \sum_{j=m+1}^{k-1} A_j^* \;. \qquad \text{(A.12)}$$

Evaluation of the polynomial matrix $A(z)$ at point $z=0$ returns its normalization $A(0)=I$, and evaluation at $z=1$ the total impact $A(1) = I - \Sigma_{i=1}^{k} A_i$. The auxiliary polynomial matrices $A^*(z)$ and $A^{**}(z)$ are again linked to their original: the first derivative of $A(z)$ at $z=1$ is given by the mean lag $A^*(1) = -\Sigma_{i=1}^{k} i\, A_i$, and the second derivative at this point is similarly given by $A^{**}(1) = \Sigma_{j=1}^{k-1} j\, A_j^* = -\frac{1}{2}\Sigma_{i=2}^{k}(i\text{-}1)\, i\, A_i$.

The $p \times p$ parameter matrices $A^{\{i\}}$ in the factorization (A.10) are defined as $A^{\{0\}} \equiv I - \Sigma_{i=1}^{k} A_i$ for the first index, and as $A^{\{i\}} \equiv \Sigma_{m=1}^{i} b_m^i\, A^{(m)}$ for the higher order indices. The latter expression, in turn, is defined using the matrices $A^{(m)} \equiv \Sigma_{i=1}^{k} i^m A_i$ and the recursively constructed constants $b_{m<i}^i \equiv (i\text{-}1) b_m^{i-1} / i - b_{m-1}^{i-1} / i$ and $b_{m=i}^i \equiv (-1)^{i+1} / i!$. Evaluation of these admittedly somewhat cumbersome expressions reveals that $A^{\{0\}} = A(1)$, $A^{\{1\}} = -A^*(1)$, and $A^{\{2\}} = A^{**}(1)$. These relations suggest using the factorization (A.10) for a partial expansion of $A(z)$ around $z=1$. In particular, employing but the first factors in (A.10) and combining the remainder into a suitably defined polynomial matrix gives

$$A(z) = A^{\{0\}} - (1-z)\, A^*(z) \tag{A.13}$$

$$= A^{\{0\}} + (1-z)\, A^{\{1\}} + (1-z)^2 A^{**}(z)\ , \tag{A.14}$$

where $A^*(z) = -\sum_{i=1}^{k} A^{\{i\}}\,(1-z)^{i-1}$ and $A^{**}(z) = \sum_{i=2}^{k} A^{\{i\}}\,(1-z)^{i-2}$ combine the respective higher order factors in (A.10). This expansion, restated in (3.16), is a multivariate version of (A.4) and (A.4). Consequently, there also exist multivariate versions of (A.6) and (A.8), which yield the vector interim multiplier representations (3.24) and (3.31). The latter in turn are the basis for the reduced rank regression models (3.36) and (3.47), respectively.

The characteristic polynomial of the vector model, i.e, the determinant $\det A(z)$, is a pk-th order scalar polynomial in z normalized on $\det A(0) = 1$. The characteristic equation of the system, $\det A(z) = 0$, therefore has pk solutions which are called latent roots of $A(z)$. From the above discussion of scalar polynomials it follows that $\det A(1) = 0$ if at least one latent root is equal to unity, and that $\det A(1) > 0$ if all latent roots are stable. Moreover, the larger $\det A(1)$ the more stable the latent roots. As a convenient way to explicitly calculate these latent roots, the general VAR(k)-model (3.15) is rewritten as a VAR(1), as $w_t = A_c\, w_{t-1}$, using the definitions

$$\underset{pk\times 1}{w_t} = \begin{bmatrix} x_t \\ x_{t-1} \\ \vdots \\ x_{t-k+1} \end{bmatrix} , \qquad \underset{pk\times pk}{A_c} = \begin{bmatrix} A_1 & A_2 & \cdots & A_{k-1} & A_k \\ I & 0 & \cdots & 0 & 0 \\ \vdots & \vdots & \ddots & \vdots & \vdots \\ 0 & 0 & \cdots & I & 0 \end{bmatrix}$$

The matrix A_c is called the *companion matrix* of $A(z)$. The companion matrix satisfies $\det(I - A_c z) = \det A(z)$. Recall that the latent roots of $A(z)$ are defined as the solutions of $\det A(z) = 0$. Therefore the pk eigenvalues of the companion matrix, i.e., the solutions of $\det(A_c - zI) = 0$, equal the reciprocals of the pk latent roots of the polynomial matrix, i.e., the solutions of $\det A(\frac{1}{z}) = 0$. Requiring all latent roots of $A(z)$ to lie *outside* the unit circle is thus equivalent to requiring all eigenvalues of A_c to lie *inside* the unit circle. This condition guarantees the stability of the (discrete linear) system; see Barnett/Storey (1970, p.79). Sometimes the characteristic equation of the system is defined as $\det[Iz^k - A_1 z^{k-1} - \ldots - A_k z^0] = 0$. In this notation the eigenvalues of the companion matrix coincide with the latent roots, and stability results if all latent roots lie inside the unit circle; see Gandolfo (1996, Section 9).

A.2 Granger Representation Theorem

This appendix details the derivation of a multivariate moving-average representation for a cointegrated VAR. The original (and namesaking) derivation of such a representation is given in Engle/Granger (1987) and relies on certain expressions for the determinant and adjoint of singular polynomial matrices. The present derivation follows Johansen (1991). It relies on the expansion of a polynomial matrix $A(z)$ as defined by (A.10) and (A.13) before.

In a first step, the factorization $A(1) = -\alpha\beta'$ motivated in (3.25), and the definitions of generalized inverse and orthogonal complement given in (3.26), are used to define the following polynomial matrix from the original $A(z)$:

$$\bar{A}(z) \equiv \begin{bmatrix} \bar{\alpha}' \\ \alpha_\perp' \end{bmatrix} A(z) \; [\bar{\beta} \,;\, \beta_\perp (1-z)^{-1}]$$

$$= \begin{bmatrix} \bar{\alpha}' A(z)\, \bar{\beta} & \bar{\alpha}' A(z)\, \beta_\perp\, (1-z)^{-1} \\ \alpha_\perp' A(z)\, \bar{\beta} & \alpha_\perp' A(z)\, \beta_\perp\, (1-z)^{-1} \end{bmatrix}$$

Evaluation of this polynomial matrix at $z = 1$ immediately gives

$$\bar{A}(1) = \begin{bmatrix} I & -\bar{\alpha}' A^*(1)\, \beta_\perp \\ 0 & -\alpha_\perp' A^*(1)\, \beta_\perp \end{bmatrix}$$

Taking determinants in the definition and in the evaluation gives

$$\det \bar{A}(z) = \begin{cases} \det[\,\bar{\alpha}\,;\alpha_\perp]' * \det A(z) * \det[\,\bar{\beta}\,;\beta_\perp] * (1-z)^{r-p} \\ \det\,[\alpha_\perp' A^*(1)\, \beta_\perp] * (-1)^p \end{cases}$$

The first line of this expression is nonzero for all $|z| < 1$ since $A(z)$ has no explosive latent roots inside the unit circle (cf assumption 2). The second line in this expression is nonzero if the matrix $\Gamma \equiv \alpha_\perp' A^*(1)\, \beta_\perp$ is nonsingular, that is, if $A^*(z)$ has no unit roots over the null space of $A(z)$. Under this additional condition (cf page 47) the polynomial matrix $\bar{A}(z)$ therefore has only stable latent roots. A vector autoregressive sequence with VAR-operator $\bar{A}(L)$ is then integrated of order zero. This property can now be used to derive certain stationary transformations of the original sequence $A(L)x_t = e_t + d_t$ defined in (3.17).

The stationary transformations of $\{x_t\}$ are conveniently derived from the second identity in (3.26), application of which gives

$$x_t = [\bar{\beta} \,;\, \beta_\perp\, (1-L)^{-1}] \begin{bmatrix} \beta' \\ \bar{\beta}_\perp'(1-L) \end{bmatrix} x_t \;.$$

Inserting this identical decomposition for x_t into the original representation $A(L)x_t = e_t + d_t$, and premultiplying $[\,\bar{\alpha}\,;\alpha_\perp]'$ then gives

$$\bar{A}(L) \begin{bmatrix} \beta' \\ \bar{\beta}'_{\perp}(1-L) \end{bmatrix} x_t = \begin{bmatrix} \bar{\alpha}' \\ \alpha'_{\perp} \end{bmatrix} (e_t + d_t) \ . \tag{A.15}$$

Since $\bar{A}(L)$ contains only stable roots this sequence is integrated of order zero, and can be inverted for a moving average representation:

$$\begin{bmatrix} \beta' \\ \bar{\beta}'_{\perp}(1-L) \end{bmatrix} x_t = \bar{A}(L)^{-1} \begin{bmatrix} \bar{\alpha}' \\ \alpha'_{\perp} \end{bmatrix} (e_t + d_t) \ . \tag{A.16}$$

From this expression it follows immediately that the transformations $\{\beta' x_t\}$ and $\{\bar{\beta}'_{\perp} \Delta x_t\}$, in words: the cointegration relations and the differenced stochastic trends, are integrated of order zero. Differencing the sequence in all directions gives, via premultiplication of $[\bar{\beta}(1-L) \, ; \beta_{\perp}]$ in (A.16), a moving average representation also for the original sequence:

$$\begin{aligned} \Delta x_t &= [\bar{\beta} \, ; (1-L)\beta_{\perp}] \ \bar{A}(L)^{-1} \begin{bmatrix} \bar{\alpha}' \\ \alpha'_{\perp} \end{bmatrix} (e_t + d_t) \\ &\equiv C(L) \, (e_t + d_t) \ . \end{aligned}$$

Evaluation of the moving-average matrix $C(L)$ implicitly defined in this expression allows to express the $p \times p$ long-run impact matrix $C(1)$ in terms of original autoregressive parameters as

$$\begin{aligned} C(1) &= [0 \, ; \beta_{\perp}] \begin{bmatrix} I & -\bar{\alpha}' A^*(1) \, \beta_{\perp} \, (\alpha'_{\perp} A^*(1) \, \beta_{\perp})^{-1} \\ 0 & -(\alpha'_{\perp} A^*(1) \, \beta_{\perp})^{-1} \end{bmatrix} \begin{bmatrix} \bar{\alpha}' \\ \alpha'_{\perp} \end{bmatrix} \\ &= -\beta_{\perp} \, [\alpha'_{\perp} A^*(1) \, \beta_{\perp}]^{-1} \, \alpha'_{\perp} \ . \end{aligned}$$

Considering the nonsingular $p{-}r \times p{-}r$ matrix $\Gamma \equiv \alpha'_{\perp} A^*(1) \, \beta_{\perp}$ immediately reveals that $\operatorname{rk} C(1) = p{-}r$. This was also stated in equation (3.27) in section 3.2.2.

A.3 Concentration of Likelihoodfunction

This appendix details the concentration of the likelihood function for a VAR model. Such concentrations are extensively used within Johansen's maximum likelihood procedure. The present example produces reduced-rank regression implementing the generic over-identifying hypothesis $\mathcal{H}_2(r,i)$ in chapter 4. The reduced-rank regression implementing the just-identifying hypothesis $\mathcal{H}(r,i)$ in chapter 3 emerges as a special case.

Using the data matrices defined for the I(1)-model in section 3.2.3, the Gaussian-normal likelihood function analyzed here is expressed as

$$l\,(\alpha_u, \beta_u\,;\, G, \Omega, \alpha_k, \beta_k) \;=\; -pT/2\,\ln(2\pi) \;-\; T/2\,\ln|\Omega| \;-\; 1/2\,\mathrm{tr}[\,e'\,\Omega^{-1}e\,] \tag{A.17}$$

where the innovation matrix is defined by the following, slightly extended version of the interim multiplier representation (3.24):

$$\underset{p\times T}{e} \;\equiv\; \underset{p\times T}{X_d} \;-\; \alpha_u\,\beta_u'\,\underset{p\times T}{X_l} \;-\; \alpha_k\,\beta_k'\,\underset{p\times T}{X_l} \;-\; G\,\underset{n\times T}{X}\;. \tag{A.18}$$

Besides the data matrices of first differences (X_d), lagged levels (X_l), and lagged first differences (X) this expression includes the parameter matrices G ($p\times n$) for the short-run dynamics and Ω ($p\times p$) for the innovation variance. Moreover, the long-run is governed by a parameter matrix Π_1 which is here already factorized and partitioned as

$$\underset{p\times p}{\Pi_1} \;=\; \underset{p\times r}{\alpha}\;\underset{r\times p}{\beta'} \;=\; \begin{bmatrix} \underset{p\times r_u}{\alpha_u} & \underset{p\times r_k}{\alpha_k} \end{bmatrix} \begin{bmatrix} \underset{r_u\times p}{\beta_u'} \\ \underset{r_k\times p}{\beta_k'} \end{bmatrix}\;.$$

Suppose now that the matrix β_k is known, either by hypothesis or by previous estimation in some switching algorithm. Suppose further that the unknown matrices of interest are α_u and β_u. This suggests to first concentrate the likelihood with respect to the remaining uninteresting parameters G, α_k and Ω. To obtain likelihood-maximizing estimators for them, the derivatives of $l(\cdot)$ with respect to these parameters have to be calculated. For this calculation, the definition $X_d - \alpha_u\beta_u'\,X_l \equiv u$ is introduced to save notation. Using some basic properties of the trace, the last term in (A.17) can be written as

$$\begin{aligned} -\tfrac{1}{2}\mathrm{tr}[e'\,\Omega^{-1}e] \;=\;& \\ &-\tfrac{1}{2}\mathrm{tr}[XX'G'\Omega^{-1}G] \;+\; \mathrm{tr}[X\,u'\Omega^{-1}G] \\ &-\tfrac{1}{2}\mathrm{tr}[\beta_k'X_lX_l'\,\beta_k\alpha_k'\Omega^{-1}\alpha_k] \;+\; \mathrm{tr}[\beta_k'X_l\,u'\Omega^{-1}\alpha_k] \;-\; \mathrm{tr}[\beta_k'X_lX'G'\Omega^{-1}\alpha_k] \\ &-\tfrac{1}{2}\mathrm{tr}[u'\Omega^{-1}u]\;. \end{aligned}$$

Using this expression and some basic rules of matrix differentation gives the following first derivatives of the likelihood function (A.17):

$$\frac{\partial l}{\partial G} = -\tfrac{1}{2}\left\{(\Omega^{-1})'G(XX')'+\Omega^{-1}G\,XX'\right\} + (X\,u'\Omega^{-1})' -(X\,X_l'\beta_k\alpha_k'\Omega^{-1})' = \Omega^{-1}\,e\,X'$$

$$\frac{\partial l}{\partial \alpha_k} = -\tfrac{1}{2}\left\{(\Omega^{-1})'\alpha_k(\beta_k'X_lX_l'\beta_k)'+\Omega^{-1}\alpha_k(\beta_k'X_lX_l'\beta_k)\right\} + (\beta_k'X_l\,u'\Omega^{-1})' - (\beta_k'X_lX'G'\Omega^{-1})' = \Omega^{-1}\,e\,X_l'\beta_k$$

$$\frac{\partial l}{\partial \Omega} = -\tfrac{T}{2}\,(\Omega')^{-1} + \tfrac{1}{2}\,(\Omega^{-1}ee'\Omega^{-1})' = \tfrac{T}{2}\,\Omega^{-1}\left(\tfrac{1}{T}\,ee'\Omega^{-1} - I\right)$$

Using these derivatives, the likelihood function can be maximized with respect to G, α_k and Ω. Setting the respective derivatives equal to zero yields the orthogonality conditions

$$\begin{aligned}
\tfrac{\partial l}{\partial G} = 0 \quad &\Leftrightarrow \quad eX' = 0 \quad \Leftrightarrow \quad G = (u - \alpha_k\,\beta_k'X_l)\,X'\,(XX')^{-1}\\
\tfrac{\partial l}{\partial \alpha_k} = 0 \quad &\Leftrightarrow \quad eX_l'\,\beta_k = 0 \quad \Leftrightarrow \quad \alpha_k = (u - GX)\,X_l'\,\beta_k\,(\beta_k'X_lX_l'\beta_k)^{-1}\\
\tfrac{\partial l}{\partial \Omega} = 0 \quad &\Leftrightarrow \quad \Omega = \tfrac{1}{T}\,ee'
\end{aligned} \tag{A.19}$$

These simultaneous equations determine the likelihood-maximizing values of G, α_k, Ω for any choice of the remaining parameters. To obtain a reduced form, two $T \times T$ projection matrices (P and Q) and several $p \times p$ sample moment matrices (S_{ij} and $S_{ij.u}$) are defined as follows:

$$\begin{aligned}
P &\equiv I - X'(XX')^{-1}X\;,\\
Q &\equiv I - \tfrac{1}{T}P\,X_l'\beta_k\,(\beta_k'X_lPX_l'\beta_k)^{-1}\beta_k'X_l\;,\\
S_{ij} &\equiv \tfrac{1}{T}\,X_iP\,X_j'\;,\\
S_{ij.u} &\equiv \tfrac{1}{T}\,X_iQP\,X_j' = S_{ij} - S_{il}\,\beta_k(\beta_k'S_{ll}\beta_k)^{-1}\beta_k'\,S_{lj}\;.
\end{aligned}$$

The indices $i, j = \{l, d\}$ here denote all possible constellations of X_d and X_l. Note that S_{ll} is symmetric and of full rank, whereas $S_{ll.u}$ is also symmetric but of reduced rank.[4] Note further that the projection matrices are idempotent in that $QPP'Q' = QP = PQ'$. Their mathematical task is to concentrate

[4] Postmultiplying $S_{ll.u}$ by β_k reveals its r_k-dimensional null space and, hence, its reduced rank $p - r_k$.

the model: the matrix P concentrates out the entire short-run, whereas the matrix Q concentrates out the known cointegration relations. Using these matrices now produces, from the likelihood-maximizing value for G in (A.19), the expression

$$u - GX \quad = \quad (u - \alpha_k \beta_k' X_l)\, P \; + \; \alpha_k \beta_k' X_l \quad . \tag{A.20}$$

Inserting this expression into the likelihood-maximizing value for α_k gives a reduced-form expression for this parameter. Inserting the latter back into (A.20) then gives a reduced-form expression for G. Inserting the reduced-form expressions for α_k and G into the definition of e produces $e = uQP$, which finally allows to solve for Ω. In summary, the simultaneous system of derivatives (A.19) produces the following reduced form:

$$\begin{aligned} G &= u\,Q\,X'\,(XX')^{-1} \\ \alpha_k &= u\,P\,X_l'\,\beta_k\,(\beta_k' X_l P X_l' \beta_k)^{-1} \\ \Omega &= \tfrac{1}{T}\,u\,Q P\,u' \quad . \end{aligned} \tag{A.21}$$

Recalling that $u \equiv X_d - \alpha_u \beta_u' X_l$, these expressions maximize the likelihood function for arbitrary values of α_u and β_u. Inserting (A.21) into the orginal likelihood (A.17) therefore produces a concentrated likelihood which depends only on the remaining unknown parameters α_u and β_u , namely

$$l\,(\alpha_u, \beta_u) \quad = \quad -pT/2\,\ln(2\pi) \quad - \quad T/2\,\ln|\Omega| \quad - \quad 1/2\,(Tp) \quad . \tag{A.22}$$

The likelihood depends on the unknown parameters via the covariance matrix Ω. Using the relation $e = uQP$ and the definition $u \equiv X_d - \alpha_u \beta_u' X_l$ this covariance matrix can explicitly be written as

$$\begin{aligned} \Omega &= \tfrac{1}{T}\,e\,e' \; = \; \tfrac{1}{T}\,u\,QP\,u' \\ &= S_{dd.u} - S_{dl.u}(\alpha_u \beta_u')' - \alpha_u \beta_u' \, S_{ld.u} + \alpha_u \beta_u' \, S_{ll.u}(\alpha_u \beta_u')' \; . \end{aligned}$$

Using the definition $u \equiv X_d - \alpha_u \beta_u' X_l$ in the first line of this expression also shows that the innovation matrix in the concentrated likelihood (A.22) is represented by the model

$$X_d Q P \quad = \quad \alpha_u \beta_u' \, X_l Q P \; + \; e \quad , \tag{A.23}$$

which is simply the concentrated version of (A.18). This is also the reduced rank regression (4.20) implementing hypothesis $\mathcal{H}_2(r, i)$ in chapter 4. In the special case $r_k = 0$ the derived data matrices collapse into $Q = I_{T \times T}$ and $S_{ij.u} = S_{ij}$. The estimator for α_k then vanishes so that $\alpha_u \beta_u' = \alpha \beta'$, and the estimators for G and Ω simplify accordingly. The model (A.23) then collapses into the reduced rank regression (3.36) implementing hypothesis $\mathcal{H}(r, i)$ in chapter 3. Its further maximization with respect to α_u and β_u is detailed in section 3.2.3.

A.4 Aggregation of Indices

This appendix details the construction of an European Paasche price index (PPI) from available national indices (PPI_n), leading to equation (5.16) in section 5.2.2. The construction also highlights the consistency-in-aggregation property of this index, which was stated in section 5.2.1.

Let the vectors $\mathbf{p}_t$ and $\mathbf{q}_t$ contain the prices p_t^i (denominated in a common currency) and quantities q_t^i from all transactions $i \in \mathbb{I}$ recorded in Europe within a certain time period. Let similarly the vectors $\mathbf{p}_{nt}$ and $\mathbf{q}_{nt}$ contain the prices (denominated in the common currency) and quantities from the subset of transactions $i \in \mathbb{I}_n$ recorded in the n-th country. Let finally e_n denote the exchange rate converting the respective national currency into the common denomination.

Any Paasche price index can be expressed as a weighted harmonic mean of its constituent price relatives. For the European deflator this gives

$$PPI \;\equiv\; \frac{\mathbf{p}_t\,\mathbf{q}_t}{\mathbf{p}_0\mathbf{q}_t} \;=\; \left(\sum_{i\in\mathbb{I}} \frac{p_0^i\,q_t^i}{\mathbf{p}_t\mathbf{q}_t}\right)^{-1} \;=\; \left(\sum_{i\in\mathbb{I}} w_{it}\,(p_t^i\,/\,p_0^i)^{-1}\right)^{-1} ,$$

where the weight $w_{it} \equiv p_t^i q_t^i \,/\, \mathbf{p}_t\,\mathbf{q}_t$ denotes the current value share of the i-th transaction in European nominal output. To derive an alternative expression of this index in terms of Paasche subindices, these value shares are simply decomposed into, first, the value share of the i-th transaction in national output and, second, the value share of national output in European output. This gives:

$$\sum_{i\in\mathbb{I}} w_{it} \;\equiv\; \sum_{i\in\mathbb{I}} \frac{p_t^i q_t^i}{\mathbf{p}_t\mathbf{q}_t} \;=\; \sum_{n=1}^{N} \frac{\mathbf{p}_{nt}\mathbf{q}_{nt}}{\mathbf{p}_t\mathbf{q}_t} \sum_{i\in\mathbb{I}_n} \frac{p_t^i\,q_t^i}{\mathbf{p}_{nt}\mathbf{q}_{nt}} \;\equiv\; \sum_{n=1}^{N} w_{nt} \sum_{i\in\mathbb{I}_n} w_{it}(n) ,$$

where as defined w_{nt} is the current European value share of national output, and similarly $w_{it}(n)$ the current national value share of the i-th transaction. Using this decomposition the above European deflator can be expressed as

$$\begin{aligned} PPI \;&=\; \left(\sum_{n=1}^{N} w_{nt}\,\frac{e_{n0}}{e_{nt}} \sum_{i\in\mathbb{I}_n} w_{it}(n) \left(\frac{p_t^i}{e_{nt}} \,/\, \frac{p_0^i}{e_{n0}}\right)^{-1}\right)^{-1} \\ &=\; \left(\sum_{n=1}^{N} w_{nt} \left(\frac{e_{nt}}{e_{n0}}\right)^{-1} PPI_n^{-1}\right)^{-1} , \end{aligned}$$

where PPI_n is the national index compiled from national prices denominated in national currency. The two equivalent expressions for PPI depict the consistency-in-aggregation property of the Paasche index: the European deflator can be expressed either directly as a harmonic mean of all European price relatives (weighted by w_{it}), or indirectly as a harmonic mean of converted national price indices (weighted by w_{nt}) which themselves in turn are harmonic means of all national price relatives. In a similar way it can be shown that the European Laspeyres quantity index can be expressed either directly as an arithmetic mean of all European quantity relatives (weighted by w_{i0}), or indirectly as an arithmetic mean of national quantity indices (weighted by w_{n0}).

A.5 Identification of Cointegration Vectors

This appendix checks the identification scheme applied in section 6.3.2 to European cointegration relations for compliance with the generic identification condition (4.11). Specifically, for the present 5 variables $x = [m, p, y, is, il]$ linked by $r = 3$ cointegration relations, the design matrices H_i implementing the identification scheme are given, as in equation (6.3), by

$$H_1 = \begin{bmatrix} -1\,0\,0 \\ 1\,0\,0 \\ 1\,0\,0 \\ 0\,1\,0 \\ 0\,0\,1 \end{bmatrix} , \quad H_2 = \begin{bmatrix} 0\,0\,0 \\ 0\,0\,0 \\ 1\,0\,0 \\ 0\,1\,0 \\ 0\,0\,1 \end{bmatrix} , \quad H_3 = \begin{bmatrix} 0\,0\,0 \\ 1\,0\,0 \\ 0\,0\,0 \\ 0\,1\,0 \\ 0\,0\,1 \end{bmatrix} . \tag{A.24}$$

An identification scheme can alternatively be expressed in terms of restriction matrices R_i which are orthogonal complements to the design matrices such that $R_i' H_i = 0$. The restriction matrices corresponding to (A.24) are

$$R_1' = \begin{bmatrix} 1\,0 & 1\,0\,0 \\ 0\,1 & -1\,0\,0 \end{bmatrix} , \quad R_2' = \begin{bmatrix} 1\,0\,0\,0\,0 \\ 0\,1\,0\,0\,0 \end{bmatrix} , \quad R_3' = \begin{bmatrix} 1\,0\,0\,0\,0 \\ 0\,0\,1\,0\,0 \end{bmatrix} .$$

Each restriction matrix R_i imposes 2 restrictions on the corresponding i-th cointegration vector. The design matrix H_i combines the remaining 3 freely varying parameters φ_i. That is, the i-th structural cointegration vector b_i is required to satisfy $R_i' \, b_i = 0$ or equivalently $b_i = H_i \, \varphi_i$, as stated in condition (4.9). In the present case the matrix H_1 restricts the coefficients on $-m$ and y to equal that on p. The matrix H_2 restricts the coefficients on m and p to zero. The matrix H_3 imposes a similar exclusion restriction on m and y.

In the present case ($r = 3$) the generic identification condition (4.11) requires that $\text{rk}\,(R_i' \, H_{j_1}) \geq 1$ and $\text{rk}\,(R_i' \, [H_{j_1}; H_{j_2}]) \geq 2$ for all possible indices $i \neq j_1 \neq j_2$. Applied to the first of the above restriction matrices, namely R_1, these rank requirements are indeed satisfied:

$$\text{rk}\,(R_1' H_2) = \text{rk} \begin{bmatrix} 1\,0\,0 \\ -1\,0\,0 \end{bmatrix} = 1 \ , \quad \text{rk}\,(R_1' H_3) = \text{rk} \begin{bmatrix} 0\,0\,0 \\ 1\,0\,0 \end{bmatrix} = 1 \ ,$$

$$\text{rk}\,(R_1' [H_2; H_3]) = \text{rk} \begin{bmatrix} 1\,0\,0\,0\,0\,0 \\ -1\,0\,0\,1\,0\,0 \end{bmatrix} = 2 \ ,$$

where $\text{rk}\,(\cdot)$ refers to the row-rank. In a similar fashion the rank requirements for the restriction matrices R_2 and R_3 are satisfied. The restrictions implied by (A.24) are therefore generically identifying. Since precisely $r{-}1 = 2$ restrictions are imposed on each cointegration vector, the restrictions are moreover just-identifying in that their imposition does not change the long-run matrix $\Pi_1 = \alpha\beta'$ and, hence, also not the likelihood function (3.43).

As a simple extension, consider the case of over-identifying restrictions, whose imposition changes the long-run matrix $\Pi_1 = \alpha\beta'$ and hence also the likelihood function (3.43). For example, the additional restriction that the two interest rates enter the first cointegration relation only as a spread $(il - is)$ is here implemented by the matrices

$$R_1' = \begin{bmatrix} 1\,0 & 1\,0\,0 \\ 0\,1 & -1\,0\,0 \\ 0\,0 & 0\,1\,1 \end{bmatrix} \quad , \qquad H_1 = \begin{bmatrix} -1 & 0 \\ 1 & 0 \\ 1 & 0 \\ 0 & 1 \\ 0 & -1 \end{bmatrix} ,$$

leaving the other matrices unaffected. In this case the rank requirements implied by the generic identification condition (4.11) are still satisfied:

$$\mathrm{rk}\,(R_1'H_2) = \mathrm{rk}\begin{bmatrix} 1\,0\,0 \\ -1\,0\,0 \\ 0\,1\,1 \end{bmatrix} = 2 \ , \quad \mathrm{rk}\,(R_1'H_3) = \mathrm{rk}\begin{bmatrix} 0\,0\,0 \\ 1\,0\,0 \\ 0\,1\,1 \end{bmatrix} = 2 \ ,$$

$$\mathrm{rk}\,(R_1'[H_2;H_3]) = \mathrm{rk}\begin{bmatrix} 1\,0\,0\,0\,0\,0 \\ -1\,0\,0\,1\,0\,0 \\ 0\,1\,1\,0\,1\,1 \end{bmatrix} = 3 \ .$$

The modified identification scheme thus imposes a total of $r(r-1)$ just-identifying and 1 over-identifying restrictions.

As another extension, consider the case where the same restriction is imposed on all cointegration relations, i.e., on the whole cointegration space. This modification renders the design matrices H_i, and consequently also the restriction matrices R_i, plainly identical over $i = 1, ..., r$. For example, the restriction that in all cointegration relations the interest rates enter but as a spread $(il - is)$, and that similarly money and prices enter but as real money $(m - p)$, is here implemented by the matrices

$$H_i = H = \begin{bmatrix} -1\,0 & 0 \\ 1\,0 & 0 \\ 0\,1 & 0 \\ 0\,0 & 1 \\ 0\,0 & -1 \end{bmatrix} \quad , \qquad R_i' = R' = \begin{bmatrix} 1\,1\,0\,0\,0 \\ 0\,0\,0\,1\,1 \end{bmatrix} \ ,$$

for all indices $i = 1, 2, 3$. In this case of identical design matrices H_i the generic identification condition (4.11) clearly fails. The reason is that the imposed restrictions are simply not just-identifying since they cannot uniquely distinguish the individual cointegration relations. However, since the cointegration space as a whole is nevertheless affected these restrictions are over-identifying in that their imposition changes the long-run matrix $\Pi_1 = \alpha\beta'$, and hence also the likelihood function (3.43). As a result, one arrives at the over-identifying hypothesis $\mathcal{H}_1(r, i)$, which is formulated by (4.17) and tested by (4.18) in section 4.2.

A.6 Invalid SECM for Germany

To illustrate the qualitative differences between German and European money demand, the particular just- and overidentifying restrictions structuralizing the European data in table 6.16 are in this appendix *imposed* onto the German data. The resulting SECM is statistically not valid, but serves an useful illustrative purpose.

Conditioned Variables	$\hat{a}$			$\hat{b}'$					$W(\hat{\delta}_i)$
				m	p	y	is	il	
Germany									
Δp	0.01	*	*	−1	1	1	0.195	−0.125	4.7
Δy	*	−0.01	*	*	*	1	−0.500	0.334	1.0
$\Delta$is	*	*	−0.24	*	−2.57	*	1	−0.685	11.8

Critical value (5%) of Wald-statistic $W(\hat{\delta}_i)$ is 14.4 (Boswijk 1994, Table B.2).

Table A.1. Invalid Structural ECM for Germany

In terms of economic interpretability, the equilibrium relations for Δp (money demand) and for Δy (the IS-curve) in this SECM are not entirely implausible: the long-run coefficients all have economically 'correct' signs, even though the interest rate elasticities are fairly high. However, the response of the conditioned variables to these structural relations is simply negligible, as evidenced by the low adjustment coefficients and the insignificant Wald statistics. Rather, these statistics imply that the underlying CVAR for the conditioned variables $y = [p, y, is]$ is dynamically unstable. As a complement result, the likelihood ratio testing weak exogeneity of $z = [m, il]$ for the parameters $\hat{a}$ and $\hat{b}$ is given by $\chi^2(6) = 37.3$, which decidedly rejects the null. In summary, the identification scheme which worked well for the European data is simply invalid for the German data.

A.7 Data Sources

This appendix details the data set for the empirical analysis in chapter 6. The data set includes national time series for Austria, Belgium/Luxemburg, Denmark, France, Germany, Ireland, Italy, Netherlands, Spain, and Portugal (Euro10). For each country, the data set includes quarterly time series on narrow and broad money, nominal and real output, a short-maturity and long-maturity interest rate, and the national exchange rate to the US-Dollar.

Pending on data availability, output is measured by either GDP or GNP. The short-term interest rate is usually some 1- to 3-month money market rate, and the long-term interest rate a 5- to 10-year government bond yield. Narrow money comprises currency outside banks plus sight deposits, whereas broad money comprises narrow money plus time- and savings-deposits plus similar short-term liabilities of commercial banks. It is noted that the definitions of money are not necessarily cross-country consistent in that they may either exclude or double-count cross border deposits (CBD's). This problem is discussed in section 5.2.2, but it appears that the impact of CBD's is empirically negligible.

The raw data were taken from the International Financial Statistics (IFS) database at the International Monetary Fund, Washington, from the Main Economic Indicators (MEI) database at the Organization for Economic Co-operation and Development, Paris, and from the National Accounts database at the Deutsches Institut für Wirtschaftsforschung (DIW), Berlin. The data series for Germany (cf section 6.1) are summarized in the following table:

Variable	Data Series	Description
Money	IFS, Series 134_39mcc	Broad money M3, national definition
	IFS, Series 134_34b	Narrow money, IMF definition
Output	DIW, Series WH31016B	GNP in current prices (West)
	DIW, Series GH31016B	GNP in current prices (Unified)
	DIW, Series WH12012B	GNP in 1991 prices (West)
	DIW, Series GH12012B	GNP in 1991 prices (Unified)
Long Rate	IFS, Series 134_61	Government Bond Yield
Short Rate	IFS, Series 134_60b	Money Market Rate

Table A.2. Data Series for Germany

The raw data series on money from the IFS database date the German reunification break at 91:1. To reconcile the break with history it is here shifted back to 90:3. The missing entries for 90:3 and 90:4 for unified Germany calculated from data published in the Bundesbank's Monthly Reports.

The data series for Europe (cf section 6.2) are summarized in the following table:

Variable	Data Series	Countries
Broad Money	IFS, Series ***_39mcc MEI, Series ***_4831	France, Germany, Netherlands, Portugal Austria, Belgium, Denmark, Ireland, Italy, Spain
Narrow Money	IFS, Series ***_34b IFS, Series ***_39mac	Euro10 except France France
Real Output	IFS, Series ***_99br MEI, Series ***_0031 Other	France, Italy, Netherlands Austria, Denmark, Portugal, Spain Belgium (n.a.) Germany (DIW), Ireland (n.a.)
Nom. Output	IFS, Series ***_99bc MEI, Series ***_0030 Other	France, Italy, Netherlands Austria, Denmark, Portugal, Spain Belgium (n.a.) Germany (DIW), Ireland (n.a.)
Long Rate	IFS, Series ***_61	Euro10
Short Rate	IFS, Series ***_60b	Euro10
US$-Rate	IFS, Series ***_rf	Euro10

The wildcards (***) in the series-labels denote the respective country code.

Table A.3. Data Series for Europe

As reflected by these diverse data sources, the data quality in the IFS and the MEI databases is surprisingly poor. The most disappointing examples are Belgium and Ireland, where quarterly output series were not available at all, and Austria, where this series was not available over 96:1 to 98:3. The same problem was encountered by Kremers/Lane (1990). Following their solution, the quarterly index of industrial production (IFS, Series ***_66b) is therefore used to interpolate the available yearly series on real output. The quarterly consumer price index (IFS, Series ***_64) is then used to represent the deflator of nominal to real output. Quarterly series on real output were also incomplete for Portugal, where the IFS-series had to be used until 87:4 and the MEI-series from 88:1 onwards. Similarly, the series on broad money for Denmark was partially empty, so that narrow money (IFS, Series ***_34b) plus quasi-money (IFS, Series ***_35) had to be used to interpolate the missing values.

The raw series referenced in tables A.2 and A.3 were, if necessary, adjusted or rescaled to achieve standardized dimensions. In particular, money is here measured by quarterly average stocks in billions [10^9] of national currency. Output is measured by quarterly flows, multiplied by 4, in billions of national currency. Real output is always expressed in 1979-prices, so that the ratio of nominal to real output produces a quarterly Paasche price index (deflator) whose average over 1979 equals 100. The interest rates are measured by quarterly average returns annualized as percents per year. The US-Dollar exchange rate is simply a quarterly average of daily market rates. The implied cross-rates to the Deutsche Mark are used to convert all national series on money and nominal output into a common denomination (compare equations (5.14) and (5.15) in section 5.2.2). Graphs of the resulting standardized data series are given in chapter 5 (figure 5.5 and figure 5.6) and in chapter 6 (figure 6.1 and figure 6.5).

List of Abbreviations

Abbreviations defined in the text:

ADF	page 36	Augmented Dickey-Fuller
ADL	page 64	Autoregressive Distributed Lag model
AR	page 29	scalar AutoRegressive model
CBD	page 106	Cross Border Deposits
CBT	page 107	Cross Border Transactions
CVAR	page 63	Conditional Vector AutoRegressive model
DGP	page 13	Data Generation Process
ECM	page 46	Error Correction Model
GNC	page 75	Granger NonCausality in the long run
GUM	page 26	General Unrestricted Model
ID	page 121	Impulse Dummy
LQI	page 106	Laspeyres Quantity Index
MA	page 32	Moving Average model
ME	page 55	Maximal Eigenvalue statistic
PPI	page 106	Paasche Price Index
SECM	page 70	Structural Error Correction Model
SGM	page 15	Statistical Generating Mechanism
TR	page 55	TRace statistic
VAR	page 41	Vector AutoRegressive model

Other abbreviations:

ARCH	AutoRegressive Conditional Heteroscedasticity
ARIMA	AutoRegressive Integrated Moving Average
CPI	Consumer Price Index
CV	Critical Value

DM	Deutsche Mark
ECB	European Central Bank
ECU	European Currency Unit
EMS	European Monetary System
EMU	European Monetary Union
ERM	Exchange Rate Mechanism
EU	European Union
GDP	Gross Domestic Product
GLS	Generalized Least Squares
GNP	Gross National Product
LM	Lagrange Multiplier test
OLS	Ordinary Least Squares
PPP	Purchasing Power Parity
SR	Short Run
SURE	Seemingly Unrelated Regression Equations

List of Mathematical Symbols

α, a	Matrix of Adjustment-Coefficients (statistical, structural)
adj M	Adjoint matrix of a square matrix M
β, b	Matrix of Cointegration-Vectors (statistical, structural)
Δ	Difference operator
diag$(\cdot)$	Diagonal matrix operator
det M	Determinant of a square matrix M
$Cov_N[\cdot,\cdot]$	Covariance w.r.t. Normal distribution $N(\cdot)$
d, $\hat{d}$	Order of integration (true, estimated)
$E_F[\cdot]$	Expectation w.r.t. some distribution $F(\cdot)$
$E_H[\cdot]$	Expectation w.r.t. Haavelmo distribution $H(\cdot)$
$E_N[\cdot]$	Expectation w.r.t. Normal distribution $N(\cdot)$
$E[\cdot \mid \mathcal{I}]$	Expectation conditioned on σ-field $\mathcal{I} \subset \mathcal{F}$
$I(d)$	Integration of order d
λ	Sample eigenvalue from reduced rank regression
L	Lag operator $Lx_t = x_{t-1}$
$M_{p\times r}$	Any matrix M having p rows and r columns
M_{ij}	Element in i-th row and j-th column of matrix M
$n_x(x_t \mid \cdot)$	Conditional Normal density of random variable x_t
$n_T(X_1^T)$	Joint Normal density of random variables $x_1, ..., x_T$
$o_p(\cdot)$	Order in probability for stochastic convergence
r, $\hat{r}$	Rank of cointegration (true, estimated)
rk M	Rank of a square matrix M
$\sigma(X_1^T)$	σ-field generated by random variables $x_1, ..., x_T$ in event space
$V_N[\cdot]$	Variance w.r.t. Normal distribution $N(\cdot)$
$V[\cdot \mid \mathcal{I}]$	Variance conditioned on σ-field $\mathcal{I} \subset \mathcal{F}$
$x_t \sim I(d)$	Stochastic sequence $\{x_t \,;\, t \in \mathbb{Z}\}$ integrated of order d
X_{t-k}^{t-1}	Sample of random variables $x_{t-k}, ..., x_{t-1}$

References

1. **Aigner, D.; Goldfeld, S. (1974):** 'Estimation and Prediction from Aggregate Data when Aggregates are measured more accurately than their Components', *Econometrica*, 42, 113-134.
2. **Aldrich, J. (1994):** 'Haavelmo's Identification Theory', *Econometric Theory*, 10, 198-219.
3. **Alogoskoufis, G.; Smith, R. (1991):** 'On Error-Correction Models: Specification, Interpretation, Estimation', *Journal of Economic Surveys*, 5, 97-128.
4. **Anderson, T. (1984):** *An Introduction to Multivariate Statistical Analysis.* Wiley & Sons, New York.
5. **Angeloni, I.; Cottarelli, C.; Levy, A. (1994):** 'Cross-Border Deposits, Aggregation, and Money Demand in Transition to EMU', *Journal of Policy Modeling*, 16, 27-54.
6. **Arnold, I. (1992):** 'The Derivation of the Liquidity Ratio in the EMS', *IMF Staff Papers*, 39, 195-202.
7. **Artis, M. (1996):** 'Currency Substitution in European Financial Markets', Ch.8, 139-154, in Mızen, P.; Pentecost, E. (Eds.): *The Macroeconomics of International Currencies*, Edward Elgar, Cheltenham.
8. **Artis, M.; Bladen-Hovell, R.; Zhang, W. (1993):** 'A European Money Demand Function', Ch.9, 240-263, in Masson, P.; Taylor, M. (Eds.): *Policy Issues in the Operation of Currency Unions*, Cambridge University Press, Cambridge.
9. **Balk, B. (1989):** 'On van Ijzeren's Approach to International Comparisons and its Properties, *Statistical Papers*, 30, 295-315.
10. **Balk, B. (1995):** 'Axiomatic Price Index Theory: A Survey', *International Statistical Review*, 63, 69-93.
11. **Banerjee, A.; Dolado, J.; Galbraith, J.; Hendry, D. (1993):** *Cointegration, Error-Correction, and the Econometric Analysis of non-stationary Data.* Oxford University Press, Oxford.
12. **Banerjee, A.; Dolado, J.; Mestre, R. (1998):** 'Error-Correction Mechanism Tests for Cointegration in a Single-Equation Framework', *Journal of Time Series Analysis*, 19, 267-283.
13. **Bank of England (1997):** 'The Information in Money', *Bank of England Quarterly Bulletin*, 37, 174-180.
14. **Bank of England (1999):** 'The Transmission Mechanism of Monetary Policy', *Bank of England Quarterly Bulletin*, 39, 161-170.
15. **Barndorff-Nielsen, O. (1978):** *Information and Exponential Families.* John Wiley, Chichester.
16. **Barnett, S.; Storey, C. (1970):** *Matrix Methods in Stability Theory.* Barnes & Noble, New York.

17. **Barr, D. (1992):** 'The Demand for Money in Europe', *IMF Staff Papers*, 39, 718-729.
18. **Beveridge, S.; Nelson, C. (1981):** 'A new Approach to Decomposition of economic Time Series into Permanent and Transitory Components with particular Attention to Measurement of the Business Cycle', *Journal of Monetary Economics*, 7, 151-174.
19. **Bayoumi, T.; Kenen, P. (1993):** 'How useful is an EC-wide Monetary Aggregate as an Intermediate Target for Europe?', *Review of International Economics*, 1, 209-220.
20. **Beyer, A. (1998):** 'Modelling Money Demand in Germany', *Journal of Applied Econometrics*, 13, 57-76.
21. **Bini-Smaghi, L.; Vori, S. (1991):** 'Currency Substitution, Monetary Stability and European Monetary Unification', *Rivista Internazionale di Scienze Sociali*, 37, 45- 68.
22. **Blough, S. (1992):** 'The Relationship between Power and Level for Generic Unit Root Tests in Finite Samples', *Journal of Applied Econometrics*, 7, 295-308.
23. **Boswijk, H. (1994):** 'Testing for an unstable root in Conditional and Structural Error Correction Models', *Journal of Econometrics*, 63, 37-60.
24. **Boswijk, H. (1995):** 'Efficient inference on cointegration parameters in Structural Error Correction Models', *Journal of Econometrics*, 69, 133-158.
25. **Box, G.; Jenkins, G. (1976):** *Time Series Analysis.* Holden-Day, Oakland.
26. **Breusch, T.; Pagan, A. (1980):** 'The Lagrange Multiplier Test and its Applications to Model Specification in Econometrics', *Review of Economic Studies*, 47, 239-253.
27. **Brillinger, D. (1975):** *Time Series.* Holt, Rinehart & Winston, New York.
28. **Brunner, K. (1984):** 'Monetary Policy and Monetary Order', *Aussenwirtschaft*, 39, 187-206.
29. **Bundesbank (1992):** 'Zum Zusammenhang zwischen Geldmengen- und Preisentwicklung in der Bundesrepublik Deutschland', *Monatsberichte der Deutschen Bundesbank*, 44, Nr.1, 20-29.
30. **Bundesbank (1997):** 'Überprüfung des Geldmengenziels', *Monatsberichte der Deutschen Bundesbank*, 49, Nr.8, 17-32.
31. **Bundesbank (1998):** 'Geldpolitische Strategien in den Ländern der Europäischen Union', *Monatsberichte der Deutschen Bundesbank*, 50, Nr.1, 33-47.
32. **Burke, S. (1996):** 'Some Reparameterizations of Lag Polynomials for Dynamic Analysis', *Oxford Bulletin of Economics and Statistics*, 58, 372-389.
33. **Campos, J.; Ericsson, N.; Hendry, D. (1996):** 'Cointegration Tests in the Presence of Structural Breaks', *Journal of Econometrics*, 70, 187-220.
34. **Cassard, M.; Lane, T.; Masson, P. (1994):** 'ERM Money Supplies and the Transition to EMU', *IMF Working Paper*, No 94/1.
35. **Cassard, M.; Lane, T.; Masson, P. (1997):** 'Core ERM Money Demand and Effects on Inflation', *The Manchester School*, 65, 1-24.
36. **Chan, N. (1989):** 'Asymptotic Inference for Unstable Autoregressive Time Series with Drifts', *Journal of Statistical Planning and Inference*, 23, 301-312.
37. **Chan, N.; Wei, C. (1988):** 'Limiting Distributions of Least Squares Estimates of Unstable Autoregressive Processes', *The Annals of Statistics*, 16, 367-401.

38. **Cheung, Y.; Lai, K. (1993):** 'Finite-Sample Sizes of Johansen's Likelihood Ratio Test for Cointegration, *Oxford Bulletin of Economics and Statistics*, 55, 313-328.
39. **Cheung, Y.; Lai, K. (1995a):** 'Lag Order and Critical Values of the Augmented Dickey-Fuller Test', *Journal of Business and Economic Statistics*, 13, 277-280.
40. **Cheung, Y.; Lai, K. (1995b):** 'Lag Order and Critical Values of a Modified Dickey-Fuller Test', *Oxford Bulletin of Economics and Statistics*, 57, 411-419.
41. **Chipman, J. (1975):** 'The Aggregation Problem in Econometrics', *Advances in Applied Probability*, 7 (Supplement), 72-83.
42. **Choi, I. (1993):** 'Asymptotic Normality of the Least Squares Estimates for Higher Order Autoregressive Integrated Processes with some Applications', *Econometric Theory*, 9, 264-282.
43. **Claassen, E. (1977):** 'Weltinflation bei flexiblen Wechselkursen', *Kredit und Kapital*, 10, 18-43.
44. **Clements, M.; Mizon, G. (1991):** 'Empirical Analyis of Macroeconomic Time Series', *European Economic Review*, 35, 887-932.
45. **Cochrane, J. (1991):** 'A Critique of the Application of Unit Root Tests', *Journal of Economic Dynamics and Control*, 15, 275-284.
46. **Cook, S.; Hendry, D. (1994):** 'The Theory of Reduction in Econometrics', *Poznan Studies in the Philosphy of the Sciences and the Humanities*, 38, 71-100.
47. **Cooley, T.; LeRoy, S. (1981):** 'Identification and Estimation of Money Demand', *American Economic Review*, 71, 825-844.
48. **Cuthbertson, K.; Taylor, M. (1992):** 'A Comparison of the Rational Expectations and the General-to-Specific Approaches to Modelling the Demand for M1', *The Manchester School*, 60, 1-22.
49. **Davidson, J. (1991):** 'The Cointegration Properties of Vector Autoregression Models', *Journal of Time Series Analysis*, 12, 41-62.
50. **Davidson, J. (1994):** *Stochastic Limit Theory.* Oxford University Press, Oxford.
51. **Davidson, J.; Hendry, D.; Srba, F.; Yeo, S. (1978):** 'Econometric Modelling of the aggregate Time-Series Relationship between Consumers Expenditure and Income in the United Kingdom', *The Economic Journal*, 88, 661-692.
52. **Davidson, J.; Hall, S. (1991):** 'Cointegration in Recursive Systems', *Economic Journal,* 101, 239-251.
53. **Dickey, D.; Fuller, W. (1979):** 'Distribution of the Estimators for Autoregressive Time Series with a Unit Root', *Journal of the American Statistical Association*, 74, 427-431.
54. **Dickey, D.; Fuller, W. (1981):** 'Likelihood Ratio Statistics for Autoregressive Time Series with a Unit Root', *Econometrica*, 49, 1057-1071.
55. **Dickey, D.; Pantula, S. (1987):** 'Determining the Order of Differencing in Autoregressive Processes', *Journal of Business and Economic Statistics*, 5, 455-461.
56. **Diewert, W. (1995):** 'Axiomatic and Economic Approaches to Elementary Price Indices', *NBER Working Paper* No. 5104.
57. **Doan, T. (1995):** *Users Manual RATS for Windows.* Estima, Evanstown.
58. **Doornik, J. (1998):** 'Approximations to the Asymptotic Distributions of Cointegration Tests', *Journal of Economic Surveys,* 12, 573-593.

59. **Doornik, J.; Hendry, D. (1997):** *Modelling Dynamic Systems using Pc-Fiml for Windows.* International Thomson Business Press, London.
60. **Eichengreen, B. (1997):** *European Monetary Unification: Theory, Practice, and Analysis.* MIT Press, Cambridge (Mass.).
61. **Eichhorn, W. (1978):** *Functional Equations in Economics.* Addison-Wesley, Reading Mass..
62. **Elliot, G.; Rothenberg, T.; Stock, J. (1996):** 'Efficient Tests for an Autoregressive Unit Root', *Econometrica,* 64, 813-836.
63. **Engle, R.; Granger, C. (1987):** 'Co-Integration and Error Correction: Representation, Estimation, and Testing', *Econometrica,* 55, 251-276.
64. **Engle, R.; Hendry, D.; Richard, J. (1983):** 'Exogeneity', *Econometrica,* 51, 277-304.
65. **Engsted, T; Haldrup, N. (1997):** 'Money Demand, Adjustment Costs, and Forward Looking Behavior', *Journal of Policy Modeling,* 19, 153-173.
66. **Ericsson, N. (1995):** 'Conditional and Structural Error Correction Models', *Journal of Econometrics,* 69, 159-171.
67. **Ericsson, N. (1998):** 'Empirical Modeling of Money Demand', *Empirical Economics,* 23, 295-315.
68. **Ericsson, N.; Hendry, D.; Tran, H. (1994):** 'Cointegration, Seasonality, Encompassing, and the Demand for Money in the U.K.', Ch.7, 179-224, in Hargreaves, C. (Ed.): *Nonstationary Time Series Analysis and Cointegration,* Oxford University Press, Oxford.
69. **European Central Bank (1999a):** 'The stability-oriented Monetary Policy Strategy of the Eurosystem', *Monthly Bulletin,* 1, Nr.1, 43-56.
70. **European Central Bank (1999b):** 'Euro-area Monetary Aggregates and their Role in the Eurosystem's Monetary Policy Strategy', *Monthly Bulletin,* 1, Nr.2, 29-46.
71. **Fagan, G.; Henry, J. (1998):** 'Long Run Money Demand in the EU: Evidence for Area-wide Aggregates', *Empirical Economics,* 23, 483-506.
72. **Falk, M.; Funke, N. (1995):** 'The Stability of Money Demand in Germany and in the EMS: Impact of German Unification', *Weltwirtschaftliches Archiv,* 131, 470-488.
73. **Florens, J.; Mouchart, M.; Rolin, J. (1993):** 'Noncausality and Marginalization of Markov Processes', *Econometric Theory,* 9, 241-262.
74. **Forni, M.; Lippi, M. (1997):** *Aggregation and the Microfoundations of Dynamic Macroeconomics.* Clarendon Press, Oxford.
75. **Frazer, R.; Duncan, W.; Collar, A. (1965):** *Elementary Matrices.* Cambridge University Press, Cambridge.
76. **Frowen, S.; Kouris, G. (1977):** 'The Existence of a World Demand for Money Function: Preliminary Results', *Kredit und Kapital,* 10, 1-16.
77. **Fuller, W. (1976):** *Introduction to Statistical Time Series.* John Wiley, New York.
78. **Fuller, W.; Hasza, D.; Goebel, J. (1981):** 'Estimation of the Parameters of Stochastic Difference Equations', *The Annals of Statistics,* 9, 531-543.
79. **Funke, M. (1991):** 'The Stability of the Demand for Money Function in Germany: Myth or Reality?', *Zeitschrift für Wirtschafts- und Sozialwissenschaften,* 116, 185-198.
80. **Gandolfo, G. (1996):** *Economic Dynamics.* 3rd Edition. Springer, Berlin.

81. **Gerdesmeier, D. (1996):** 'Die Rolle des Vermögens in der Geldnachfrage', *Volkswirtschaftliche Forschungsgruppe der Deutschen Bundesbank*, Diskussionspapier 5/96.
82. **Gihman, I.; Skorohod, A. (1974):** *The Theory of Stochastic Processes I.* Springer Verlag, Berlin.
83. **Gilbert, C. (1986):** 'Professor Hendry's Econometric Methodology', *Oxford Bulletin of Economics and Statistics*, 48, 283-307.
84. **Gilbert, C. (1989):** 'LSE and the British Approach to Time Series Econometrics', *Oxford Economic Papers*, 41, 108-128.
85. **Giavazzi, F.; Giovannini, A. (1987):** 'Models of the EMS: Is Europe a greater Deutschmark Area?', Ch.7, 237-265, in Bryant, R.; Portes, R. (Eds.): *Global Macroeconomics: Policy Conflict and Cooperation*, MacMillan Press, London.
86. **Giovannini, A. (1990):** 'Money Demand and Monetary Control in an Integrated European Economy', *European Economy*, Special Edition No.1. Reprinted as Ch.10, 259-285, in Giovannini, A. (Ed.): *The Debate on Money in Europe*, MIT Press, Cambridge (Mass.), 1995.
87. **Giovannini, A.; Turtelboom, B. (1994):** 'Currency Substitution', 390-436, in Van der Ploeg, F. (Ed.): *Handbook of International Macroeconomics*, Blackwell Publishers, Cambridge (Mass.).
88. **Girton, L.; Roper, D. (1981):** 'Theory and Implications of Currency Substitution', *Journal of Money, Credit, and Banking*, 13, 12-30.
89. **Giucca, P.; Levy, A. (1992):** 'Monetary Aggregates and Monetary Policy Coordination on the Way to Economic and Monetary Union: The Role of Cross-Border Deposits', *Temi di Discussione*, Banca d'Italia, Roma.
90. **Gonzalo, J. (1993):** 'Cointegration and Aggregation', *Ricerche Economiche*, 47, 281-291.
91. **Gonzalo, J. (1994):** 'Five alternative Methods of Estimating Long-Run Equilibrium Relationships', *Journal of Econometrics*, 60, 203-233.
92. **Gottschalk, J. (1999):** 'On the Monetary Transmission Mechanism in Europe', *Jahrbücher für Nationalökonomie und Statistik*, 219, 357-374.
93. **Granger, C. (1980):** 'Long Memory Relationships and the Aggregation of Dynamic Models', *Journal of Econometrics*, 14, 227-238.
94. **Granger, C. (1982):** 'Generating mechanisms, models, and causality', Ch.8, 237-253, in Hildenbrand, W. (Ed.): *Advances in Econometrics*, Cambridge University Press, Cambridge.
95. **Granger, C.; Lin, J. (1995):** 'Causality in the Long Run', *Econometric Theory*, 11, 530-536.
96. **Gray, M.; Ward, R.; Zis, G. (1976):** 'The World Demand for Money Function: Some preliminary Results', 151-181, in Parkin, M.; Zis, G. (Eds.): *Inflation in the World Economy*, Manchester University Press, Manchester.
97. **Green, H. (1964):** *Aggregation in Economic Analysis.* Princeton University Press, Princeton.
98. **Grunfeld, Y.; Griliches, Z. (1960):** 'Is Aggregation necessarily bad?', *The Review of Economics and Statistics*, 42, 1-13.
99. **Gulde, A.; Schulze-Ghattas, M. (1992):** 'Aggregation of Economic Indicators across Countries: Exchange Rate versus PPP based GDP Weights', *IMF Working Paper*, No 92/36.
100. **Haavelmo, T. (1944):** 'The Probability Approach in Econometrics', *Econometrica*, 12, supplement.

101. **Haldrup, N. (1998):** 'An Econometric Analysis of I(2) Variables', *Journal of Economic Surveys*, 12, 595-650.
102. **Haldrup, N.; Salmon, M. (1998):** 'Representations of I(2) cointegrated Systems using the Smith-McMillan Form', *Journal of Econometrics*, 84, 303-325.
103. **Hall, A. (1994):** 'Testing for a Unit Root in Time Series with Pretest Data-Based Model Selection', *Journal of Business and Economic Statistics*, 12, 461-470.
104. **Hamilton, J. (1994):** *Time Series Analysis*. Princeton University Press, Princeton.
105. **Hannan, E. (1970):** *Multiple Time Series*. John Wiley, New York.
106. **Hansen, B. (1994):** 'Autoregressive conditional Density Estimation', *International Economic Review*, 35 , 705-730.
107. **Hansen, G.; Kim, J. (1995):** 'The Stability of German Money Demand: Tests of the Cointegration Relation', *Weltwirtschaftliches Archiv*, 131, 286-301.
108. **Hansen, H.; Johansen, S. (1993):** 'Recursive Estimation in cointegrated VAR-models', Preprint No.1, Institute of Mathematical Statistics, University of Copenhagen.
109. **Hargreaves, C. (1994):** 'A Review of Methods of Estimating Cointegrating Relationships', Ch.4, 87-131, in Hargreaves, C. (Ed.): *Nonstationary Time Series Analysis and Cointegration*, Oxford University Press, Oxford.
110. **Hassler, U.; Wolters, J. (1995):** 'Long Memory in Inflation Rates: International Evidence', *Journal of Business and Economic Statistics*, 13, 37-45.
111. **Hasza, D.; Fuller, W. (1979):** 'Estimation for Autoregressive Processes with Unit Roots', *The Annals of Statistics*, 7, 1106-1120.
112. **Hatanaka, M. (1996):** *Time-Series based Econometrics*. Oxford University Press, Oxford.
113. **Haug, A. (1996):** 'Tests for Cointegration: A Monte Carlo Comparison', *Journal of Econometrics*, 71, 89-115.
114. **Hendry, D. (1979):** 'Predictive Failure and Econometric Modelling in Macroeconometrics: the Transactions Demand for Money', Ch.9 in Ormerod, P. (Ed.): *Economic Modelling*, Heinemann, London. Reprinted as Ch.11, 246-269, in Hendry, D. (Ed.): *Econometrics. Alchemy or Science ?*, Blackwell Publishers, Oxford 1993.
115. **Hendry, D. (1980):** 'Econometrics - Alchemy or Science ?', *Economica*, 47, 387-406. Reprinted as Ch.1, 11-28, in Hendry, D. (Ed.): *Econometrics: Alchemy or Science ?*, Blackwell Publishers, Oxford 1993.
116. **Hendry, D. (1987):** 'Econometric methodology: A personal perspective', Ch.10, 29-48, in Bewley, T. (Ed.): *Advances in Econometrics*, Cambridge University Press, Cambridge.
117. **Hendry, D. (1988):** 'The Encompassing Implications of Feedback versus Feedforward Mechanisms in Econometrics', *Oxford Economic Papers*, 40, 132-149.
118. **Hendry, D. (1995):** *Dynamic Econometrics*. Oxford Univ. Press, Oxford.
119. **Hendry, D.; Doornik, J. (1994):** 'Modelling Linear Dynamic Econometric Systems', *Scottish Journal of Political Economy*, 41, 1-33.
120. **Hendry, D.; Ericsson, N. (1991):** 'An Econometric Analysis of U.K. Money Demand in Monetary Trends in the United States and the United

Kingdom by Milton Friedman and Anna J. Schwartz', *American Economic Review*, 81, 8-38.
121. **Hendry, D.; Neale, A. (1991):** 'A Monte Carlo Study of the Effects of Structural Breaks on Tests for Unit Roots', Ch.8, 95-119, in Hackl, P.; Westlund, A. (Eds.): *Economic Structural Change: Analysis and Forecasting*, Springer Verlag, Berlin.
122. **Hendry, D.; Richard, J. (1982):** 'On the Formulation of Empirical Models in Dynamic Econometrics', *Journal of Econometrics*, 20, 3-33. Reprinted as Ch.14, 304-334, in Granger, C. (Ed.): *Modelling Economic Series*, Clarendon Press, Oxford 1990.
123. **Hendry, D.; Richard, J. (1983):** 'The Econometric Analysis of Economic Time Series', *International Statistical Review*, 51, 111-163.
124. **Hendry, D.; Wallis, K. (Eds.) (1984):** *Econometrics and Quantitative Economics.* Basil Blackwell, Oxford.
125. **Hill, P. (1988):** 'Recent Developments in Index Number Theory and Practice', *OECD Economic Studies*, No.10, 123-148.
126. **Hubrich, K. (1999):** 'Estimation of a German Money Demand System', *Empirical Economics*, 24, 77-99.
127. **Ijiri, Y. (1971):** 'Fundamental Queries in Aggregation Theory', *Journal of the American Statistical Association*, 66, 766-782.
128. **Issing, O. (1992):** 'Theoretical and Empirical Foundations of the Deutsche Bundesbank's Monetary Targeting', *Intereconomics*, 27, 289-300.
129. **Issing, O.; Tödter, K. (1995):** 'Geldmenge und Preise im vereinigten Deutschland', 97-123, in Duwendag, D. (Ed.): *Neuere Entwicklungen in der Geldtheorie und Währungspolitik*, Duncker und Humblot, Berlin.
130. **Jarchow, H. (1998):** *Theorie und Politik des Geldes I.* 10. Aufl., Vandenhoeck & Ruprecht, Göttingen.
131. **Johansen, S. (1988):** 'Statistical Analysis of Cointegration Vectors', *Journal of Economic Dynamics and Control*, 12, 231-254.
132. **Johansen, S. (1991):** 'Estimation and Hypothesis Testing of Cointegration Vectors in Gaussian Vector Autoregressive Models', *Econometrica*, 59, 1551-1580.
133. **Johansen, S. (1992a):** 'Determination of Cointegration Rank in the Presence of a Linear Trend', *Oxford Bulletin of Economics and Statistics*, 54, 383-397.
134. **Johansen, S. (1992b):** 'Testing Weak Exogeneity and the Order of Cointegration in UK Money Demand Data', *Journal of Policy Modeling*, 14, 313-334.
135. **Johansen, S. (1992c):** 'A Representation of Vector Autoregressive Processes Integrated of order 2', *Econometric Theory*, 8, 188-202.
136. **Johansen, S. (1994):** 'The Role of the Constant and Linear Terms in Cointegration Analysis of Nonstationary Variables', *Econometric Reviews*, 13, 205-229.
137. **Johansen, S. (1995a):** 'A Statistical Analysis of Cointegration for I(2) Variables', *Econometric Theory*, 11, 25-59.
138. **Johansen, S. (1995b):** 'Identifying Restrictions of Linear Equations with Applications to Simultaneous Equations and Cointegration', *Journal of Econometrics*, 69, 111-132.
139. **Johansen, S.; Juselius, K. (1990):** 'Maximum Likelihood Estimation and Inference on Cointegration - with Applications to the Demand for Money', *Oxford Bulletin of Economics and Statistics*, 52, 169-210.

140. **Johansen, S.; Juselius, K. (1992):** 'Testing structural Hypotheses in a Multivariate Cointegration Analysis of the PPP and UIP for UK', *Journal of Econometrics*, 53, 211-244.
141. **Juselius, K. (1996):** 'An Empirical Analysis of the Changing Role of the German Bundesbank after 1983', *Oxford Bulletin of Economics and Statistics*, 58, 791-819.
142. **Kawashima, H. (1980):** 'Parameter Estimation of Autoregressive Integrated Processes by Least Squares', *The Annals of Statistics*, 8, 423-435.
143. **King, R.; Plosser, C. (1984):** 'Money, Credit, and Prices in a Real Business Cycle', *American Economic Review*, 74, 363-380.
144. **Kirman, A. (1992):** 'Whom or What does the Representative Individual Represent?', *Journal of Economic Perspectives*, 6, 117-136.
145. **Klein, L. (1946):** 'Remarks on the Theory of Aggregation', *Econometrica*, 14, 303-312.
146. **König, R. (1996):** 'The Bundesbank's Experience of Monetary Targeting', Ch.5, 107-140, in Deutsche Bundesbank (Ed.): *Monetary Policy Strategies in Europe*, Verlag Vahlen, München.
147. **Kremers, J.; Lane, T. (1990):** 'Economic and Monetary Integration and the Aggregate Demand for Money in the EMS', *IMF Staff Papers*, 37, 777-805.
148. **Kremers, J.; Lane, T. (1992a):** 'The Demand for Money in Europe: Reply to Barr', *IMF Staff Papers*, 39, 730-737.
149. **Kremers, J.; Lane, T. (1992b):** 'Derivation of the Liquidity Ratio in the EMS: Reply to Arnold', *IMF Staff Papers*, 39, 203-207.
150. **Kremers, J.; Lane, T. (1992c):** 'The Implications of Cross-Border Monetary Aggregation', *IMF Working Paper*, No. 92/71.
151. **Lai, T.; Wei, C. (1983):** 'Asymptotic Properties of General Autoregressive Models and Strong Consistency of Least-Squares Estimates of their Parameters', *Journal of Multivariate Analysis*, 13, 1-23.
152. **Laidler, D. (1982):** 'On the Demand for Money and the Real Balance Effect', 37-66 in: Laidler, D.: *Monetarist Perspectives*, Philip Allan, Oxford.
153. **Lane, T. (1990):** 'Costly Portfolio Adjustment and the Short-Run Demand for Money', *Economic Inquiry*, 28, 466-487.
154. **Läufer, N. (1990):** 'The Inefficiency of the D-Mark Standard', 1045-1058 in: Heilmann, W. (Ed.): *Geld, Banken und Versicherungen*, VVW, Karlsruhe.
155. **Läufer, N. (1992a):** 'Die relative Stabilität der europäischen Geldnachfragefunktion', 130-140 in: Bol, G.; Nakhaeizadeh, G.; Vollmer, K. (Eds.): *Ökonometrie und monetärer Sektor*, Physica Verlag, Heidelberg.
156. **Läufer, N. (1992b):** 'A Monetary Policy for Unified Germany: Europeanization of Money Supply Targetting', 46-64 in: Vosgerau, H. (Ed.): *European Integration in the World Economy*, Springer Verlag, Berlin.
157. **Läufer, N. (1995):** 'The relative Stability of the European Money Demand Function: The Portfolio Diversification Effect', Grüne Reihe SFB 178, Serie II Nr.249, University of Konstanz.
158. **Lau, L. (1982):** 'A Note on the Fundamental Theorem of Exact Aggregation', *Economics Letters*, 9, 119-126.
159. **Leamer, E. (1978):** *Specification Searches.* John Wiley & Sons, New York.
160. **Lee, H.; Siklos, P. (1995):** 'A Note on the Critical Values for the Maximum Likelihood (seasonal) Cointegration Tests', *Economics Letters*, 49, 137-145.
161. **Lee, K.; Pesaran, M.; Pierse, R. (1990):** 'Testing for Aggregation Bias in Linear Models', *The Economic Journal*, 100 (Supplement), 137-150.

162. **Lewbel, A. (1989):** 'Exact Aggregation and a Representative Consumer', *Quarterly Journal of Economics*, 104, 621-633.
163. **Lewbel, A. (1992):** 'Aggregation with Log-Linear Models', *Review of Economic Studies*, 59, 635-642.
164. **Ljung, G.; Box, G. (1978):** 'On a measure of lack of fit in Time Series Models', *Biometrika*, 65, 297-303.
165. **Lucas, R.; Sargent, T. (1981):** 'After Keynesian Macroeconomics', Ch.16, 295-319, in Lucas, R.; Sargent, T.: *Rational Expectations and Econometric Practice*, George Allen, London.
166. **Lukacs, E. (1975):** *Stochastic Convergence.* 2nd Ed., Academic Press, New York.
167. **Lütkepohl, H.; Reimers, H. (1992):** 'Impulse Response Analysis of Cointegrated Systems', *Journal of Economic Dynamics and Control*, 16, 53-78.
168. **Lütkepohl, H.; Saikkonen, P. (1999):** 'Order Selection in Testing for the Cointegration Rank of a VAR Process', Ch.7, 168-199, in Engle, R.; White, H. (Eds.): *Cointegration, Causality, and Forecasting*, Oxford University Press, Oxford.
169. **Lütkepohl, H.; Wolters, J. (1998):** 'A Money Demand System for German M3', *Empirical Economics*, 23, 371-386.
170. **MacKinnon, J. (1991):** 'Critical Values for Cointegration Tests', Ch.13, 267-287, in Engle, R.; Granger, C. (Eds.): *Long-Run Economic Relationships*, Oxford University Press, Oxford.
171. **MacKinnon, J. (1996):** 'Numerical Distribution Functions for Unit-Root and Cointegration Tests', *Journal of Applied Econometrics*, 11, 601-618.
172. **MacKinnon, J.; Haug, A.; Michelis, L. (1996):** 'Numerical Distribution Functions of Likelihood Ratio Tests for Cointegration', unpublished paper.
173. **Mann, H.; Wald, A. (1943):** 'On the Statistical Treatment of Linear Stochastic Difference Equations', *Econometrica*, 11, 173-220.
174. **Maravall, A.; Mathis, A. (1994):** 'Encompassing univariate Models in multivariate Time Series', *Journal of Econometrics*, 61, 197-233.
175. **McKinnon, R. (1982):** 'Currency Substitution and Instability in the World Dollar Standard', *American Economic Review*, 72, 320-333.
176. **McKinnon, R. (1984):** *An International Standard for Monetary Stabilization.* Institute for International Economics, Washington.
177. **McKinnon, R. (1996):** 'Concepts of international Currency Substitution', Ch.3, 44-59, in Mizen, P.; Pentecost, E.J. (Eds.): *The Macroeconomics of International Currencies*, Edward Elgar, Cheltenham.
178. **Mercenier, J.; Sekkat, K. (1988):** 'Money Stock Targeting and Money Supply: An intertemporal Optimization Approach (with an Application to Canada)', *Journal of Applied Econometrics*, 3, 215-228.
179. **Mizen, P.; Pentecost, E. (1996):** 'Currency Substitution in Theory and Practice', Ch.2, 8-43, in Mizen, P.; Pentecost, E. (Eds.): *The Macroeconomics of International Currencies*, Edward Elgar, Cheltenham.
180. **Monticelli, C. (1996):** 'EU-wide Money and Cross-Border Holdings', *Weltwirtschaftliches Archiv*, 132, 215-235.
181. **Monticelli, C.; Papi, L. (1996):** *European Integration, Monetary Coordination, and the Demand for Money.* Clarendon Press, Oxford.
182. **Monticelli, C.; Strauss-Kahn, M. (1993):** 'European Integration and the Demand for Broad Money', *The Manchester School*, 61, 345-366.

183. **Morgan, M. (1987):** 'Statistics without Probability and Haavelmo's Revolution in Econometrics', Ch.8, 171-197, in Krüger, L.; Gigerenzer, G.; Morgan, M. (Eds.): *The Probabilistic Revolution, 2,* MIT Press, Cambridge (Mass.).
184. **Muscatelli, V. (1988):** 'Alternative Models of Buffer Stock Money: An Empirical Investigation', *Scottish Journal of Political Economy,* 35, 1-21.
185. **Nankervis, J.; Savin, N. (1987):** 'Finite Sample Distributions of t and F statistics in an AR(1) Model with an Exogeneous Variable', *Econometric Theory,* 3, 387-408.
186. **Nataf, A. (1948):** 'Sur la Possibilité de Construction de certains Macromodèles', *Econometrica,* 16, 232-244.
187. **Nelson, C.; Plosser, C. (1982):** 'Trends and Random Walks in Macroeconomic Time Series', *Journal of Monetary Economics,* 10, 139-162.
188. **Ng, S.; Perron, P. (1995):** 'Unit Root Tests in ARMA Models with Data-Dependent Methods for the Selection of the Truncation Lag', *Journal of the American Statistical Association,* 90, 268-281.
189. **Nickell, S. (1985):** 'Error Correction, Partial Adjustment and all that: An Expository Note', *Oxford Bulletin of Economics and Statistics,* 47, 119-129.
190. **Nielsen, B. (1997):** DisCo Version 1.4. Nuffield College, Oxford.
191. **Osterwald-Lenum, M. (1992):** 'A Note with Quantiles of the Asymptotic Distribution of the Maximum Likelihood Cointegration Rank Test Statistics', *Oxford Bulletin of Economics and Statistics,* 54, 461-471.
192. **Pantula, S. (1989):** 'Testing for Unit Roots in Time Series Data', *Econometric Theory,* 5, 256-271.
193. **Park, J.; Sung, J. (1994):** 'Testing for Unit Roots in Models with Structural Change', *Econometric Theory,* 10, 917-936.
194. **Parkin, M. (1977):** 'World Inflation, International relative Prices, and Monetary Equilibrium under fixed Exchange Rates', Ch.13, 220-241, in Aliber, R. (Ed.): *The Political Economy of Monetary Reform,* MacMillan Press, London.
195. **Paruolo, P. (1996):** 'On the Determination of Integration Indices in I(2) Systems', *Journal of Econometrics,* 72, 313-356.
196. **Paruolo, P. (1997):** 'Asymptotic Inference on the Moving Average Impact Matrix in Cointegrated I(1) VAR Systems', *Econometric Theory,* 13, 79-118.
197. **Perron, P. (1988):** 'Trends and Random Walks in Macroeconomic Time Series', *Journal of Economic Dynamics and Control,* 12, 297-332.
198. **Perron, P. (1989):** 'The Great Crash, the Oil Price Shock, and the Unit Root Hypothesis', *Econometrica,* 57, 1361-1401.
199. **Perron, P.; Campbell, J. (1993):** 'A Note on Johansens Cointegration Procedure when Trends are Present', *Empirical Economics,* 18, 777-789.
200. **Pesaran, M.; Pierse, R.; Kumar, M. (1989):** 'Econometric Analysis of Aggregation in the Context of Linear Prediction Models', *Econometrica,* 57, 861-888.
201. **Phillips, P. (1986):** 'Understanding spurious Regressions in Econometrics', *Journal of Econometrics,* 33, 311-340.
202. **Phillips, P. (1987):** 'Time Series Regression with a Unit Root', *Econometrica,* 55, 277-301.
203. **Phillips, P. (1991):** 'Optimal Inference in Cointegrated Systems', *Econometrica,* 59, 283-306.
204. **Phillips, P.; Solo, V. (1992):** 'Asymptotics for Linear Processes', *The Annals of Statistics,* 20, 971-1001.

205. **Podolski, T. (1986):** *Financial Innovations and the Money Supply.* Basil Blackwell, Oxford.
206. **Pokropp, F. (1978):** 'The Functional Equation of Aggregation', 122-139 in: Eichorn, W. (Ed.): *Functional Equations in Economics,* Addison-Wesley, Reading Mass..
207. **Poole, W. (1970):** 'Optimal Choice of Monetary Policy Instruments in a Simple Stochastic Macro Model', *Quarterly Journal of Economics*, 84, 197-216.
208. **Portes, R. (1993):** 'EMS and EMU after the Fall', *World Economy*, 16, 1-15.
209. **Pu, S. (1946):** 'A Note on Macroeconomics', *Econometrica*, 14, 299-302.
210. **Ramsey, J. (1996):** 'On the Existence of Macro Variables and of Macro Relations', *Journal of Economic Behaviour and Organization*, 30, 275-299.
211. **Reimers, H. (1992):** 'Comparison of Tests for Multivariate Cointegration', *Statistical Papers*, 33, 335-359.
212. **Ringwald, K. (1980):** *A Critique of Models in linear Aggregation Structures.* Athenaeum Verlag, Königstein.
213. **Rothenberg, T. (1971):** 'Identification in Parametric Models', *Econometrica*, 39, 577-591.
214. **Russo, M.; Tullio, G. (1988):** 'Monetary Policy Coordination within the European Monetary System: Is there a Rule?', Ch.11, 292-356, in Giavazzi, F.; Micossi, S.; Miller, M. (Eds.): *The European Monetary System*, Cambridge University Press, Cambridge.
215. **Sardelis, C. (1993):** 'Targeting a European Monetary Aggregate', Economic Papers No. 102, Commission of the European Communities, Brussels.
216. **Sasaki, K. (1978):** 'An Empirical Analysis of Linear Aggregation Problems', *Journal of Econometrics*, 7, 313-331.
217. **Scharnagl, M. (1998):** 'The Stability of German Money Demand: Not just a Myth', *Empirical Economics*, 23, 355-370.
218. **Schmidt, P. (1990):** 'Dickey-Fuller Tests with Drift', Ch.6, 161-200, in Fomby, T.; Rhodes, G. (Eds.): *Advances in Econometrics, 8: Cointegration, spurious regressions, and unit roots*, JAI Press, Greenwich.
219. **Seitz, H. (1993):** 'Still More on the Speed of Adjustment in Inventory Models: A Lesson in Aggregation', *Empirical Economics*, 18, 103-127.
220. **Silvestre, J.; Rossello, A.; Ortuno, M. (1999):** 'Response Surface Estimates for the Dickey-Fuller Unit Root Test with structural Breaks', *Economics Letters*, 63, 279-283.
221. **Sims, C.; Stock, J.; Watson, M. (1990):** 'Inference in Linear Time Series Models with some Unit Roots', *Econometrica*, 58, 113-144.
222. **Spanos, A. (1986):** *Statistical Foundations of Econometric Modelling.* Cambridge University Press, Cambridge.
223. **Spanos, A. (1989):** 'On Rereading Haavelmo: A Restrospective View of Econometric Modeling', *Econometric Theory*, 5, 405-429.
224. **Spanos, A. (1990):** 'The Simultaneous Equations Model Revisited', *Journal of Econometrics*, 44, 87-105.
225. **Spanos, A. (1995):** 'On Theory Testing in Econometrics: Modelling with nonexperimental Data', *Journal of Econometrics*, 67, 189-226.
226. **Stock, J., Watson, M. (1988):** 'Testing for Common Trends', *Journal of the American Statistical Association*, 83, 1097-1107.
227. **Stoker, T. (1984):** 'Completeness, Distribution Restrictions, and the Form of Aggregate Functions', *Econometrica*, 52, 887-907.

228. **Stoker, T. (1993):** 'Empirical Approaches to the Problem of Aggregation over Individuals', *Journal of Economic Literature*, 31, 1827-1874.
229. **Theil, H. (1954):** *Linear Aggregation of Economic Relations.* 2nd printing 1965, North-Holland, Amsterdam.
230. **Tödter, K.; Reimers, H. (1994):** 'P-Star as a Link between Money and Prices in Germany', *Weltwirtschaftliches Archiv*, 130, 273-289.
231. **Tso, M. (1981):** 'Reduced-Rank Regression and Canonical Analysis', *Journal of the Royal Statistical Society B*, 43, 183-189.
232. **Tullio, G.; DeSouza, E., Giucca, P. (1996):** 'The Demand for Money Functions in Europe and in Germany before and after the Fall of the Berlin Wall', Ch.12, 310-338, in DeGrauwe, P.; Micossi, S.; Tullio, G. (Eds.): *Inflation and Wage Behaviour in Europe*, Clarendon Press, Oxford.
233. **VanDaal, J.; Merkies, A. (1981):** 'A simple Proof of Nataf's Theorem on Consistent Aggregation', *Economics Letters*, 7, 145-150.
234. **VanDaal, J.; Merkies, A. (1988):** 'The Problem of Aggregation of Individual Economic Relations: Consistency and Representativity in a Historical Perspective', 607-637 in: Eichorn, W. (Ed.): *Measurement in Economics*, Physica Verlag, Heidelberg.
235. **VanRiet, A. (1992):** 'European Integration and the Demand for Money in the EC', *Quarterly Bulletin No 92-3 (December 1992).* De Nederlandsche Bank, Amsterdam.
236. **VanRiet, A. (1993):** 'Studies of EC Money Demand: Survey and Assessment', *Quarterly Bulletin No 92-4 (March 1993).* De Nederlandsche Bank, Amsterdam.
237. **Watson, M. (1994):** 'Vector Autoregressions and Cointegration', Ch.47, 2843-2915, in Engle, R.F.; McFadden, D.L. (Eds.): *Handbook of Econometrics*, IV, Elsevier Science, Amsterdam.
238. **Wesche, K. (1997):** 'The Stability of European Money Demand: An Investigation of M3H', *Open Economies Review*, 8, 371-391.
239. **West, K. (1987):** 'A Note on the Power of Least Squares Tests for a Unit Root', *Economics Letters*, 24, 249-252.
240. **West, K. (1988):** 'Asymptotic Normality when Regressors have a Unit Root', *Econometrica*, 56, 1397-1417.
241. **White, H. (1994):** *Estimation, Inference and Specification Analysis.* Cambridge University Press, Cambridge.
242. **Wickens, M. (1996):** 'Interpreting Cointegrating Vectors and Common Stochastic Trends', *Journal of Econometrics*, 74, 255-271.
243. **Wolters, J.; Lütkepohl, H. (1997):** 'Die Geldnachfrage für M3: Neue Ergebnisse für das vereinigte Deutschland', *IFO-Studien 1/1997*, 35-54.
244. **Wolters, J.; Teräsvirta, T.; Lütkepohl, H. (1998):** 'Modeling the Demand for M3 in the Unified Germany', *The Review of Economics and Statistics*, 80, 399-409.
245. **Zellner, A. (1962):** 'An Efficient Method of Estimating Seemingly Unrelated Regressions and Tests for Aggregation Bias', *Journal of the American Statistical Association*, 57, 348-368.
246. **Zellner, A. (1969):** 'On the Aggregation Problem: A new Approach to a troublesome Problem', 365-374 in: Fox, K.; Sengupta, J.; Narasimham, G. (Eds.): *Economic Models, Estimation and Risk Programming*, Springer, Berlin.

Contributions to Economics

Nikolaus Thumm
Intellectual Property Rights
2000. ISBN 3-7908-1329-X

Max Keilbach
Spatial Knowledge Spillovers and the Dynamics of Agglomeration and Regional Growth
2000. ISBN 3-7908-1321-4

Alexander Karmann (Ed.)
Financial Structure and Stability
2000. ISBN 3-7908-1332-X

Joos P. A. van Vugt/Jan M. Peet (Eds.)
Social Security and Solidarity in the European Union
2000. ISBN 3-7908-1334-6

Johannes Bröcker/Hayo Herrmann (Eds.)
Spatial Change and Interregional Flows in the Integrating Europe
2001. ISBN 3-7908-1344-3

Kirstin Hubrich
Cointegration Analysis in a German Monetary System
2001. ISBN 3-7908-1352-4

Nico Heerink et al. (Eds.)
Economic Policy and Sustainable Land Use
2001. ISBN 3-7908-1351-6

Friedel Bolle/Michael Carlberg (Eds.)
Advances in Behavioral Economics
2001. ISBN 3-7908-1358-3

Volker Grossmann
Inequality, Economic Growth, and Technological Change
2001. ISBN 3-7908-1364-8

Thomas Riechmann
Learning in Economics
2001. ISBN 3-7908-1384-2

Miriam Beblo
Bargaining over Time Allocation
2001. ISBN 3-7908-1391-5

Peter Meusburger/Heike Jöns (Eds.)
Transformations in Hungary
2001. ISBN 3-7908-1412-1

Claus Brand
Money Stock Control and Inflation Targeting in Germany
2001. ISBN 3-7908-1393-1

Erik Lüth
Private Intergenerational Transfers and Population Aging
2001. ISBN 3-7908-1402-4

Nicole Pohl
Mobility in Space and Time
2001. ISBN 3-7908-1380-X

Pablo Coto-Millán (Ed.)
Essays on Microeconomics and Industrial Organisation
2002. ISBN 3-7908-1390-7

Mario A. Maggioni
Clustering Dynamics and the Locations of High-Tech-Firms
2002. ISBN 3-7908-1431-8

Ludwig Schätzl/Javier Revilla Diez (Eds.)
Technological Change and Regional Development in Europe
2002. ISBN 3-7908-1460-1

Alberto Quadrio Curzio/Marco Fortis (Eds.)
Complexity and Industrial Clusters
2002. ISBN 3-7908-1471-7

Friedel Bolle/
Marco Lehmann-Waffenschmidt (Eds.)
Surveys in Experimental Economics
2002. ISBN 3-7908-1472-5

Pablo Coto-Millán
General Equilibrium and Welfare
2002. ISBN 7908-1491-1

Wojciech W. Charemza/Krystyna Srzala (Eds.)
East European Transition and EU Enlargement
2002. ISBN 3-7908-1501-2

Natalja von Westernhagen
Systemic Transformation, Trade and Economic Growth
2002. ISBN 3-7908-1521-7

Josef Falkinger
A Theory of Employment in Firms
2002. ISBN 3-7908-1520-9

Econometrics
and Formulas for Economists

B.H. Baltagi

Econometrics

This textbook teaches some of the basic econometric methods and the underlying assumptions behind them. Some of the strengths of this book lie in presenting difficult material in a simple, yet rigorous manner.

3rd ed. 2002. XVI, 401 pp. 48 figs., 41 tabs. Softcover * **€ 42,75**; sFr 68,50 ISBN 3-540-43501-8

B. Luderer, V. Nollau, K. Vetters

Mathematical Formulas for Economists

The present collection of formulas has been composed for students of economics or management science at universities, colleges and trade schools. It contains basic knowledge in mathematics, financial mathematics and statistics in a compact and clearly arranged form.

Table of Contents available:
http://www.springer.de/books/toc/3540426167-c.pdf

2002. X, 186 pp. 58 figs., 6 tabs. Softcover * **€ 19,21**; sFr 31,- ISBN 3-540-42616-7

K. Sydsaeter, A. Strom, P. Berck

Economists' Mathematical Manual

This volume presents mathematical formulas and theorems common to economics. The volume is the first grouping of this material for a specifically economist audience. This third edition is extensively revised and contains more than 250 new formulas, as well as new figures.

3rd rev. and enlarged ed. 1999. Corr. 2nd printing 2000. XII, 206 pp. 63 figs. Hardcover * **€ 24,02**; sFr 38,50 ISBN 3-540-65447-X

*Suggested retail price

Visit our homepage:
http://www.springer.de/economics

Please order from
Springer · Customer Service
Haberstr. 7
69126 Heidelberg, Germany
Tel.: +49 (0) 6221 - 345 - 217/8
Fax: +49 (0) 6221 - 345 - 229
e-mail: orders@springer.de
or through your bookseller

Die €-Preise für Bücher sind gültig in Deutschland und enthalten 7% MwSt.
Die mit * gekennzeichneten Preise sind unverbindliche Preisempfehlungen inkl. 7% MwSt. Preisänderungen und Irrtümer vorbehalten. d&p · BA 44002/2

Springer

GPSR Compliance

The European Union's (EU) General Product Safety Regulation (GPSR) is a set of rules that requires consumer products to be safe and our obligations to ensure this.

If you have any concerns about our products, you can contact us on ProductSafety@springernature.com

In case Publisher is established outside the EU, the EU authorized representative is:

Springer Nature Customer Service Center GmbH
Europaplatz 3
69115 Heidelberg, Germany

Batch number: 10725973

Printed by Printforce, the Netherlands